Mary MacKillop Unveiled

'The story told on the following pages ... ~y the stuff of some of our best rebels and fighters. It is a marvellously rich tapestry of guts, impulsiveness, grit, compassion and dreams. It is a story that takes in some of the biggest myths of our culture ... The more I read of her history, the more she encapsulates something quintessentially Australian ... The "unveiled" Mary emerges as magnificent.'

GERALDINE DOOGUE
From the Foreword

'What an outstanding and extraordinary woman! I feel a great sense of pride that she was a woman of such determined devotion to God who showed such dedication to the poor, the homeless, the migrant, the sick and the aged, but above all to the education of children. Lesley O'Brien presents a very good, down-to-earth understanding of the difficulties Mary MacKillop had to endure. I feel that past pupils of the Josephites, like myself, as well as many other readers will be delighted with this account of such a great life.'

GABI HOLLOWS

'Mary MacKillop and her sisters speak with their own voices in this revealing biography. Lesley O'Brien has gone to the letters and diaries of the time to give us an authentic portrait of the first Australian saint. The result is an intimate conversation with one of the great women of our history and an honest account of her difficulties in the Australian Church.'

EDMUND CAMPION
Author of *Rockchoppers* and *Australian Catholics*

' "The life and death of each of us has its influence on others" ' (Romans 14:7). In *Mary MacKillop Unveiled*, Lesley O'Brien tells us of a life and a death. Then simply and with great skill, she allows that life and death to influence the reader. As one who has "known" Mary MacKillop for many years, I have discovered in Lesley's narration a new insight into Mary's character, and a profound appreciation of what it takes to be "Australian" and at the same time a "saint". I hope this will be the experience of all who read this book.'

MARY CRESP RSJ
Former Congregational Leader
Sisters of St Joseph

'How appropriate that Australia's first official saint should be a woman, and a woman who gave the Church a hard time at that! The beatification of Mary MacKillop should encourage all women who struggle to be heard in the Church today. Lesley O'Brien's biography tells the story of the difficulties this remarkable pioneer woman had to overcome to create a unique Australian Order which has done so much for the poor in this country. Mother MacKillop's triumphant vindication is surely a sign of hope.'

MURIEL PORTER
Author of *Women in the Church*

' "The closer people are to God, the closer they come to one another; and the closer they are to one another the closer they come to God." The life of Mary MacKillop was typical of the lives of many Australians in the 19th century who battled to make decent lives for themselves and for others. To Mary, education was the key, and she gave her life to educating the children of the outback. The God she loved called her to love and to love most especially those who were poor and without power. That love is what makes her a saint. Paradoxically, it also means that she often had to battle Church officials. Indeed, prophets are often uncomfortable. The triumph of Mary MacKillop is a triumph for all Australians.'

VERONICA BRADY
Author of *Caught in the Draft*

'Lesley O'Brien's *Mary MacKillop Unveiled* is an excellent biography of Mary MacKillop. Through her skilful use of contemporary documents, the writer has brought her characters to life and given a clear picture of the era. It is history at its best — accurate, honest, and withal, eminently readable.'

MARIE FOALE RSJ
Author of *The Josephite Story*

'An account of the life of Mary MacKillop, written by a woman who is neither a religious sister nor a professional Church historian, is a valuable addition to the literature emerging now that the date of beatification is close. Lesley O'Brien's view is taken at some distance from convent life and Church politics, so that her perspective brings both a freshness and a unique insight into the story: that of one woman appraising the qualities of another.'

MARGARET PRESS RSJ
Author of *Julian Tenison Woods: 'Father Founder'*

Mary MacKillop
Unveiled

LESLEY O'BRIEN

johngarrattpublishing

Published in Australia by
John Garratt Publishing
32 Glenvale Crescent
Mulgrave Vic 3170

First published 1994 By Harper An imprint of HarperCollins Melbourne
ISBN 978-1-920721-62-6.

Original layout and typesetting by William Hung

Cover design by Lynne Muir
Print coordinated in Australia by Advent Print Management

Photographs are used with the permission of the
Mary MacKillop Archive (North Sydney) maintained by the Trustees of the
Sisters of St Joseph.
Mary MacKillop Unveiled is an official publication of the
Mary MacKillop Secretariat of the Sisters of St Joseph, the
Religious Order founded by Mary MacKillop.

CONTENTS

FOREWORD

THESE days I sense a considerable hunger for good stories about people, stories that unfold episodically and reveal lives marked by passion, struggle and a sense of integrity. There is simply nothing as captivating as the tale of a person who develops before one's very eyes. A person who is exposed to challenges that threaten the core of their personality. A person called upon to display both heroism and submission. In effect, one who is called upon to undergo a classic death-and-resurrection metamorphosis.

The thrill of exploring any character undergoing one of life's great tests is a major by-product of good literature. When the tale being told is true and the material, though of the past, has such relevance to the present, it becomes a rare quinella for the writer and the reader. This is the case with the story of Mary MacKillop. For some time now, I have sensed that the prospect of sainthood – a 'first' in Australian history – has tended to swathe Mary in an untouchable glow. She has been dubbed one of our 'worthies', admirable naturally and an exemplar of all the virtues we inherently admire: self-sacrifice and commitment to the underprivileged and the vulnerable. She has received the status of 'good woman'.

However, the 'hero' status we accord to those we genuinely love in Australia and in whom we revel, has somewhat eluded Mary. Yet the story told on the following pages is surely the stuff of some of our best rebels and fighters. It is a marvellously rich tapestry of guts, impulsiveness, grit, compassion and dreams. It is a story that takes in some of the biggest myths of our culture: the 'small person' versus the authorities; pragmatism; loneliness; engagement with the awesome power of the Australian landscape; and survival against some of the most potent weapons available to those in power, including excommunication.

This is the story of a remarkable woman who worked out how her life would have meaning. True, she did not display the larrikinism and rat-baggery with which Australians feel so comfortable deep down, and which probably ensures entry to our 'pantheon of stars'. But Mary did it hard. Her path was tortuous. She never stopped questioning her motives. She constantly sought to 'target' her energies best. She made mistakes and she knew it. She was not a piously holy icon, though her impact on others was indescribable. And the more I read of her history, the more she encapsulates something quintessentially Australian – the monumental struggle to create structures that safeguard the precious ethic of egalitarianism, fairness by any other name. By this dream shall we know Mary MacKillop, one of the tallest of our poppies. She lived out her faith in a way that thousands of her compatriots can use as a model of modern witness.

In hearing her full story, the 'unveiled' Mary emerges as magnificent.

GERALDINE DOOGUE

PROLOGUE

THE sixth of July 1993, the day that Pope John Paul II announced from Rome that Mary MacKillop would be made Australia's first saint, signalled the end of a long wait for the country's four-and-a-half million Catholics. It was 67 years, in fact, since the first tentative steps were taken in what became a slow, complicated and controversial process.

To mark the Papal announcement, it was decided to especially open the Mary MacKillop Commemorative Chapel in Mount Street, North Sydney (it had been temporarily closed for renovations), on 8 July 1993, just two days after the announcement. The occasion was the hour-long 'Pilgrimage Mass' held each month in honour of Mary. Though the weather had been fine for weeks on end, leaden cloud closed over the night before the Mass, bringing with it torrential rain, whipped up by cold, gusty winds. The grounds of the Commemorative Chapel were muddied and littered with the sopping building debris of the renovations, the front of the chapel was boarded up, and there was a steady dripping through the gabled roof of the foyer.

But the miserable weather and work-in-progress did nothing to dampen the enthusiasm of Mary's faithful supporters. At the appointed time, while the rest of North Sydney hid indoors during the usually frenetic lunch hour, Mount Street fairly bustled with bobbing umbrellas. All were heading towards the Commemorative Chapel, a neat and quietly majestic structure set amongst the spindly shadows of high-rise buildings and the hum of freeway traffic.

Inside the chapel, an eclectic set of men and women lined the pews – nuns, mothers with children, businessmen in suits, the sick, the elderly, slickly dressed women, and teenagers – several hundred in all. Yet they all came together with a common purpose: to pray for a miracle in the name of Mary MacKillop; for themselves, for a relative, or for the person beside them. They voiced their appeals during the Prayers of the Faithful – for a daughter with leukaemia, a father with Parkinson's disease, a sister with cancer; as well as for problems in the trouble spots of the world.

That Mary could deliver on these seemingly impossible requests, they had few doubts. We have all had the experience of turning to a friend for help in times of difficulty, possibly even asking them to support us with their prayers. Catholics believe that we can also turn to those who have died and are now with God. In particular, the prayers of a 'saint', who we are assured is especially close to God, can result in God's action in quite extraordinary ways.

The Papal announcement that Mary MacKillop was to be made a saint followed the Catholic Church's formal recognition of her role in the miraculous cure of an Australian woman suffering from leukaemia. After being diagnosed with the disease back in 1961, the woman prayed fervently to Mary to save her life. Against the prognosis of specialists, her condition slowly began to improve. Some 30 years, and six children, later, she is not only alive, but completely healthy.

However, this was only one of many documented miracles that could have received the Papal approval necessary for recognition as a saint. The Sisters of St Joseph, the group of Australian nuns founded by Mary MacKillop, have received hundreds of letters from people who can vouch for the power of prayer. Some are truly touching in their simplicity – the woman who has been given peace of mind, the family that has been reconciled, the man who has secured a job, a crop that has been saved by much-needed rain. Others, like the woman with leukaemia, are thanking Mary for something far more precious – their lives.

Emma and Kevin (not their real names) are two such people. In amazing circumstances, both made recoveries from the brink of death that left their doctors searching for answers. The documented evidence includes letters from parents, friends and family, and official statements from doctors and specialists. Although the doctors fall short of calling the cures 'miraculous', most concede that something extraordinary did happen.

Six years ago, Emma and her twin sister were born in a delivery fraught with complications. Their mother, Sue, had been admitted to a Sydney hospital in the last five weeks of pregnancy after doctors detected problems with one of the placentas. Just days later, Sue went into labour. The first twin was delivered without difficulty, but the second baby, Emma, was starved of oxygen for 25 minutes due to a problem with the umbilical cord. After delivery, Emma had convulsions and was rushed to the neonatal intensive care unit for resuscitation. Doctors told Sue and her husband that if Emma lived, she would be severely brain damaged. For a time, things looked so hopeless that doctors all but gave up the fight to save Emma.

It was then that Emma's parents asked family and friends, including a nun from the Sisters of St Joseph, to pray to Mary MacKillop to ask God for a miracle. Emma not only pulled through, but, to her doctors' amazement, suffered no brain damage whatsoever. Tests conducted one month later showed that she was developing normally in every way, and she was discharged from hospital soon after. Emma's parents took her back to hospital for regular check-ups, to keep an eye on her development, but no problems – intellectual or physical – were ever detected. Each time, Emma continued to show normal development for her age.

Sue says, 'The doctor only sees her as a curiosity now, as he's sure he'll never find anything wrong with her.' Sue and her husband are convinced Mary heard the family's prayers and felt their anguish, and that her own prayers to God saved their daughter's life.

The second case – that involving Kevin – occurred in Queensland more than 20 years ago. Kevin, then 16, was playing football when a scrum collapsed on him, breaking his fifth and sixth vertebrae, two very sensitive and vital bones in the upper spinal column. As a result, he lost all movement in his arms and legs, and his bladder stopped functioning. Kevin was operated on, but there was no change in his condition, and his specialist informed him and his family that he would be paralysed for life from the shoulders down.

From the time of the accident, Kevin's local priest asked

Church-goers to appeal to Mary MacKillop for his recovery. Kevin had been a promising young footballer, and was well-known in the district. A Novena was held (where special prayers are said each day for nine days), attended by members of the whole community. Each person agreed to say a specially composed prayer on each of the nine days, requesting that Mary MacKillop plead with God to cure Kevin.

Meanwhile, the Sisters of St Joseph sent Kevin a photo of Mary, which was pinned to a band around his wrist. He became so attached to the photo, he would not allow it to be removed. Just 13 days after Kevin had been admitted to hospital, against all the odds and the professional opinion of specialists, he began to regain some movement of his fingers. By the time he was discharged five months later, he had movement in all muscle groups of his legs, and could walk for very short periods. There was, however, little improvement in his hands and arms.

Despite his surprising progress, Kevin's future still looked bleak. He would always require a wheelchair, would never recover the use of his arms, and his bladder would have to be mechanically emptied every two hours. Kevin was told he would be required to attend Hospital Outpatients for treatment for the rest of his life. However, time was to tell a different story. Eighteen months after the accident, Kevin no longer required a wheelchair, his bladder was functioning normally again, and his hands and arms had improved, although they were still weak. His recovery was such that he no longer even received Outpatient treatment.

Medical staff were stunned. In his final report, Kevin's doctor wrote: 'It is evident that regeneration of the central nervous system has actually taken place, this fact being in reverse to all known knowledge of medical science and contradicting the teachings and clinical findings as are going on in medicine today. It is apparent that there is no factual explanation of this change in the sensitive, vital and traumatised tissues...' Kevin has since married and had children, and leads a full – and mobile – life.

Other letters contain stories equally as poignant. More than 20 years ago, 17-month-old Samantha was rushed to hospital after swallowing 30 ml of Dieldrin, a savage neurological poison being used on pests on the family property. It was enough to kill her 14 times over. That night, the local Catholic priest suggested the family and doctor ask Mary MacKillop for a miracle. When Samantha was discharged from hospital 10 days later, she was alive, but mentally retarded. Again, the doctor and her family prayed to Mary MacKillop. Two days later, Samantha's mother phoned to say her daughter had woken that morning perfectly normal: eating, speaking and running around, just like she was before the accident. According to Samantha's doctor, 'This was a total impossibility and against the law of nature...'

For these people and many others, Mary MacKillop has held, and always will hold, a very special place in their hearts. When their needs went beyond what one can hope for in this world, Mary took their prayers to God, who answered them with a miracle.

Each month, close to 1000 people walk through the doors of the Commemorative Chapel in North Sydney to pray at Mary's tomb, asking for help or thanking her for her intercession. Some travel hundreds of kilometres – from Tamworth, Hobart, Canberra, Rockhampton, Port Augusta, Perth, even New Zealand – for this purpose alone, then return home. The Chapel Register also shows a steady stream of overseas visitors – from Japan, Canada, the United States and France – who read about Mary MacKillop in some newspaper clipping, and decided to track down her grave.

A few report remarkable outcomes from these visits – a tumour that has shrivelled up, a cure to heart problems – but most, it seems, simply come away with a renewed sense of inner peace and calm, even while there is tragedy and turmoil around them.

Perhaps surprisingly, not all who pray at Mary's tomb are Catholics. One man, who overheard a fellow visitor expressing his concerns that he was Protestant, told him, 'That doesn't matter. She brings everyone...' In fact, Mary 'brings' so many people that during recent renovations to the chapel, the Sisters of St Joseph were forced to close it temporarily.

However, it would be a mistake to think that Mary MacKillop is revered simply for being a miracle worker, because these are a very small part of what makes her so special. She is, before all else, a great Australian, a heroine who devoted her life to giving poor, sick and underprivileged Australians a better life, at a time when there were very few others willing – or able – to help. Her courage, commitment and dedication to this cause were formidable. In pursuit of it, she dared to cross the most powerful men in the land, in an era that considered women unworthy of the vote. She dared to be an Australian in a Church that still clung proudly to its European traditions. She dared to view each person as an equal, at a time when prejudice and bigotry raged in the Church and in Australia at large: Catholics versus Protestants, English versus Irish, Europeans versus Chinese, wealthy versus poor.

Mary was an exceptionally good and holy person, a philanthropist in every sense of the word. And while we can well imagine her declaring herself unworthy of the honour of being the country's first saint, she would no doubt be pleased that Australians have one of their own so close to God.

A HIGHLAND FAMILY
IN MELBOURNE

MARY was born in Fitzroy, Melbourne, on 15 January 1842, to Alexander MacKillop and Flora MacDonald, who wore a wedding ring made out of a gold coin. Both were fresh to the Australian colonies from the Scottish Highlands, Flora having arrived with her family in early 1840 and Alexander in January 1838. Three months after Flora arrived, they were married in Melbourne.

As with many families, there was some dispute over the naming of their first child, Mary. Alexander, who could speak five or six languages, including Italian and Latin, wanted her called simply Maria. However, relatives were adamant she should be called after her grandmother, Helen MacKillop. Eventually, Maria Ellen was settled on, although she was always known as Mary.

It is interesting to note that Mary's godfather was Alexander Chisholm, a relative of Mrs Caroline Chisholm, who did much to ease the way for immigrants to Australia in the 19th century. By all accounts, Mary was marked as 'special' from a very young age. In a snippet from the family memoirs, her younger sister Annie recalled with some sentimentality: 'She was a very wise and beautiful child.

People often stopped her nurse just to look at her, she was so like pictures of angels.'

Mary was the eldest of eight children, an average-sized family by colonial standards, when infant mortality ran high and couples sought the safety of numbers to ensure the family name lived to see another generation. Mary was followed by Maggie, John, Alick, Annie, Lexie, Donald and Peter. To them, big-sister Mary was like a second mother, though she was little more than a child herself. At an age when most children are totally focussed on themselves, Mary seemed to have developed an astute regard for the welfare of others. One time, when as a four-year-old she was climbing a steep hill with her mother on a scorching summer's day, Mary noticed that her mother was tired and asked her to 'take her arm'.

On another occasion, Flora came home to find 11-year-old Mary dressing baby Donald and the hired nurse nowhere to be seen. 'Where is the nurse?' her mother asked.

'I sent her away,' replied Mary. When asked why, she said, 'I sacked her. She was drunk.' Her sister, Annie, later recounted, 'Dressing a baby was much more complicated then, but it was all correctly done. Mary was a very observant child... She took charge of us all.'

By Mary's own admission, her childhood was not a particularly happy or carefree one. It was marred not only by too many responsibilities on too-young shoulders, but by death, financial ruin and the break-up of her family. From her earliest years, Mary was obliged to take life very seriously, nursing babies, keeping house and earning money. She developed into a sensitive and practical young lady, mature beyond her years. 'My life as a child was one of sorrow, my home when I had it, a most unhappy one.'

For many of these troubles, the finger was often pointed in the direction of Alexander, Mary's father. He was a passionate, head-strong young man, who acted from his heart rather than his head, to the cost of his family. Whereas Mary considered herself an Australian, Alexander was a Scot through and through. As a young boy in Achluachrach, Brae Lochaber, a district in the Scottish Highlands, Alexander was fed on the fervour of the MacKillops' proud Catholic traditions. While Scots are predominantly Protestant, the Scottish Highlands has always had a strong contingent of Catholics. The ancestors of both the MacKillops and the MacDonalds backed the Catholic 'Bonnie Prince Charlie' in his attempt in 1745 to restore his family, the Stuarts, to the British throne, after a revolt 56 years earlier against Prince Charlie's grandfather, James VII, due to his support of Catholics. After taking Edinburgh, Bonnie Prince Charlie pressed on into England, but was forced back into the Scottish Highlands, where he lost the Battle of Culloden to British troops. Prince Charlie escaped to France, with the help of the Highlanders, in particular Flora MacDonald, whom Mary's mother was named after. She provided Charlie with a passport and women's clothing for his disguise as 'the Irish spinning maid, Betty Bourke'.

This history, together with the pride that came from withstanding years of religious persecution, was passed down to generation after generation of Catholic Highlanders. Perhaps it played a part in the young Alexander MacKillop's decision to become a priest. He spent nearly eight years in training in Rome and Scotland until, quite unexpectedly, he quit. It seems that Alexander, an exceptional student and more than a little arrogant about it, was put out when he failed to receive 'star' treatment.

'After nine years in Rome,' his son Donald later wrote, 'my Dad found it cold in Scotland. He asked for a fire in his room and was refused. Now the young man who in Rome had been made much [of] fancied himself not a little, [and] no doubt when he found himself among the old Fossils of Blairs College went off in a huff to complain to the Bishop. Of course His Lordship [the bishop] advised immediate return to his College. This was too much!... He returned to his home... He had [not become a priest].'

Some years later, at 25, he migrated to Australia, 14 months before the rest of his family. He settled first in Sydney, then in Melbourne in 1839, working with the trading firm, Campbell and Sons. He met Flora MacDonald, who had recently arrived from the Scottish Highlands town of Glen Roy, with her mother, brother and sister. Her father was prevented from boarding the ship, due to some unpaid bills, and came out later. Tragically, during the 100-day voyage, one of her two brothers fell overboard and drowned while delirious with typhoid fever.

Alexander married Flora just months later, on 14 July 1840. By the time Mary was born, in early 1842, he had found success as a landholder, and was employing convict labour. The family fortunes were flowing, and they were living in a sprawling house in Brunswick Street, Fitzroy, in Melbourne. But the prosperity came too easily, and Alexander gave way to recklessness. He was a man who enjoyed the thrill of the chase, the excitement of playing for high stakes, but the truth was, although a clever man, he did not have the business instincts to carry it off.

With Mary just months old, Alexander was forced to sell the Fitzroy mansion. Word soon got around that Alexander was 'pressed', and this, together with the tight economy, saw him settle for half of what he had paid for the house. Just two years later, in 1844, Alexander was declared bankrupt.

Alexander continued to seek out money-making enterprises, but the MacKillops were never to be affluent again. The family was always on the move, mostly around Melbourne, relying on what relatives could afford to give, and Alexander's sporadic earnings from farming. But working the land did nothing to satisfy Alexander's quick mind or his fiery spirit. He enjoyed the cut and thrust of a good debate, and never missed an opportunity to have his say on the political and religious issues close to his heart.

One of his pet topics was the move throughout Australia to 'secularise' education, whereby the governments of the colonies were threatening to stop all funding to Church schools and establish their own. This occurred in South Australia in 1851 – government-run schools were set up, and any religious teaching, other than a daily reading of the Bible, was forbidden. Young Mary would have heard her father argue passionately that Catholics had a right to be taught the fundamentals of their faith, and that secularised education was a blatant attempt to stamp out Catholicism and institute a 'godless society'.

While Alexander was never one to back away from issues to which he was committed, sometimes things got too hot, even for him. In the 1843 Port Phillip election (Victoria was then known as the Port Phillip District of New South Wales), Alexander supported a Catholic candidate, Curr, against the Presbyterian minister, Reverend John Dunmore Lang. In MacKillop and Lang, you could not have got two men more diametrically opposed in their views, or more committed in their pursuit of them.

Alexander voiced his opinions in local newspapers, using the pen name, 'A Scottish Highlander', in letters laced with venom and vitriol. In the *Port Phillip Herald*, he condemned the writings of Lang as 'a tissue of glaring falsehoods, infamous scandals, bigoted opinions, egregious calumnies, and seditious satires'. In turn, Alexander was described by a Lang supporter in a letter to the *Port Phillip Patriot and Melbourne Advertiser* as having 'the disgraceful notoriety of being the FIRST person to commence a religious war in Melbourne... You would be a dangerous man, only thank God, you lack the ability...'

Alexander eventually lost the protection of his pseudonym, and with it, the job he then held; but he was never able to shake off his newfound notoriety as 'The Scottish Highlander'. Far from being disillusioned with politics, though, he contested a couple of elections himself ten years later – without success – in equally colourful campaigns.

For a time in the mid-1840s, the MacKillops lived at Darebin Creek (about 18 km north-east of Melbourne city, an area which is now suburban but was then an expansive rural district) on a property given to Alexander by his father. The family made their living by raising sheep and cattle, and growing crops. The property was quite close to Merri Creek, where Grandfather and Grandmother MacDonald, the parents of Mary's mother, Flora, lived. As a very small girl, Mary loved to sit on the creaky, sun-drenched porch with Grandfather and mimic the strange words from his Gaelic tongue. From him, and no doubt her own parents, Mary picked up the Scottish lilt, a gentle accent which stayed with her throughout her life. Her grandfather called her 'gnothach miadhail', meaning 'precious thing'.

Mary's favourite pet as a child was a calf called Blorac, given to her by Grandfather MacDonald. Tears flowed one particular day when Mary returned home to find that Blorac's calf, also called Blorac, had been taken away by an aunt-in-law, to whom Alexander had promised it. Jumping onto her pony, Mary rode quickly over to her grandfather's house, in the hope he might be able to help rescue the calf. Seeing Mary's distress, he did not hesitate in giving her the money she needed, and by afternoon, Blorac was back in the MacKillop paddock.

Sadly, this was one of the last times Mary was to see Grandfather MacDonald. One day in April 1847, Grandmother MacDonald and one of her sons walked across to the MacKillop house for a visit. Grandfather MacDonald stayed home to catch up on some jobs he had not had time to finish. Shortly before his wife and son were due home, storm clouds began to gather and, worried that they might get caught, Grandfather MacDonald set out to meet them. But he had underestimated the force of the storm, and in the blinding rain he lost his way and stumbled down the steep, slippery banks of Darebin Creek. Mother and son returned home to an empty house, and hastily convened a small search party. However, they found nothing. Some days later Alexander discovered Grandfather MacDonald's body drifting downstream towards the MacKillop home. The tragic circumstances of his drowning were reported in a short article in the newspaper, the *Port Phillip Gazette*, titled 'Melancholy Accident'. Throughout her life, Mary's fond memories of her grandfather never dimmed. Her sister Annie wrote half a century later, 'She loved him very much and even last year reminded me with tears in her eyes of his birthday...'

Just six months after her grandfather's death, Mary lost her 11-month-old brother, Alick, who had never been particularly strong or healthy. Mary loved Alick as only a five-year-old could, lavishing him with kisses and cuddles, and helping to feed and dress him, and his death affected her deeply.

Not long after Alick's death, Mary went to stay with an aunt, Mrs L'Estrange, in Melbourne. On the first night, Mrs L'Estrange went in to check on Mary, thinking she might be a bit homesick, or distressed about Alick. To her surprise, she was sitting up in bed, wide awake. 'A beautiful lady has been here, and told me she would be a mother to me always.' To her dying day, Mrs L'Estrange believed that the little girl had seen a vision of Jesus' mother, Mary. Some 20 years later, Mary wrote a prayer that seemed to confirm she had a vision that night. '...Ah, my Mother, think of the day when I knelt but a child to ask you to be my Mother and to let me love no other mother but you, and I remember your gentle whisper when you said that you marked me as your child since my birth...'

On her return home to Darebin Creek, Mary again took up her chores, helping to care for the younger children, keeping house, and doing light work on the farm. During her play time, young Mary could usually be found on the back of a horse, pretending to round up the cattle. Horse-riding was one of her passions, no doubt taught to her by her mother, Flora, who was a fearless horsewoman who, it is claimed, once rode a whole day with a broken collar-bone. As Mary's brother Donald later recalled, his sister put many of the men to shame with her riding skill. 'Mary was a good horsewoman and when young [was] fond of riding. The fate of Absalom was once nearly hers before she was twenty. We were going home from Sunday Mass and Mary was riding Donkey, a brute very fond of bolting. He had bolted with strong men,' Donald pointed out. '…Now in those days girls wore their hair in nets. Donkey tore away under [the honeysuckle], and I saw Mary's net left hanging until it was [later] retrieved…'

But Mary's abilities extended beyond the saddle. She had a bright and enquiring mind – 'why?' was a word never far from her lips. When money would allow it, Mary and her brothers and sisters attended school, and it was there that she began to show a little of her father's fire. One time, when a teacher gave a lesson on Mary Queen of Scots that didn't quite fit the facts as Mary knew them, she refused to read the textbook, for which the teacher labelled her 'a little bigot'. Mary's courage in challenging a teacher, in an era where children were seen and definitely not heard, showed her to be high-principled, confident, outspoken, and more than a little proud. A similar incident occurred while Mary was visiting Protestant friends. While looking about the house, her eyes fell upon a copy of the anti-Catholic book, *Awful Disclosures of Maria Monk*. So horrified was she by the discovery, Mary promptly tossed the offending literature into the fire!

For the most part, Mary spent very little time in school; money was too tight, and Flora needed her children's help at home. It was here that Alexander's years of study for the priesthood paid dividends. He was devoted to his children and committed to them receiving an education, so he called on all that he had learnt to give them a solid and well-rounded education. Mary, as the eldest, and an intelligent and eager student, appeared to benefit most from these informal classes.

The family had little money for books, so Mary learned by listening, and following the lessons her father prepared for her. From him, she acquired a good command of English and Gaelic, a reasonable grasp of numbers (it was as much as he could give), a fluency in letter-writing, an acute awareness of social issues, and a life-long love of God and the Catholic faith. 'From early childhood, as far back as I can remember, [I had] such a sense of [God's] watchful presence that I would feel myself reproved for my smallest faults.'

Alexander's decision to quit his studies for the priesthood was something which played on Mary's mind from a very young age. In those days, to abandon a religious life was considered something of a disgrace, and Mary felt it keenly. While still a mere child, she began to sense that God had 'called' her to take her father's place. '...From the time I came to understand that he had been intended for the Church, and had not persevered, I began to desire I could leave all I loved, and live for God alone.'

Outside lesson time, Mary was watching, and learning from, the unfolding of a very exciting period of Australian history. In February 1851, Edward Hargraves and three brothers, William, James and Henry Tom, discovered gold in Lewis Ponds Creek, north of Bathurst, New South Wales, marking the start of the gold rush in Australia.

The Victorian government, alarmed by the exodus of the best of its workforce to neighbouring New South Wales and envious of the accumulation of wealth there, offered a reward for the first gold deposit found within 320 km of Melbourne. Six months later, James Esmond took the prize after discovering gold at Clunes. Gold was subsequently found at Castlemaine, Ballarat, Bendigo and the Ovens Valley. By the end of 1851, more than 5000 men in Victoria had downed tools and headed for the goldfields, pitching their tents beside the hundreds of others in what were becoming known as 'canvas towns'. Between 1851 and 1861, with an influx of gold-seeking immigrants – including many Chinese – the colony's population swelled from 77,000 to 540,000. Little thought was given to the wives left behind on bush properties or in dismal city slums – many of whom worked night and day to earn money to feed and clothe their children. In other cases, men entrusted their families to the local priest, until they returned, sometimes years later, with their fortune...or not.

Mary heard and read about the sad predicament of many families. The misery of the deserted women and children – their loneliness, fear and abject poverty – pricked her social conscience. It was in these years that she became committed to the idea of somehow helping these struggling Australians find an easier life. This, together with her belief that God wanted her to fill the place in religious life her father had decided not to take up, led Mary to set her sights on becoming a nun.

While families throughout the country were abandoned in the quest for gold, Flora MacKillop and her five children were left by husband and father for a somewhat nobler cause. In 1851, Alexander joined a dying friend in his last visit to Scotland. While Alexander was generous to a fault and would have done as much for a friend, this little jaunt would hardly have been unappealing to him, proud Scotsman that he was. If he was concerned about how Flora would manage while he was away, and how the bills would be paid, it was not enough to change his mind.

To finance the voyage, Alexander mortgaged his property at Darebin Creek to his wealthy brother, Peter. Some of the money he gave to Flora to care for the family while he was away, although he did not tell her from where he got it. It was an irresponsible move for a man who had very little behind him, but perhaps he thought that if he got into a tight spot, his brother might forget about the loan. If this was his thinking, he was to be sadly disappointed.

Alexander stayed away for a longer-than-anticipated 17 months, and Flora, unaware of his financial arrangements, found herself in the centre of an ugly family dispute, with their family home, once again, on the line.

MARY,
THE BREADWINNER

ALEXANDER'S delayed return saw a tug-of-war begin for the Darebin property and caused a rift in the MacKillop family from which it never really recovered. Mary and the children watched helplessly as Uncle Peter and Aunt Julia moved to turn them out of the house, while MacKillop relatives took sides. However, Flora would not budge, and Mary found herself acting as the go-between. '[Father's] brother and his wife...took possession [and moved in],' Mary's sister Annie recalled, 'though our mother easily borrowed the money from her friends the Butlers as soon as she and they knew of the mortgage. It was *not accepted*, as Uncle Peter said he required the home for himself. It was conveniently situated for his wife... It was a very unhappy time for all, as our mother would not leave, and Aunt Julia always remained in her room, seeing no one but Mary...'

A grudging settlement was eventually reached when Uncle Donald MacDonald offered to provide for his sister Flora and the children at his property in Plenty, just a few kilometres away. They stayed there well after Alexander's return in 1852, earning money from farming. The family employed two women, one a dairymaid, whose fares to Australia were paid by the colony under the assisted immigration scheme set up to attract more people, especially women, to Australia. However, Alexander lacked a farmer's know-how, and this, together with the expense of buying and maintaining equipment, saw the family move to Melbourne in early 1857.

During the family's first few months in the city, there was a hint of a brighter future with Alexander being appointed Clerk of the Goldfields, through cabinet minister and future premier of Victoria, John O'Shannassy. But such hopes were soon trampled underfoot when Alexander, with his usual degree of tact and diplomacy, launched a vocal public attack on O'Shannassy's land policy. Politely but firmly, he was shown the door.

Flora, mother to seven, now accepted that Alexander would never be able to hold a job long enough to provide for the family's upkeep. Calling on her own resources, she opened a boarding house in the Melbourne suburb of Collingwood. However, keeping track of the children, boarders, expenses and income proved too much, and the boarding house closed. Flora was distraught – the family had no money, and she could no longer be consoled by Alexander's assurances that his luck was about to turn.

Mary, though still only a teenager, realised that the family's livelihood rested with her, and she began canvassing for employment. She had a knack with children (she had, after all, helped raise her six brothers and sisters), and was soon snapped up by family friends, the L'Estranges, as governess to their two young adopted children. Each week, Mary handed over her entire pay-packet to her mother, a practice she was to continue for some years. 'When I was little more than 16 years of age,' Mary later said, 'the principal care of a very large family fell upon me, and from that until I was 25 I felt its burthen yearly more and more.'

In 1858, 16-year-old Mary moved into a higher-paying job as assistant forewoman with stationers Sands and Kenny (later Sands and MacDougall) in Melbourne. Mary had a warm, genuine nature, and the owner families were instinctively drawn to her (Mrs MacDougall, in fact, had been a friend of Mary's in girlhood). The fact that none were Catholic was of no consequence to Mary – they were better people than many so-called 'Churchgoers', a conviction born out with time, and each was to remain her life-long friend.

As for the job itself, Mary found it 'revolting' – it was a long way from the charitable work she hoped to perform as a nun. What is more, she was distressed by the way in which she, a mere 'shop-hand', was treated by some of the more well-to-do customers. Mary abhorred the notion that people could be judged by their social status, race, religion, occupation, or the size of their bank balance.

When she herself was the victim of this type of thinking, it was her pride that suffered the most, as one incident recalled by her brother Donald showed: 'A Belgian aristocrat called once at Sands and MacDougalls and it happened to be Mary who had to show him around. Not long after this, a Mr Keogh gave an evening party and this Belgian was one of the guests. Mary was a guest also... Now this was too awful for the aristocrat,' Donald continued. 'To have to acknowledge thus a factory girl! The ass showed himself a snob and Mary left the room. Mr Keogh followed and found her crying in her own room. He prevailed upon her to return saying he would fix things up. He got back to the company first and quietly passed the word round. When Mary returned, she was made the centre of attraction, Queen of the evening in fact. The Belgian took the hint and soon departed... Ah, well, she was young, in the full flush of her teens – from all accounts a very prepossessing and high-spirited girl, with a pedigree to be proud of, and the Belgian was very rude.'

Sands and Kenny paid Mary a good salary, and the relief it brought to her family overshadowed her misgivings about the job. However, she could not help but think of the work she might have been doing as a nun, helping those struggling Australian families she grew up amongst. This was her dream, but she had little idea about how to make it a reality, even if it were within her power. The fact was, while she knew she wanted to become a nun, the idea of joining the Sisters then in Australia did not appeal to her. They were from Europe – mostly Ireland – and Mary doubted whether they could address the needs of a country which was so different to their own. She only hoped that, with time, new opportunities would present themselves. In the meantime, she continued with her work at Sands and Kenny, until at age 18, she was offered a position as governess to her cousins, John, Sarah, Mary and Lexie Cameron, in Penola, South Australia, which she gladly accepted.

South Australia was different from other Australian colonies in that it was settled by free immigrants. Most of the colony was virtually uninhabitable but wheat and sheep did well in the settled areas, although frequent droughts and a shortage of labour made farming a hazardous business. Penola, about 160 km from Portland and 12 km from the Victorian border, was a small town. Like most country centres, it had a public house, a post office, a church, a blacksmith and a handful of shops. Rail lines between major country centres did not open until the 1880s, so the yawning miles were covered on horseback, or in a trap or coach. Roads were no more than crude cuts through scraggly bush, worn deep time and time again by Cobb & Co coaches loaded with passengers (up to 16), goods and mail.

Mary moved from Melbourne to Penola to take up her new post in 1860, the year that famous Australian explorers Burke and Wills made their disastrous expedition from Melbourne to the Gulf of Carpentaria at the northern tip of the continent. The move to Penola exposed Mary to the perils of life in the Australian bush. Hot, dry and vast, it seemed to capture the best, and worst, of nature – strangely beautiful, with its majestic gum trees and gloriously coloured wild flowers, and yet cruel, unforgiving and dangerous. To Australians, each day in the bush was a lottery – droughts, bushfires, dust storms, floods, disease and unbearable heat – no one dared guess what the new dawn would bring. Bush men lived hard, rugged lives, many spending all their wages on alcohol, living on tea and damper, and getting about half-dressed, unwashed and unshaven.

To a large extent, this social degeneracy was a legacy of the gold-rush era. Between 1851 and 1861, with the huge influx of immigrants to the goldfields, Australia experienced a population explosion. When it all ended, many were left dirt-broke, requiring food, clothing, shelter and employment.

Some of those who managed to make money out of the gold rush opened up their own businesses; others took advantage of land selection programs, whereby a person could buy a piece of Crown land in a rural area, farm it, and pay for it over a number of years. The program was designed to reduce overcrowding in the cities, and curb the power of squatters. Squatters were graziers who occupied Crown land illegally and, with the high price that wool then demanded, often made their fortune in the process (wool commanded about 10 times the price of wheat).

Overall, however, land selection failed. The 'selectors' often lacked the necessary skills and equipment, and many tried to apply British farming techniques, obviously developed for an entirely different climate and environment. Often, too, the land was not suitable for small-scale farming, with its dried-out soil, irregular rainfall and insect plagues. Near the rivers, while the soil was fertile, there was the danger of flooding, which could wipe out not only crops but homes and livestock as well.

Women played a vital role in this pioneering era of Australia, keeping house, caring for the family, managing the farm and educating the children, amidst great adversity. During the first few months on the land, the family often lived in a tent, while the men built a house, usually from timber or bark, filled in with mud to keep out the wind and rain, with a sheet of corrugated iron for the roof. Wallpaper was whitewashed newspaper or wattle-and-daub, hessian bags covered the windows, and a mud-like cement, baked by the sun, often hid the dirt floor. 'Toilets' were nothing more than a hole dug in the ground, some distance from the house.

The kitchen consisted of a fireplace of stone or brick. With no 'convenience' products, women called on their initiative. The clothes were all hand-washed, with soap made from tallow and caustic soda, lime and resin from a gum tree, and lighting provided by candles made from mutton fat and string, or kerosene lamps. Another chore was waterproofing boots, using warmed beeswax and mutton fat, and making the butter (kept cool in a dug-out cellar covered with thatch or wood). Old clothes became patchwork quilts, curtains or stuffing for pillows.

With the hot weather, food did not stay fresh for long, so each day brought with it long hours of cooking, 'salting' meat (to preserve it), tending and collecting vegetables grown in the garden (if the land would yield) and crushing grain to make flour. Potatoes, peas and beans were commonly served with the meat, and dessert was often rice or bread-and-butter pudding with treacle.

Because many properties were so isolated, stores were usually ordered every six months or so. Between times, small items were bought from travelling hawkers, who peddled their wagonload of goods – clothes, food, spices, 'medicines' (rum, most often), tobacco, sweets, pots and pans – from farm to farm. These visits provided women with some welcome company, as the hawker invariably brought with him gossip and local news.

There is little question that while life was tough in the bush, it was toughest in the colony of South Australia. While New South Wales and Victoria had each reaped the financial and economic benefits of having a gold rush, South Australia was left behind. Although there was an increased demand for its grain products coinciding with the growth in Australia's population, it lost the bulk of its workforce to the goldfields during the 1850s and 1860s. This had a disastrous impact on business and trade. When drought ruined the wheat crop in 1860, the struggling colony was pushed even deeper into recession. Rising unemployment forced many South Australian families into the city to secure work on

government projects; those that remained looked to the
Church for some relief. However, South Australia had few
priests and, in 1860, no nuns to assist in social welfare.

This was the environment in which Mary took up her new
duties as governess in the Cameron household. Her new
parish at Penola, with its 1500 Catholics strewn across an
expansive district, was served by Father Julian Tenison
Woods, an English-born priest. From their earliest meetings,
Mary and Father Woods seemed to connect on an
intellectual level, both being humanitarians, devoutly
religious and committed to giving ordinary Australians a
better life. As a priest, Father Woods had found an avenue
from which he could do this, but Mary was still searching.
During their meetings, after Mass or during one of his visits
to the Cameron house, Father Woods became a mentor to
Mary, nurturing her desire to become a nun and to help the
underprivileged. A priority to them both was the provision
of a Catholic-based education to children of poor families,
from which they would acquire a knowledge of God, and an
opportunity to improve their lot in life. In this, Mary was
carrying on a battle fought valiantly by her own father in
many a political skirmish.

When he met Mary, Julian Woods was a young man of 28,
with only three years' experience as a priest. Like her, he had
had a long struggle to follow his vocation. At first Julian
followed in his father's steps as a journalist, working in
London for *The Times*. But he became disenchanted with
the attitudes of his Protestant workmates, and resigned just
two years later. He joined the Passionist Order, but poor
health forced him to leave, as it also did when he joined the
Marist Order in France.

In spite of these setbacks, he continued to travel and to

study, taking a keen interest in both theology and science. He was back in London again in 1854 when he met an Australian bishop, Robert Willson, who offered to take Julian with him to Van Diemen's Land (Tasmania). 'Up to that time,' Father Woods candidly wrote, 'I had regarded exile to the colonies, as I called it, with the greatest aversion.'

As it turned out, 'the colonies' lived up to his worst expectations: he thought Australia a horrible place, and not two months later, was making efforts to earn his return fare to England. He moved to Adelaide, South Australia, where his brother, James, lived, and took a job with the Adelaide *Times*. There he met a young lady who, for a very short while, distracted him from thoughts of becoming a priest. There were two quite conflicting accounts of this affair; one told by Mary, who no doubt heard it from Father Woods himself, and the other by his niece, Mechtilde. Mary's account was definitely the more romantically inspired... '[Father Woods] certainly knew he was not disagreeable to her [the woman in question]; and, as he was invited to spend an evening at her home...he determined he would...decide the important matter,' Mary recalled. 'When the appointed evening came, it brought a grand thunderstorm; heavy rain deluged the streets, and made going out an impossibility. After waiting a considerable time for the rain to cease, the thought occurred to the young man: "It is not the will of God for me to go there". When too late to attempt going, the storm cleared away and a beautiful evening set in.'

However, Mechtilde Woods' report seems a little more likely: 'As the obstacles to his becoming a priest now seemed insurmountable, Julian now thought that it must be God's will that he should enter the married state and he became engaged to a lady whom all his friends thought suitable; but she, after a month's engagement, broke it off and married someone else...' The broken engagement renewed Julian's zeal for the priesthood, and he resumed his studies, this time with Jesuit teachers at Sevenhill, 120 km north of Adelaide. He was made a priest six months later, in January 1857.

Father Woods was assigned to work in Penola, then one of the most isolated districts in the colony and an overwhelming task for any priest. From the abandoned shop that became both church and home, Father Woods composed this honest, but none too flattering, portrait of Penola in *Ten Years in the Bush*: 'You must suppose a place without what you would consider houses. Of course people don't exactly live in caves and holes, but there are no houses; bark huts, slab huts, log huts and weather-boarded huts – but no houses...

'There are no fences,' he wrote. 'A post and rail you did see now and then but generally only a fence of dead trees. What we called a road was a dray track sometimes clear and distinct, but often so flat that you had to use all your ingenuity to keep the course, especially when the grass began to shoot up in the spring.' Another time, he wrote with dry humour, 'If anyone wants to know what the Egyptian must have suffered, let him go to Australia – it does not matter much *where*, for the Australian mosquito defies any attempt at sleep – on land.'

A Jesuit friend, Father Joseph Tappeiner, sensed Father Woods' despondency at the job ahead of him, and tried to offer him some encouragement: 'Your letter looks so gloomy – why that? What reason have you to fear? I see none. The finest country, the best people in the world – what do you want more?' But Father Tappeiner had little to fear – Father Woods' sanguine nature would not allow him to take up this new work with anything but eagerness and enthusiasm. The district he served was large, an area of 51,800 square kilometres and including the townships of Robe, Mount Gambier and Penola. With only a horse for transport, he was often away for weeks at a time. He and Mary kept in touch by letter, although she was much more diligent about it than he. In fact, Father Woods, a man with some wit, had a hard time convincing Mary that the long silences at his end were not a sign that he was unhappy with her.

'I think I have told you about 100 times that if I have much to do and cannot write, you mustn't think that I am in a huff. I think also I have said, say half as many times, that if I should be offended with you, I should tell you so without loss of time... Think of me up to my knees in unopened letters,' Father Woods wrote, 'up to my elbows in ink, up to my eyebrows in postage stamps – obliterated of course – and out of my wits trying to understand where I am, who I am, and how I am to satisfy all. But an end must come. Who knows but I shall be found lifeless at my desk with an epitaph just finished – "He answered his letters – the mail is now closed."' Then, thinking that Mary may be taking his letter too seriously, he finished, 'I give you leave to read this to [your sister] Maggy [sic], for perhaps you may misunderstand, and she will laugh...'

In Father Woods, Mary found an idealist like herself – someone in whom she could confide all her dreams. She told him of her search for a way in which she could leave her family provided for, so that she could follow her 'calling' and become a nun. 'He told me that for a time longer my duty was to them,' Mary said, 'but reassured me as to my vocation, and gave me certain rules for my spiritual guiding. This was Father Woods...my Director...' Mary, too, was an inspiration of sorts to Father Woods, giving new impetus to a plan that had been brewing in his mind for some time. He had long been concerned that the children of his parish had no access to a formal Catholic education, and were growing up strangers to God.

This was a problem which extended far beyond Penola – all the Australian colonies were facing a similar crisis, following the introduction of legislation to curtail the funding received by religious schools. From the 1850s, there was a strong move by the colonial governments to take sole control of education by closing down religious schools and providing government-run schools in their place.

South Australia led the way in this, with its Education Act of 1851 marking the end of funding to religious schools. Government money was only distributed to licensed schools in which non-denominational religious instruction was given (for example, Bible reading, without any interpretation from the teacher). At the time of Mary's arrival in Penola, South Australia's Education Act of 1851 had had its impact. The Catholic Church struggled to keep open a few of its schools in the colony, but in 1858, only two remained.

By 1870, all the other colonies (except Western Australia) had begun to move in the same direction, with Church schools having to comply with increasingly stringent conditions, usually relating to the teaching of religion, the school's position (they were not allowed to be too close to government schools) and size. School fees were subsidised for poorer families, but the stigma attached to such 'handouts' was reason enough for many parents to keep their children at home.

This backlash against religious schools created a number of quite serious problems. Firstly, it denied families the right to give their children a Catholic education. Consequently, there was the quite legitimate fear that it was the beginning of the end of Catholicism in Australia. As well, colonial governments did not have the teachers, buildings, finances or resources to provide proper schools for Australia's very mobile and scattered population. New settlements and remote bush areas were particularly neglected, largely because properly trained teachers just did not want to work there. These areas were frequently served by provisional schools, which had temporary, and often untrained, teachers, sometimes as young as 14.

Even after the introduction of compulsory, 'free', secular education, these problems did not ease. This legislation was introduced in Victoria in 1872, Queensland and South Australia in 1875, New South Wales in 1880, Tasmania in 1885 and Western Australia in 1895. Religious instruction in government-funded schools was banned, though religious denominations had access to children, and although it was supposedly 'free' education, fees were still charged, at least for some subjects. This prevented many poor children from attending. As well, children living more than a few kilometres from the nearest school (a sizeable number in some rural districts) were exempt from compulsory education, allowing parents to keep them at home to help run the properties.

In some colonies, though not in South Australia, rich children in government schools were taught – and played – in separate areas to poor children, and some subjects, such as history, were reserved for rich children only. In this way, genteel Australians could be assured that their children were not being 'corrupted' by the common element. So while colonial governments had policies of universal education and equal educational opportunity, in practice they fell a long way short of such ideals.

The fact that Catholic children were being denied the opportunity to learn about their faith, and that many poor children were not attending school, or were being discriminated against when they did, were problems of which both Mary and Father Woods were very aware. Father Woods considered bringing in teaching nuns from Europe, but South Australia's extreme poverty and harsh conditions, together with its relatively small proportion of Catholics (only 10 percent of its population), made this difficult to afford. By 1860, every colony except South Australia had at least one group of nuns providing lessons to children and welfare to the needy. What was required, Father Woods decided, was a well-educated, cheap, portable and committed teaching force, who were prepared to live as paupers.

He often recalled the teaching Sisters of Auvergne, France, whom he spied while in Europe. They lived simple lives in the barest poverty, teaching basic skills to the village peasants. That such a group of Sisters could work here was an idea 'so wild...so utterly impractical [that Father Woods] scarcely ever spoke of it to anyone'. He had pushed the thought to the back of his mind, but found himself returning to it again and again. This could well be the solution to his problem – to start up a group of Sisters specially designed for Australian conditions. He mentioned his idea to Mary, but warned her not to get too excited about it as he had a lot of thinking to do yet.

In the meantime, Mary improved her teaching skills with the Cameron children then in her care, in preparation for her time ahead as a nun. According to one of the Cameron children, Mary always strove to get the best out of her students. 'You could not face cousin Mary with ill-done work; she would give you a look you couldn't forget.' Mary stayed with the Camerons for about two years, after which time they no longer needed her and she returned to her family in Melbourne.

Within a matter of weeks, however, she was called into action again, this time as governess to some distant relatives, also named Cameron, who lived in the Victorian sea-side town of Portland. This post proved more of a challenge to 20-year-old Mary, as the children were used to having the run of the house, and would not respond to discipline. Worse, there seemed little prospect of her ever being able to leave her family to become a nun. For no want of trying, her father, Alexander, had been unable to find a secure job, and so the pressure on Mary to provide a stable, regular income remained.

In July 1862, with Mary settled in Portland, Alexander decided to try his luck on the goldfields. He headed off to the South Island of New Zealand with his son John, convinced that this time he would make his fortune. However, Flora had seen enough of Alexander's hare-brained ideas not to get overly excited by this one. John wrote to his mother: 'You say that you fear that you will never come over here at all; if such will be the case I am sure it will be no fault of Papa's for he is doing his best and I have not seen him groggy since I left Melbourne...'

The suggestion that Alexander was a little heavy-handed with alcohol was backed up in later years by Annie. 'I believe that he did speculate a lot, and he took too much spirits.' Although occasional bouts of drinking probably did nothing for the MacKillops' fragile family life, there is no evidence that Alexander was an alcoholic. His public antagonists called him many things – but not 'drunkard'.

Alexander's nine-month sojourn in New Zealand turned out to be fruitless: the pickings were not easy, and he ultimately returned home without John, sad and disillusioned.

TEACHING
IN PORTLAND

WHILE Alexander was in New Zealand, and well after his return, Mary continued to support the family, still in Melbourne, through her work as a governess. During her few months in the Cameron household, Mary found the children more than a handful. They were unmanageable and unwilling to learn, and she could do little with them. Accordingly, she began casting her eye around for other prospects. In October 1863, she was offered a job as a teacher in Portland's Catholic Denominational School, which she accepted gladly. Her sister Annie began teaching there a short time later, after the entire MacKillop family moved from Melbourne to Portland in 1864.

Although she was pleased with her new job, Mary had hoped to be made a teacher at a Catholic school Father Woods was planning to take over in Penola. The school was then being run by a Miss Johnson, who held classes at her own home and was charging fees. Father Woods wanted to convert it to a 'free' school, which all children – not just the rich ones – could attend. 'I like the idea [of you teaching at the Penola school] very well,' Father Woods told Mary, 'and would give you all the assistance in my power but I dread very much the presence of your father, to break up your little home again if you made one. I think you should make it understood that he is not to come. As yet, however, there is no knowing when Miss Johnson will give it up.'

Father Woods was long familiar with the 'Alexander' factor: he viewed him as a time-bomb set to go off at any time, and saw no point tip-toeing around the issue for the sake of family pride. On Mary securing the Portland teaching job, Father Woods warned: 'You won't forget that your father is an unfortunate manager and might embarrass your position very much should he get into dispute with ...anyone...in the town whose influence it is in your interests to keep... You may soon be in a position where any indiscretion on his part would bring absolute ruin upon you all.' Mary was not oblivious to her father's faults; in fact, at times, she found it difficult to hide her exasperation with him. Although she only ever spoke of her father in kindness, she told her mother she regretted 'all the impatience and irritability I gave way to so often, particularly towards poor Papa'.

Upon their move to Portland, the family took out a lease on a rambling old guesthouse – Bay View House. With many large rooms spare, Flora thought she would turn it into a 'Seminary for Young Ladies' and try to earn some extra money. Flora did the housework, Mary's sister Maggie taught the three boarders, and Mary and Annie helped out after school.

On finishing all her work, Mary could usually be found praying in the local church. One evening, Mary had her family very worried when she did not return home at the usual time. It turned out that she had been in such deep prayer, she did not hear the church being locked for the night, so she was forced to make a bed for herself on one of the pews. While Mary was at church, the family usually spent their evenings reading, listening to music or dancing. '[Mary] would come in about nine or half-past to find Maggie, Mrs Finn [a family friend] and others practising the latest dances, in which she had no time to join,' Annie recalled. 'And she used to be very sorry for me, as I generally had to play [the piano] the whole evening [for them].'

Although the boarding house drained more funds than it created, it brought the family together in such a way that, for once, it could actually be described as a happy home. Maggie wrote: 'I like Portland very much. Perhaps I would not care for it so much, if we were not all together and in a home of our own at last. Oh! it is so pleasant to have Papa with us. He is so nice, kind and good to us all... I trust in God that we will be able to go on smoothly and keep down our little debts which I have no doubt we will as long as poor Papa keeps as he is doing.'

For Mary, Portland posed the same old problems, and some new ones. While she was glad her family was finally pulling together, the day when she might finally leave them to become a nun seemed more remote than ever. What is more, the Portland people – one in particular – loved her too much to lose her to religious life. '[Mary had]...many difficulties to overcome,' Father Woods' niece, Mechtilde, wrote, 'and suffered through the attention paid to her by a gentleman of wealth and position who desired to wed the virtuous maiden. But Mary had determined to give herself to God alone, and resisted all his overtures.'

Mary's stay in Portland was eventually brought to a close by a disastrous affair in the classroom, precipitated by a visit from the school inspector who was due to examine the children. His visit had been eagerly awaited, because at that time, the level of a teacher's salary depended on the students' results. Mary had worked hard to bring her class up to the mark, and both she and her parents fully expected that she would take home a heavier purse for her efforts.

'Mary...took a great pride in her classes,' Annie wrote, '...and was getting them ready for the Inspector. I had a small class too...and we were getting on famously, when, shortly before the Inspector was expected, Mr Cusack, the head Master, took for himself the classes we had taken such pains with and gave us the backward ones he had had...' Mr Cusack then proceeded to help these 'backward' students through the exam, by furtively holding the answers up on a slate. 'Mary felt it dreadfully and our father was furious when he heard of it...'

Alexander had a stormy meeting with the priest in charge of the school, demanding Mr Cusack be sacked for such blatant deceit. In protest, he also forced Annie to give up her job. Tensions ran high in the little community, as conflicting stories of what exactly had happened in the classroom that day began to emerge. It became so vicious that Alexander lodged a legal complaint against a number of boys who were taunting him in the street. He said if the law would not stop the boys, he would 'bring a case of pistols loaded with green pease [sic] and drive it amongst them'.

When Mr Cusack was at last dismissed, Mary, of all people, was blamed. Amazingly, as her good name and reputation were dragged through the mud, she saw in it the hand of God, giving her the opportunity to finally break with Portland, and begin exploring ways in which she could leave her family and take up a religious life. 'In one short week or more...a storm burst, fearful while it lasted, but it

Mary, aged in her 50s, around the time of her serious illness in Melbourne.

Mary's mother,
Flora MacDonald MacKillop
(1816–1886), would die a tragic death
at age 69.

Photo: Mary MacKillop Archive, North Sydney, NSW.

Mary's father,
Alexander MacKillop (1812–1868),
whose recklessness spelt ruin for the
MacKillop family.

Photo: Mary MacKillop Archive, North Sydney, NSW.

Mary's sisters Lexie (right) and
Maggie (left), around 1870.
Photo: Mary MacKillop Archive, North Sydney, NSW.

Mary's brother Peter and mother
Flora MacKillop, in the mid-1860s.
Photo: Adelaide Catholic Archive.

Royal Oak Hotel, Penola, 1866. Mary stayed here on her arrival in Penola.
The licensee was her uncle Donald MacDonald.
Photo: Mary MacKillop Archive, North Sydney, NSW.

The first school of the Sisters of St Joseph was in Penola, South Australia. It was a converted horse stable. This photo was taken in the 1890s.

Photo: Mary MacKillop Archive, North Sydney, NSW.

This stone schoolhouse in Penola replaced the Stable schoolhouse in 1867 after one year.

Photo: Mary MacKillop Archive, North Sydney, NSW.

Julian Tenison Woods (1832–1889). Father founder of the Sisters of St Joseph and mentor to Mary. Photographed after his ordination in 1857 at age 25.

Photo: Mary MacKillop Archive, North Sydney, NSW.

Father Woods, aged about 34, photographed during his Penola days.

Old Penola homestead, once the home of Mary's uncle and aunt, Alexander ('The King') Cameron and Margaret MacKillop. Mary lived here when 18 years old as governess to their youngest children.

Photo: Arthur Photographic Studio, Mount Gambier, SA, courtesy of Mrs Rymill, Old Penola Station.

The major players: Adelaide priests with Bishop Sheil, September 1866.

Standing: Fathers C.A. Reynolds, P. Hughes, J.E.T. Woods, M.O'Connor, T. Dowling, T. Bongaerts, C.Van der Heyden, F. Byrne, S. Carew, A. Kranewitter SJ. *Seated*: J. Smyth (Vicar General), Bishop L.B. Sheil, J. Tappeiner SJ, P. Russell.

Old church and presbytery at Penola, South Australia, where Father Woods was based in the 1860s.

Photo: Mary MacKillop Archive, North Sydney, NSW.

Bishop's House and 'old' St Patrick's Church in Adelaide, in Bishop Sheil's time, around 1869.

Photo: Adelaide Catholic Archive.

The convent of the Dominican Sisters in Franklin Street, Adelaide, in the 1880s. From 1869 until 1871, the Sisters of St Joseph occupied the buildings to the left and the Dominicans those to the right of the telegraph pole. The tower of St Patrick's Church may be seen in the centre background.

Photo: Adelaide Catholic Archive.

Mary MacKillop aged about 60.

Photo: Mary MacKillop Archive, North Sydney, NSW.

did its work for me... God permitted a very bitter enemy to rise up against me, who said such things of me that all I cared most for, turned against me... The people, even those who strove at first not to believe the things said, took my silence as a confirmation of them, and treated me as an impostor and a traitor.' Years later, Mary spotted Mr Cusack waiting for a ferry at Sydney's Circular Quay. Old, crippled and in rags, he was obviously living a miserable life. Mary was touched and, at once forgetting the past, offered him the little money that she had with her.

Father Woods had been following Mary's misfortunes in Portland, and decided that now was the time for her to move back to Penola and begin preparations to become a nun. Once there, he wanted Mary to take over the Catholic school, as Miss Johnson had since married and given up her job as teacher, and many of the local children were no longer attending classes. She would be the first nun in a group he was planning to set up, who would be solely committed to helping the poor children of the district. However, he knew Mary would never agree to all this unless her family was left financially secure. Somehow, he had to find a solution.

The problem, however, was larger than Father Woods could ever have anticipated. The MacKillops' debts had slowly mounted over the years, not helped by the loss of Annie's income from teaching. They had also unwittingly incurred a fairly substantial debt for a piano. Their music tutor had offered to sell them the instrument, and Mary, knowing how her sister Annie loved to play, wrote to Grandfather MacKillop asking for his help. The money was sent, but Alexander mistakenly believed it was meant for him, and spent the lot.

Father Woods was frustrated that these money matters should stand in the way of his grand plans, so rashly guaranteed to see all the family's debts settled. In her relief and gratitude, Mary gave no thought as to how Father Woods, a poor priest in an even poorer parish, might do this. 'Father Woods will see those dreadful debts paid,' Mary soothed in a letter to her mother, 'not yet for he cannot, but sooner than I could by remaining in this world and earning money for that purpose alone...'

Father Woods could see only one other problem – Alexander. He would have to be put out of harm's way if the family was to have any chance of surviving without Mary. It was agreed Alexander would move to the Hamilton property of his brother, Peter MacKillop, about 80 km north of Portland. Flora would stay on in Portland with her sons Donald and Peter, to tie up loose ends. Maggie would live with Peter MacKillop and his wife, Julia, at one of their other properties at Duck Ponds, near Geelong; and John, who had since returned from New Zealand, would continue looking for a job. Mary and her sisters Annie and Lexie would all go with Father Woods to Penola to assist with the new school.

'At last I began to think that my obligations to my family were nearly fulfilled,' Mary wrote, 'that others could now take the place I had held, and that I could freely turn to God alone.' She was not entirely easy in her mind, however, about Father Woods' plans to split her family – in effect, it amounted to the separation of her parents – and questioned whether it was really necessary. But Father Woods counselled, 'I do really think that [Alexander] should be left to himself even if [it means] the family be broken up. For after all Mary, can your Mamma be trusted to keep things straight with your Papa when you are away? I think not, and the question which remains is, is not her happiness best consulted by breaking up even though she may think it the worst?'

Mary was evidently convinced of the wisdom of Father Woods' words, for she wrote to her mother soon after, 'Though I do feel for [Papa's] lonely state, I hope that much good may be derived from it. In his sad and lonely moments [Papa] must think more of the future...'

These days in Portland were the last that Alexander was to spend with his family. He died on his brother's property at Hamilton some three years later on 19 December 1868, aged 56. 'Though I know nothing of the particulars of poor Papa's death, yet it was a joy above all joys to know that he had been duly prepared,' Mary consoled her mother. Then, in a significant statement on their unhappy homelife, she added, '...The happiness he is now in a fair way of enjoying might have been denied him but for the humiliations and sorrows of the past two or three years... I am sure that you cannot regard Papa's death as a trial.'

SISTER MARY
OF THE CROSS

After all this planning, Penola's school was in fact taken over by Mary's younger sister Annie, then just 17. Annie set out alone for Penola in late 1865 at the request of Father Woods, who was in desperate need of a teacher but could not have Mary because she still had business to clear up in Portland. To ensure she was quick about it, Father Woods told her that while Annie was adequate, 'the school could not be properly conducted until you come up yourself'.

Mary, 24, and Lexie, 15, set out for Penola by coach in January 1866. To Mary's mind, she was making fresh beginnings. The journey symbolised her exit from family life, with all its cares and troubles; at the other end, she hoped to find a peaceful, spiritually fulfilling life as a nun in which she could set about helping impoverished Australians. The three girls rented out a spartan little house, Winella Cottage, which doubled as Penola's new Catholic school for the poor. Both Father Woods and Mary had agreed that lack of money should not prevent any child from attending the school, so fees were paid only by those who could afford them. This was, in fact, a significant breakthrough (the

South Australian colony was still some 10 years off introducing 'free' education) and it went some way towards addressing the needs of poor families, especially Catholics who were mostly Irish labourers, battling to feed and clothe their families, let alone educate them. In adopting this policy, Mary and Father Woods showed their commitment to the education of *all* children, regardless of wealth or social standing.

School lessons were split between two rooms in Winella Cottage and the church. Mary had been keeping an eye out for something more suitable, but money was scarce and rents were high. She then recalled seeing a deserted old stable on the outskirts of town. If she could convince the owner to lease it for a reasonable price, she was sure that it would be just the thing. It was tired and shabby, and in desperate need of repair, but the symbolism of such a beginning could not be ignored. The owner was more than willing to earn a bit of money from what was otherwise useless to him, and he happily leased it to Mary for next-to-nothing. Mary's brother John, a carpenter by trade and eager to help out, set to work to make the old shack weatherproof and more 'school'-like. He used the timber from the horse stalls for doors and windows, patched up the rotted wood, and covered the dirt and hay with floorboards.

From this draughty, rickety old horse house emerged the very first school of what was to become the Institute (or Order) of the Sisters of St Joseph of the Sacred Heart (also known as the Sisters of St Joseph, or colloquially as the Josephites). It opened to the local children in January 1866. Two months later, on 19 March, Mary decided to publicly declare her commitment to becoming a nun and living a life of sacrifice, devoted entirely to God. She emptied her wardrobe of everything except a simple black dress and hat, and began signing her letters 'Mary, Sister of St Joseph'. That day, when Mary unofficially became a Sister of St Joseph, has since been regarded as the birthday of the Institute of the Sisters of St Joseph of the Sacred Heart.

A religious Order (which may also be known as an Institute or Congregation) is a religious community of men (Brothers or priests) or women (Sisters) who share a desire to live their lives solely for God. Many priests, Brothers or Sisters are committed to a particular task or ministry, for example, helping the poor, teaching young children, or nursing the sick. Members of an Order take vows or make promises to God and to their religious authorities relating to the principles they will adhere to throughout their life. Most 'religious' take vows of obedience, chastity and poverty in special ceremonies, somewhat like the vows exchanged at a wedding. Breaking any vow, including that of obedience, is considered an extremely grave matter.

The vow of obedience requires a Sister to obey those to whom she is responsible in the Order or in the wider Church, with those in authority understood to have been put in that position by God. Authority in the Catholic Church stems from the Pope in Rome who, as 'chief bishop', has supreme jurisdiction over the Church. The Pope is advised by high-ranking members of the Church, who also reside in Rome. As such, Rome is the central governing body of the Church; the top rung of a hierarchy that is spread throughout the world. Mary recognised and respected this chain of legitimate authority, and believed it provided the parameters of religious life.

Church men and women consider that they have a duty to obey instructions issued from the Pope or his delegated authority. Each part of the Church throughout the world is divided into a 'diocese'. Dioceses are led by bishops, archbishops or cardinals (on increasingly higher rungs of the hierarchical ladder), depending on the size and prestige of the diocese. In turn, each diocese in divided into the local community or parish, generally led by a priest. It is deeply ingrained in Catholics, particularly among those in religious Orders, that individuals obey their religious leaders, especially bishops and priests. Authority in religious Orders varies according to whether the Order is set up under its own head and governed centrally by its own members with the approval of Rome, or whether its members come under the control of the local bishop in whose diocese they reside.

Each religious Order has a set of rules or a Constitution. This sets out the aims of the Order and the way in which its members should live their lives and perform their duties so as to best achieve their goals. The Constitution enshrines the heart, soul and spirit of an Order. The first Constitution of the Sisters of St Joseph was drawn up by Father Woods, and both he and Mary regarded its provisions as crucial to their newly formed Order. To tamper with the Constitution could, in effect, completely redefine who the Sisters were and what they were all about. In the early days, Father Woods, Mary and the Sisters referred to the document as the Rule. After 1875, when the Church authorities in Rome revised the original Rule, it was referred to as the Constitution. (To avoid confusion, this book uses the term Constitution throughout.)

The name of the Order, the Sisters of St Joseph, was decided on by Father Woods, who was well known for his devotion to St Joseph, the husband of Mary, the mother of Jesus. At one time Father Woods bought two almost life-size statues of the saint for the church and school in Penola. The Sisters of St Joseph were not the first Australian Order of nuns (the Sisters of the Good Samaritan were founded in 1857). However they were the first Order of nuns founded specifically to teach Australia's poor, and they were the first prepared to move out of the cities to serve any need.

For at least the first few years, Father Woods made all the important decisions regarding the Sisters of St Joseph. He considered the Order his special charge, and although Mary was its first member and nominal head, it was he who exercised the final authority.

The fact was, the Sisters of St Joseph would never have come into existence without Father Woods. The Catholic Church was very much a male domain, and the idea that an Order of Sisters could fall under the authority of a woman was considered unwise. It was believed that men occupied a 'higher' place with God, and that Orders of religious women required a man to properly interpret spiritual and theological matters and offer guidance. The Sisters of St Joseph needed Father Woods to gain recognition within the Church – with Mary alone, the Sisters would never have been taken seriously. As such, Father Woods became known as the Director of the Order.

Many young girls joined the newly formed Order, helped along in no small way by Father Woods' winning ways with the opposite sex. He had charisma, a beguiling manner, and a very persuasive personality, which many men found unsettling, but most women found charming. Father Woods also had a certain sex appeal, and there is no doubt that some girls responded to this, joining the Sisters so as to be closer to this most captivating man and to play a part in his grand vision. Mary once said that parents did not like their daughters to talk to the tall, handsome priest with the beautiful voice and witty conversation, lest he might talk them into becoming nuns. 'He would coax a bird off a bush,' said one. 'No woman could resist him,' said another, shaking her head.

There is no doubt that Father Woods was the type of man who could make people do the unexpected. If he were around today, you could well imagine him heading one of those motivational courses which turn out pumped-up, chanting, wild things able to walk across hot coals in their bare feet.

When, one year later, people began to comment on the number of girls Father Woods was inducing to become nuns, one old Presbyterian noted, 'Well now, I think the fashionable girls (and their mothers) ought to be greatly *obleeged* to him for taking so many nice, young, good-looking ones out of the way; there is a better chance for the rest, and dear knows, we have too many old maids already.'

Mary gladly followed the direction set by Father Woods. He was her mentor and her spiritual guide, and for the first few years at least, she never ventured to take a step without his approval. In those days, nuns replaced their surname with a name of religious significance, to symbolise the cutting of ties with the outside world. Father Woods encouraged Mary to take the name 'Mary of the Cross', overriding her personal choice of 'Mary of the Sacred Heart'. The Cross represents the Cross of Jesus and the term is also used to refer to any problems, trials or burdens encountered in daily life, thought to have been sent by God to 'test' a person's character.

It may surprise us now, but Mary saw it as a great privilege to be sent these 'crosses' and to bear them bravely.

She believed that through suffering, she was brought a little closer to God. Even at just 24, Mary had already had her fair share of 'crosses', such as the unexpected deaths of her brother and Grandfather, and her unhappy home life. Years later, during some of the most turbulent times of her life, Mary was able to write: 'The Cross is my portion – it is also my sweet rest and support. I could not be happy without my cross – I would not lay it down for all the world could give. With the Cross I am happy, but without it would be lost.' It is also interesting to note that the Melbourne priest who married her parents gave to Mary's mother, Flora, a tiny sliver of wood believed to be from the cross on which Jesus was crucified. Given this history, Mary of the Cross was certainly an apt name for Mary to take.

In becoming a nun, Mary was required to cut all emotional attachments with her family and friends, so that she would be free to travel to where her work took her. This was a painful process for both Mary and her family, particularly for her mother, who would have been devastated to read the following words from her eldest daughter, not long after she left home: 'I entreated [God] never to let religion cool my great love for you and Uncle – but to permit me to live as though I had forgotten you all – or at least as though completely dead to all I ever loved.'

In the early years, Mary and Father Woods shared a single vision for the Sisters of St Joseph. It seemed logical to them both that the best thing they could do for poor Australians was to give the children an education so they at least had an opportunity of making a better life for themselves. Both wanted the Order and its schools to be totally without pretension, devoted to the education of the poor. 'St Joseph's schools are humble,' Mary wrote, '...intended only for the humble poor and have nothing to do with the great and learned.' Accordingly, Josephite schools broke with the tradition of educating girls and boys to be fine ladies and gentlemen, accomplished in languages, music and the classics. What good would such high-brow skills be, Mary thought, to children who may never see a piano or travel beyond the next township? Every minute in the schoolroom was precious; far better that they learn basic living skills, like how to write a letter and add up a grocery bill. Children were also taught religion, poetry, hymns, grammar, spelling, sewing, geography, English history, Irish history, ancient history, weights and measures and multiplication.

In Josephite schools, every child, regardless of wealth, social position or race, was as special as the other. This was a policy that Mary strictly applied, no matter who it offended: '[In] the early days in Adelaide, Mrs John George Daly desired to send her little son to the Hall school thinking the Governor's grandson would give a tone to the school,' Mary told a friend some years later. 'She requested that her son might be permitted to have a seat near my desk [and a screen put around him to separate him from the other children], but I declined to make any distinctions...'

With an Australian as its founding member, the Josephite Order reflected those qualities at the very heart of the colonial spirit: justice, equality and a fair go for all. There was no room for superior airs and graces – here, the land could make or break a person in a day, and no one knew this better than Mary, who well remembered her own family's fluctuating fortunes. She and Father Woods took extraordinary measures to ensure that all the Josephite Sisters, regardless of their background, were considered on an equal footing. Sisters were forbidden to talk about their former lives, family or childhood experiences, in case some should be considered 'better' than others.

This egalitarian approach to religious life was to upset quite a few priests and bishops, who clung to a tradition in which Sisters were usually the daughters of well-to-do families who brought a handsome dowry for their support. In return, Sisters received a 'gentlewoman's' education and a respectable life, spending their days engaged in quiet prayer, fine needlework and gentle talk. Such Sisters were known as teaching or 'choir' Sisters. There were also 'lay' Sisters, from poorer families, who did the domestic work. This was the way in which other Orders of Sisters operated. However, Mary's vision for the Sisters of St Joseph was different. Family lineage, wealth and education had no bearing on who could join the Order; in fact, some of the Sisters had previously been servants and had never seen the inside of a schoolroom. For some status-conscious Churchmen, this was a bitter pill to swallow. Mary recalled how one priest was most upset because a certain Sister had once been his own servant, and he 'therefore could not understand how she was fit for the school'. Another priest remembered one of the Sisters living 'very humbly', and could not now 'respect her as a teacher for their children'.

Mary was determined that the Sisters of St Joseph were to be no different to other Australians. They would come from ordinary families, they would face the same hardships, the same struggle for survival. Unlike members of other Orders, the Sisters would not hide behind high walls of city convents. They would live anywhere. If the work was in the bush, this was where the Sisters would be sent. They would live in twos and threes, in makeshift huts and shacks of wattle and daub, bark and iron, or whatever was on hand. There would be no homely comforts – they would live day to day, like the people they served. They would take solace from the inner peace and spiritual fulfilment which came from a life devoted to God.

Mary's first taste of 'convent' life at Penola's Winella Cottage, which she shared with Lexie and Annie from 1866, was a long way from the spiritually calm existence she had envisaged. Her sisters were always pulling pranks, designed to distract her from her prayers, if not scare her half to death. 'There were quite a number of snakes in the district,' Annie wrote, 'and one of the tricks [we] played was to put the tail of an ox into Mary's bed to make her think there was a snake there. [We] were delighted with her cries of alarm.'

Another time, Mary told Annie of a dream she had in which she was a sheep being 'dipped' by the bishop. Far from being sympathetic, Annie saw it as a great opportunity for a laugh at Mary's expense. Playing 'bishop', she dressed up in a sheet, taking a broom for a crosier. As she expected, she found Mary at her prayers. With great theatrics, she began prodding her with the broom, then washing her down with the wet bristles. She was disappointed, but not surprised, when Mary refused to take the bait, and continued, head down, with her fervent murmurings.

Despite Annie and Lexie's frivolous ways, Father Woods never gave up trying to convince them to become nuns. Annie did not believe she was pious enough for the austere convent life, but with young Lexie, Father Woods had more success. Lexie was an impressionable teenager, and was somewhat in awe of this man with the grand plans and the sparkle in his eye. Inspired by his enthusiastic talk, she soon joined Mary in becoming a 'postulant' (a trainee nun). Each was addressed as 'Sister', and they wore black dresses, with rosary beads looped at their waist.

Next to join was Blanche Amsinck, a highborn Englishwoman whose family disinherited her on discovering she had become a Catholic. Father Woods assigned Blanche and Lexie to run a school in Mount Gambier, 50 km to the south of Penola. For spiritual guidance, he gave them a short list of rules to follow. However, things seemed to go wrong for Blanche and Lexie from the start. Lexie still had doubts about whether she really wanted to be a nun, and Blanche seemed unable, or unwilling, to shed her grand English airs. She was bossy and overbearing, and off-loaded a lot of her duties onto Lexie. Reports soon got back to Mary, not to mention the MacKillop family, who were less than impressed with the way in which Lexie had been coaxed and cajoled by Father Woods into taking a decision they believed she was not ready for.

The girls' mother, Flora, was particularly critical, saying Lexie was too young to hand her life over to Father Woods and his madcap schemes. She also resented the pressure being put on Annie to become a nun, and this, together with talk from her son Donald that he was going to become a priest, left her bitter and angry. 'Mamma's first letter was a very unkind, or as I thought, unjust one,' Mary protested to Father Woods, 'and she blamed me for the way I was bringing Annie up and objected to her remaining here any longer...'

It is easy to understand Flora's frame of mind. Living apart from Alexander, she had no one to provide or care for her. Now, with most of her surviving children 'deserting' her for a religious life, she no doubt saw herself old and unloved, with no grandchildren to dote over, left to live out a meagre, lonely life. Mary tried to offer some reassuring words: 'Do not, dearest Mamma, wish that Lexie should see more of the world. When I was her age I began first to long for a religious life...', but she was only dragged deeper into what had become quite a vicious family squabble. Mary received a letter from Aunt Julia and Uncle Peter MacKillop 'which certainly does not deserve an answer...' They pitied her 'infatuation', and told her it was 'like her impudence' to think she could start a new Order of Sisters.

Convinced that Lexie was intended by God to be a nun, Mary kept up efforts to win her mother around: 'Do not, I beg, try to put her against leading a religious life. There is so much we might do for God, and yet it is so easy to overlook these things...for the sake of following or being led by the practice of...a very sinful and silly world.' It all came to a head when Father Woods decided to pay a visit to Aunt Julia, Uncle Peter, and Mary's sister Maggie, at Duck Ponds near Geelong, to see if he could smooth things over. Not surprisingly, he got a sharp reception. Wincing, he heard himself described as an 'imaginative enthusiast not overblessed with candour and sincerity'. He reported to Mary: 'Maggy [sic] privately opened her batteries about Lexie and said that they were determined to have her away from Mount Gambier... They dread her future unhappiness if she were not permitted to choose what she might when older repent of... They...plainly gave me to understand that they mistrusted me, and could not think that I was dealing candidly and sincerely with them, that I was using my influence over Lexy [sic] in a way which would prevent her having the courage to differ from me...'

Lexie had had her misgivings about the whole business from the start, and her family's staunch opposition was all she needed to pull out and return home. Surprisingly, just four years later in 1871, Lexie joined another Order, the

Sisters of the Good Shepherd, in Melbourne, where she remained all her life. The desire to become a nun had obviously been there all along, but had been obscured by family tensions, the constant pressure applied by Father Woods, and possibly the prospect of living in the shadow of her high-profile sister.

With Lexie's sudden departure from the fledgling Sisters of St Joseph, a new postulant, Rose Cunningham, moved to Mount Gambier to take her place. Rose also had a 'will-I-won't-I' attitude towards joining the Order and required a few firm prods from Father Woods before finally agreeing. Like Lexie, Rose was not one of the Order's success stories. She had a mental breakdown only a few years later and, although she remained a Sister all her life, she spent her last 47 years in a mental asylum. Neither Mary nor Father Woods were disconcerted by these early setbacks, and never stopped to consider whether they may, in fact, have been a little overzealous in their 'recruitment campaign'. By 1871, just over 120 girls, with an average age of 23, had taken their vows as Sisters of St Joseph.

There were many different reasons girls joined the Order. Although it was emphasised that becoming a nun was not a way in which to escape an unhappy or lonely life, it almost certainly was for some. Girls from dirt-poor families, with little or no education, were desperate not to follow in the footsteps of their mothers, who were often left to run the farm, pay the bills and raise a horde of children while their husbands went off to earn money, droving, gold-digging or perhaps working on the new railway lines. For those with no prospect of a 'good' marriage, who may otherwise have ended up as domestic servants or factory hands, joining the convent was viewed as a very respectable alternative.

Others were captivated by the charisma and vision of Father Woods, or by the selflessness and dedication of Mary. They thought that by living like them, they could perhaps *be* like them and 'absorb' some of their very special qualities. However, most believed they had been 'called' by God to take up a religious life. They joined the Sisters of St Joseph because they shared a commitment to easing the burden of poverty in Australia by teaching poor children. These girls also believed that in devoting their lives to the work of God, they were securing a place for themselves in heaven.

If a girl thought she was intended by God to lead a religious life, then Mary and Father Woods were quite determined that no obstacles should be put in her way. 'I met Mother Mary [the name by which Mary was to become known to the Sisters] for the first time when she was visiting the schools in South Australia,' one nun, Sister Josephine, recalled. 'I was then a girl of nearly 15 and had just returned to school after being ill with typhoid fever. Mother Mary gave us an instruction in the school and at its close she said she was on the lookout for girls who would be willing to come and serve our Lord.

'Up to that time I had no intention of becoming a nun,' Sister Josephine admitted. 'There and then I made up my mind to go with Mother Mary. I went home and told my parents. Father sent for the doctor and asked him if it would be all right for me to go so soon after the fever. The doctor said, "Man, are you mad? Where is this Mother Mary? I'll see her."

'So Mother was sent for,' Sister Josephine continued, 'and when she came into the doctor's presence, he said, "You wouldn't be foolish enough to take that child into your convent, would you?" Mother Mary said, "Yes, doctor."

'"But," said he, "you'll be responsible for her death."

'"There'll be no death," said Mother Mary. "She'll grow stronger and do a lot of work for God..." So Mother took me with her and as she said I grew stronger every day...'

Fortunately for Mary and Father Woods, their determination to make a success of the Sisters of St Joseph was matched by that of the bishop of Adelaide, Bishop Sheil, who headed the diocese, or church district, to which Penola belonged. He was impressed with the work of the Sisters there, and was keen to move them into the rest of South Australia. Accordingly, the bishop invested Father Woods with significant powers, appointing him his secretary, and Director General of Catholic Education, Chairman of the Board and Inspector of the Schools.

In early 1867, while most of Australia was absorbed in the coming colony-by-colony tour of Queen Victoria's son, Prince Albert, Father Woods was preparing to leave Penola to take up his new duties in Adelaide. In his role as head of Catholic education in the colony, Father Woods began a blitzkrieg through South Australian schools which left teachers and fellow priests speechless. He reported that he was less than satisfied with the overall standard of Catholic education, and unceremoniously sacked 'unqualified' teachers and closed many of the smaller schools. While Penola had learned to tolerate this high-handed, autocratic style of Father Woods, it did not go down well with the Adelaide clergy. They considered Father Woods arrogant and impetuous, and believed he would be the ruin of the Catholic education system.

The ill-feeling escalated when Father Woods began replacing 'unfit' teachers with Sisters who were not yet properly trained themselves. In many cases, teenage girls were taken into the convent one day, and were standing before a classroom the next. Many of these untrained Sisters were unproductive in the classroom, a drain on precious funds and an embarrassment to the Church. Another problem was that when a Sister had finally settled in to a new school, it often happened that Father Woods would uproot her and send her somewhere else. Soon, Adelaide priests were murmuring amongst themselves about the 'erratic' Father Woods and his incompetent nuns.

Meanwhile, the Sisters were having their own problems coping with Father Woods' whimsies. One nun recalled that if Father Woods met a novice and greeted her, he would reprove her for breaking silence if she answered him, and for disrespect if she did not. Another remembered how he tore up a letter a Sister received from her family because, in her excitement for permission to open it, she had dared to ask if he had noticed it on the table. For his own part, Father Woods could not understand why he had engendered so much animosity. He wrote to Mary of 'the constant opposition the attempt to establish education meets from even the good and pious... I was attacked in the papers, and though that is a mere trifle, yet I feel deeply, that my efforts are not believed in, by those whose aid would be most valuable to me.'

For all the legitimate complaints against Father Woods and the Sisters, in some cases criticisms were prompted by the deep-seated chauvinism and elitism of European-bred Churchmen. 'What can you expect from colonial girls without any knowledge of a religious life and no one to train them?' a few muttered disparagingly amongst themselves. It was an attitude Mary was to encounter innumerable times throughout her life.

Despite the hostility, Father Woods pushed on with plans to introduce the Order to the rest of South Australia. Mary and Rose Cunningham would set up a school in Adelaide, he decided, while Annie stayed behind in Penola to manage the school. In preparation for the move, Mary began to piece together the uniform or 'habit' the Sisters would wear. Uncharacteristically, Father Woods left this matter entirely in Mary's hands, although he did insist that whatever she chose, she should be sure it did not 'frighten the children'. After much thought, Mary decided on a black alpaca dress (alpaca was the cheapest and hardiest material then available) with a full skirt gathered at the waist, a small white gimp (a heavily starched bib which fitted snugly around the neck and fell to just above the waist), a black veil, a thick black leather belt buckled at the back, a crucifix and rosary beads. This was the traditional dress of nuns in the 19th century. Both Father Woods and Mary believed that this style of dress would make the Sisters more acceptable to the Adelaide Catholics.

The choice of habit was probably not one of Mary's better decisions. The only evidence that there was flesh and blood under all that billowing material was the tiny face that peeped out from the white, starchy stuff that gripped the neck. The habit was restrictive and suffocatingly hot, and of such an out-of-this-world design that the children were probably not so much frightened as terrified. After the Second Vatican Council in the 1960s, the habit was slowly modified to something less intimidating and more suited to the Australian climate.

For the time being, however, the Sisters were stuck with their habit, which they began wearing on reaching Adelaide in mid-1867. Just a few months later, they changed over from black to brown alpaca, because it was more readily available. At Father Woods' suggestion, the Sisters also cut their hair very short, for practical reasons more than anything else. At the time, it was the fashion for women to wear their hair long. However, as the Sisters' hair would not be on show – this was considered a sign of vanity and immodesty – it would be easier to keep neat and clean if it was cut short.

The move to the bustling centre of Adelaide was a significant one for the Josephites, but Mary was adamant that there should be no change to their humble lifestyle. She wrote to Father Woods: 'Please do not let the young lady who is furnishing the home for us forget that we must be very poor... I hope she is not getting any carpets or nice window curtains... We can, however, have everything neat and clean.'

On arriving in Adelaide, Mary and Rose settled first in a tiny cottage in Grote Street, then in Franklin Cottage in Franklin Street, which became the Adelaide convent. They had little money, slept on straw beds, and went begging for food. '[The Sisters] used to go out carrying large carpet bags in which they placed the alms given them,' one nun later recalled, 'and then carried them home, often panting and exhausted from the load they had to carry... Sometimes, on these begging expeditions, the Sisters had to suffer severe insults...' Many priests were embarrassed by such a shameful display of poverty, and told the bishop of Adelaide, Bishop Sheil, that they thought this was totally inappropriate behaviour for women of the Catholic Church. Bishop Sheil, however, remained firm in his support for the Sisters.

After Mary had been in Adelaide about a month, Father Woods told her that she was now ready to take her first vows to become a fully fledged Sister. On 15 August 1867, probably in a room at the back of the Grote Street Cottage, Mary made her promises of obedience, chastity and poverty, adding a fourth vow, to promote the love of Jesus Christ in the hearts of children. In the ceremony, carefully devised by Father Woods, Mary wore a crown of thorns on her head and a cross on her shoulders, as a reminder of the way in which Jesus died on the cross and to reinforce Mary's duty to suffer gladly for God.

Trembling, 25-year-old Mary left the cottage that day as the very first Sister of St Joseph.

CHAPTER 5

THE FIRST SISTERS
OF ST JOSEPH

MARY spent her early months in Adelaide trying to make a success of the Order's first school there. It had got off to a sluggish start, with an enrolment of just 60 students – the locals were naturally cautious, and wanted a chance to observe these strange-looking women for themselves. However, confidence in the Sisters grew each day, and just six months later there were 200 students on the roll, as well as quite a few new members for the Order.

Unlike many other Orders then in Australia, the work of the Sisters of St Joseph extended beyond the school gates, and included visiting hospitals, sick-rooms and gaols, and sheltering the homeless. By July 1868 there were 30 Sisters and 8 Josephite schools in South Australia, as well as a Josephite orphanage and a home for women in 'moral danger', known as The Refuge, which took in former gaol inmates, former prostitutes and unmarried mothers. However, even with these charitable institutions, there were still many people left on the streets. Government welfare was practically non-existent in Australia before the 1900s, and in Adelaide, the Destitute Asylum was the only place which provided care and shelter for the homeless. People relied on family, friends and neighbours to get them through times of crisis, but others had no help at all. To offer some relief, Mary and Father Woods decided to open up another crisis accommodation centre.

Despite a drastic shortage of money, the Sisters of St Joseph started up The Providence in Adelaide in 1868. It would cater for neglected children, young people in 'moral danger', old people and homeless migrant women, of all races and religions. The name, Providence, was chosen because the Sisters relied entirely on God to provide the resources needed to keep it open. They went out door-knocking each day to collect donations – food, clothing, money – from residents in neighbouring areas. They also did plain sewing for a small payment. Initially, The Providence was not a mixed house – it provided accommodation for women only. The Sisters helped men with food and clothing, but they had to find their own accommodation. Six months after opening, The Providence had helped 100 women and children with emergency short-term accommodation. Mostly, people stayed at The Providence while looking for work or a permanent home, but they could come and go as they pleased. Many died there, and the Sisters always scraped together enough money to give each person a proper funeral.

In 1869, the Sisters opened The Solitude in Adelaide, to provide care and accommodation for the aged, the terminally ill, and alcoholics. There were then 72 Sisters and 21 schools throughout South Australia. Life for the Sisters was hard and demanding, and Mary always kept in mind how difficult the adjustment to convent life could be, particularly for the youngest girls. She knew all the Sisters' names, and wrote regularly to each and every one of them.

A friend and confidante, Mary was able to provide the Sisters with the encouragement and support they needed to cope with the fears and uncertainties of their new lifestyle. She was generous with her praise and gentle with her reprimands, and demanded no less of herself than she did of others.

In these early years, the Sisters quickly established themselves in the hearts of the local people, who were ever-thankful that their children were at last receiving a Catholic education. (Admittedly though, some of the Sisters' practices, such as marching the students home in a procession, did raise some eyebrows. The latter was soon stopped because it was impractical.) But the Sisters also had their detractors – ironically, from within the Catholic Church itself. Many priests thought the Order was expanding too quickly, and were quite vocal in their opposition. But while ever they had Adelaide's Bishop Sheil on their side, Father Woods and the Sisters were untouchable. In an address, Bishop Sheil gratefully acknowledged that 'the untiring zeal and ardent self-devotion of the Very Reverend Father Woods have relieved me from all anxiety of providing for the Catholic education of the humbler classes...'

To protect the Sisters from unwanted interference from disgruntled priests, Father Woods thought it would be wise for the bishop to endorse the Order's Constitution, the document which enshrined the spirit of the Sisters of St Joseph, setting out the rules and principles they were to follow in their day-to-day lives. Two of the main rules were that the Sisters should live in poverty and have no possessions, and that they were to be governed by a head Sister, accountable to Church authorities in Rome and not under the control of the local bishop. This was known as central government, and was to prove extremely controversial. The reason for central government was mainly the vast distances between the colonies in Australia, and the difficulty of building a united Order if local bishops could impose their own rules on the scattered convents.

Mary and Father Woods felt equally passionate about the other key issue in the Constitution – poverty. Mary wanted the poverty provision of the Constitution to include the most specific details, like, the Sisters should sleep on wooden stretchers for beds instead of iron bedsteads, and use unbleached calico for sheets and nightdresses. Today, in an era of rampant consumerism, it is difficult to understand this uncompromising commitment to poverty. Why were Mary and Father Woods so determined to own nothing and survive on charity? Surely it would have been easier to help those in need if they were not so much in need themselves?

Poverty has, in fact, been a central element in the Constitutions of a number of religious Orders through the centuries. Perhaps the most famous example of all is St Francis of Assisi and his founding Order, the Friars Minor, also known as the Franciscans. Francis, who lived in Italy in the Middle Ages, was born into a wealthy family, but was sickened by the contrast of his life to the squalor, disease and misery he saw all around him. Inspired by the words of Jesus he decided to give up all possessions – his money, fine clothes and grand house – to live in the bleakest poverty, sheltering in doorways, caves and hovels, and surviving on scraps.

The Sisters of St Joseph and the Friars Minor were founded on similar principles – both served and lived amongst the poor and sick, and led austere lives. The Friars went barefoot, and wore clothes made from rags or sack-cloth. They were forbidden to carry anything with them on their journeys through the Italian countryside, as these were considered possessions; and they were never to handle money – they could accept only food or shelter as 'payment' for their work.

Francis was dedicated to a life of poverty in imitation of Jesus and because he believed that through suffering he would become more like Jesus. He viewed material possessions as a distraction from the real work that needed to be done amongst the sick and poor, and an obstacle between people and God. Francis also believed that with possessions came power and pride, and that you could only truly serve the poor once you had experienced their pain. Mary and Father Woods shared these beliefs, but also maintained that if the Sisters owned property they would not be free to move around the countryside as they were required. They also believed that in becoming attached to money, property and other material possessions, the Sisters would lose interest in serving the poor. It is relevant to note that one of the Sisters' most ardent supporters, Bishop Sheil, was a Franciscan, and no doubt these shared ideals had some part in his support of the Josephites. He gladly signed their Constitution, lending it the weight of his personal approval, on 17 December 1868. Ten months later, in 1869, Bishop Sheil left for Europe, where he stayed for almost 18 months. In his absence, Father John Smyth who, as Vicar General, assisted in the administration of the diocese, was left in charge.

During the late 1860s, news from the MacKillop homefront was not good. Late in 1867, Mary's 22-year-old brother John, who had returned to New Zealand, died after falling from a horse and developing tetanus poisoning. Mary was shocked and saddened by her brother's death – she had always been close to John, who had helped her set up the 'stable' schoolhouse in Penola. Mary's mother, Flora, fell into a kind of depression on hearing the news, made worse by mounting financial pressures. She still owed tradesmen about one hundred pounds from the family's days in Portland, and had written to Father Woods over and over again, urging him to fulfil his promise to see her debts paid. 'I have been refused meat and bread unless I paid so much of the old account,' Flora told him. 'Indeed several threatened to take me to court. All this I concealed from Mary as I felt the poor girl was overtaxed. So dear Father Woods, you can hardly blame me for giving way to lowness of spirit.'

In the end, Flora's debts were covered from money Grandfather MacKillop had left to charity in his will, and an inheritance to Mary from her father's sister, Anne. Father Woods did not pay a cent, not because he chose to dishonour a promise, but because, quite simply, he was stony broke (arguably something he should have thought of beforehand). 'God will always take care of you...,' he wrote to Flora. 'Ask [God] to detach you from the world... I agree with you perfectly in thinking that you are not long for this world but that is no sad news to anyone.' Reading these words a century later, they sound quite heartless, but for Father Woods there was no kinder thought than wishing someone dead (and, presumably, with God).

For all his foibles, Father Woods could only be applauded for his efforts in supporting and promoting the Sisters of St Joseph. At a meeting of Australian bishops held in Melbourne in 1869, Bishop James Quinn of Brisbane (the Brisbane diocese took in all of Queensland) said he was interested in trying out the Sisters in his diocese. Father

Woods jumped at the opportunity of sending the Sisters into another colony, and began making arrangements.

The group, which included Mary, arrived in Brisbane in December 1869 as the mercury was peaking, and with troublesome mosquitoes in plague proportions. The Sisters lived in a breezy old building, formerly a pub, that offered no protection against the nightly raids of what Mary described as her 'little tormentors'. The first two nights, the mosquitoes had a feast, but on the third night, the Sisters decided that prayer was their best weapon. 'On the third night and since the prayer has been said, though the room is full of them we all sleep in peace.'

The move to Brisbane was like starting all over again – the Sisters were a bit of a mystery to the community, and it took time to gain their support. When the money ran dry, as it often did, the Sisters relied on God to put food on their table. 'When Mother Mary was in Queensland and had no food,' one Sister recalled, '…she put the statue of St Joseph on the window-sill asking for him to provide food. A good Catholic lady was out shopping for her family, and the thought passed through her mind that those "poor strange nuns" might be in their convent without anything to eat. She took them a basket of provisions and kept up the practice as long as the Sisters were in that part of Brisbane.'

The Sisters' residence – a hotel – shocked the locals, not because it had at one time been a trading house for the 'devil's drink', but because it was believed to be haunted. Mary was quietly amused by their superstitions, but never gave them a second thought…until something started going bump in the night. 'Since our retreat,' she wrote to Father Woods, 'we have not been a night free from disturbances in the Convent. Sometimes the most unearthly noises, sometimes the Sisters are violently shaken in their beds. Other times nearly smothered, but nothing is seen all the while. Sometimes awful noises like thunder, and one night we really thought some part of the house would come down there was such racing all over it.' Another time, she wrote: 'I am sure Horney [her nickname for the ghost] was at work there, the noises, screams and pattering of bare feet was something dreadful to those who heard them. As for me, I did not hear either the pattering or scream but I did hear the rest. The Sisters say it all seemed to come from our door, that is, the door of the room in which Sister Josephine and I sleep...'

A few months later, Mary jotted nervously at the end of a letter, 'I must stop for tonight. It is getting near the time for Master Horney's visits, and I have not courage enough to stay up late.' These letters appear to have been written in earnest, and for level-headed Mary to be so shaken, someone – or something – was clearly making mischief.

While the Sisters' nights were disrupted by Horney's eerie visits, their days were up-ended by the crazy doings of Mary Joseph, a homeless girl who had accompanied them from Adelaide because Father Woods believed she was 'saintly'. Mary Joseph's wild rampages were a constant theme in Mary's letters to Father Woods in early 1870, where she tried again and again to convince him that a convent was not the place for a person who was obviously insane:

> '[She] has an unearthly appearance that often terrifies those who see her. Her eyes are so wild and vacant – and her ideas sometimes sweetly beautiful – and perhaps in the next moment extremely dangerous...'

'She has a mania for secreting knives and any sharp instrument which she can on her person or in her bed, and with these she says she must kill the big people. Sometimes she says Sister Clare and I must die…'

'She is like a perfect fiend let loose in the house – cunning and untruthful in the extreme at times – and heartlessly selfish as well. I am often for days together obliged to remain in the house to prevent some glaring mischief or scandal…'

'No one about her thinks her quite sane, and were it not for that and the charity of the people, we might have the convent forced open sometimes to see what could be the matter. She screams and kicks and uses the most dreadful language to the Sisters…'

'She publicly disgraced herself and us last Sunday… She went out on the green field in front of the Convent and in the face of a number of people…waded in and out, over and over again, through the water which the heavy rains had caused to lodge there. Then she sat down under the heavy rain… She continued thus all day…'

'I had to get a Catholic policeman…to come and frighten her into a sense of what she was doing… [but] she was so hardened and impudent that she made him cry.'

However, Father Woods insisted that Mary Joseph stay on at the convent. He believed God had given him a special ability to see into the future, and in the first of many dreadfully misguided predictions he was to make in his life, he said Mary Joseph was a saint in the making. 'Her wonderful sanctity will yet astonish you all. She won't, however, see fullness of age. She will perform miracles both before and after death.' He then doled out some harsh words for pragmatic Mary: 'I fear (a little, just a little) that sometimes you look too humanly at things and people and their motives and conduct.' After a number of months, Mary Joseph no longer figured in Mary's letters. Surprisingly, she did eventually join the Josephites at Bathurst – no doubt at Father Woods' insistence – but how her mental health bore up is difficult to say, as there is very little on record about this period of her life. When an offshoot Order, the diocesan Sisters of St Joseph, also known as the Black Josephites, was formed in Bathurst, Sister Mary Joseph joined them. She remained there until her death, and is buried in the Sisters' plot.

Back in 1869, at the time of the Sisters' arrival in Queensland, James Quinn was the bishop of Brisbane. His younger brother, Matthew, was the bishop of Bathurst, New South Wales. Over the coming years they were to play a large part in Mary's life and in the controversial shaping of the Josephites.

The Quinn brothers were members of a powerful contingent of Irishmen who basically ruled the Church in 19th century Australia. Most of this group, including James and Matthew, studied together in Rome, and from this developed a bond of loyalty that rendered them a formidable force. Many of these leading Churchmen were also blood relations – the Quinn brothers, for instance, were also cousins of New South Wales' bishop of Maitland, Dr Murray, who was the grand-nephew of the archbishop of Dublin.

James Quinn was appointed the first bishop of Brisbane six years before his younger brother, Matthew, was made the first bishop of Bathurst. Both were strong-minded men, who ruled their districts with an arm of steel. Of the two, James was by far the more dangerous. He was intelligent, graceful and outwardly charming, yet could turn at the merest hint of opposition. Mary was always cautious with the bishop, who she described as 'a terrible man', and yet 'most winning' and 'hard to resist'.

For the duration of Mary's stay in Queensland, from December 1869 to early 1871, Bishop James Quinn was away in Europe. However, he had left his administrator, the Vicar General, Dr Cani, with strict instructions on how to handle the Sisters. They were a little too feisty for his liking, particularly when it came to defending their Constitution. There were several points in the Josephite Constitution with which James Quinn vehemently disagreed, such as their refusal to accept government grants for education (a condition of such grants was a restriction on the teaching of religion in the classroom, to which Father Woods and Mary would never agree) and the fact that they were centrally governed, answerable to a head Sister rather than the bishop. He was convinced that these untenable rules were merely the whim of a woman who did not know any better, and that a show of strength on his part would quickly resolve the problem.

However, Bishop Quinn failed to realise what a formidable opponent he had in Mary. She made it clear to Bishop Quinn's Vicar General, Dr Cani, that the Constitution was non-negotiable, and she would rather see the Order disbanded than change it. 'He [Dr Cani] told me he thought there was a great deal of selfishness in this,' Mary reported to Father Woods, 'and wondered that we could think of objecting to anything the Bishop approved of... I told him I could not understand how the Bishop, in his conversation with you in Melbourne, had not clearly seen the spirit of our [Order] in this matter... My opinion is that they both understood it, but thought we would not be particular in opposing the Bishop's wishes,' Mary noted astutely.

This was, in fact, quite true. The bishop knew exactly what the Sisters were about long before they arrived in Brisbane – in fact, he had promised Father Woods 'that the [Constitution] should not be interfered with'. Mary realised she was being bullied, and quietly determined that she would not allow the Constitution to be pushed aside. In a letter to Father Woods five months later, she wrote '...I think there is every likelihood that our [Constitution] will be much interfered with in Queensland... [Dr Cani] does not seem to think that I have any right to wish to carry things out in any way but as seems best to himself and the Bishop.'

The friction with Dr Cani over the Constitution made life very difficult for the Brisbane Sisters. He was the only priest allowed to hear the Sisters' confessions and offer spiritual guidance, and yet he managed to visit them just once a month. When he did stop by, he was peevish and aloof. 'I feel so powerless, so utterly unable to represent anything clearly to [Dr Cani],' Mary told Father Woods. 'He silences me at once when I try by saying that I am too self-sufficient, that it is my own way I am seeking, and more that I cannot remember. I feel that he gives me only what I deserve, and that is contempt...'

Mary tried to keep her problems with Dr Cani in perspective, at times managing even a touch of humour: 'I think him a truly holy man,' she once wrote, 'one whose virtues are little known excepting to heaven...' On one level, Mary actually felt sorry for Dr Cani and the rest of the Brisbane clergy, as she sensed that their working relationship with Bishop James Quinn was quite strained. All, she believed, were intimidated by him. 'I think Dr Quinn must have a very determined will. All seem so afraid of crossing him.'

Despite these political tensions, Mary remain focussed on the work at hand, which was to bring free Catholic education to children of the poor in Queensland. Within just three months, the Sisters had opened three schools in Brisbane with more than 300 students.

In many ways, Mary's year-long stay in Brisbane marked a 'coming of age'. For once, she began to taste a little independence, and act without the guidance of Father Woods. The conflict with Dr Cani, although unpleasant, left her mentally stronger and more confident, and somewhat wiser to the politics of the Church. Mary was sensitive by nature and hated confrontation, but realised that in standing firm on the issues that were important to the Sisters, she would come under fire. If the Order was to survive, she would have to grow a tough shell, and close her mind to everything but the welfare of the Sisters and the people they served.

Because it was her first long absence from Adelaide, at times Mary found herself feeling quite lonely and despondent. She missed the Sisters, and eagerly awaited the bundle of letters they sent each week. It was the little everyday things she liked to hear about – the doings of some mischievous child at school, how such and such a Sister had mended a hole in the roof, or how they had all begged and scraped to meet this month's rent.

Father Woods also wrote. but Mary found his letters unsettling. It appeared that two of the Sisters, Sister Ignatius (who was in charge in Adelaide while Mary was away) and Sister Angela, had convinced Father Woods that they were 'mystics', and that God was acting through them.

Father Woods was most excited by all this, and eagerly relayed to Mary the latest 'proof' of their powers: 'S. Ignatius was ill,' he wrote, 'and Sister Angela has been visited again in a very trying manner. Sister Clare heard her moaning last night and found a great log of wood lying across her neck... it was an hour before she and Sisters Ignatius and Clare could restore her to consciousness. I saw the log of wood and didn't know whence the devil could have brought it... There were two this time,' Father Woods marvelled, 'one like a serpent and another like an ape. Sister Ignatius saw one but he was like a cat... On Monday one threw S. Angela down and tore her habit in many places by beating her chest very much and trampling upon her. He also tore her chest very much and made it bleed...'

Several months later, Mary received an update: 'Sister Angela's bed was set on fire last night and her clothing burnt but she was unimpaired.' And again, 'Last night the devil heated a saucepan of boiling grease and threw it over S. Ignatius as she was in bed and asleep... She is very much scalded about the head, hands and face, but not dangerously.'

Mary, ever the realist, believed it was all nonsense, harmful nonsense at that, and that Father Woods was being led by the nose by two very cunning Sisters. She suspected Ignatius and Angela were trying to outdo each other, to establish themselves as Father Woods' 'favourite', and that they would go to ever-greater lengths to achieve this end. Mary's confidence in Father Woods was shaken, and for the first time she began to harbour serious concerns about the direction in which he was leading the Sisters.

THE 'MYSTICS' FIASCO

THE fanatical displays of the Adelaide 'mystics' did nothing for the little credibility Father Woods had left with Adelaide priests. Most shook their heads and deplored his lack of 'proper training' in spiritual and theological matters, and acknowledged among themselves that the Sisters of St Joseph were doomed under his directorship. Mary herself had similar fears and would have recalled, with some pain, his own words to her: 'I never read a spiritual book now, especially those which treat of supernatural things. I don't know anything about the theory and I dread to learn.' She determined that no matter what the consequences, it was her duty to alert Father Woods to the possibility that he was being fooled by the 'mystics'.

Mary's time in Brisbane allowed her to view her mentor a little more objectively. From a distance, ironically, his flaws had begun to come into view – his gullibility, his self-righteousness, his dogmatism, his fanaticism. As well, she had developed more confidence in her own judgement and, as a result, began to question his. However, when the time came for her to speak her mind on the 'mystics' affair, she was not as brave as she would have liked. Though Father

Woods' star now shone a little less brightly, he was still a powerful figure in her life, and she did not yet have the temerity to seriously challenge him. In a somewhat meek letter, Mary put to him that he occasionally made slight mistakes in the way he looked at things, and that she wished he was 'more prudent and more simply distrustful' in some things than he naturally was.

But nothing could shake Father Woods' confidence in the 'mystics' – he believed he had been chosen by God to guide these two 'saintly' women, and he was hurt, disappointed and 'greatly pained' that Mary could call his judgement into question. 'Let me also impress on you,' he told her, 'that anything tending to make you lose confidence in your Director and Superior must be a temptation.' As Mary was to discover, the merest hint on her part that Father Woods was mishandling affairs would always be dismissed as a 'temptation' to sin against God.

By this time, life in the convent at Franklin Street, Adelaide, was something of a fiasco, with nights and days disrupted by Sisters Ignatius and Angela's dalliances with 'supernatural' forces. Each week, Mary received letters from Sisters alarmed by what was going on, and surely wondering what sort of Order they had joined. Some also probably felt a twinge of resentment, as Ignatius and Angela used the power that came with being Father Woods' 'pets' to bend the rules in their own favour.

Isolated in Brisbane, Mary felt utterly powerless, and with every mail she hoped would come a letter from Father Woods requesting her return to Adelaide so that she could try to sort out the mess. Even at this stage, when she had such grave doubts about Father Woods' direction of the Sisters, Mary was unable, or unwilling, to run counter to him. He was Director of the Order, and she felt bound to obey him.

There was another aspect of Father Woods' behaviour that was worrying Mary, and that was his preoccupation with gazing into the future. Mary read through page after page of his rambling 'predictions', on anything from the date and circumstances of a Sister's death to that of his own gloomy end. 'I shall be accused of a great crime,' he wrote, 'and shall be tried in a most ignominious matter. I even think I shall be found guilty and sentenced to death.' The MacKillop family also appeared in his visions. 'Peter [Mary's youngest brother] would become a priest and a bishop,' Father Woods predicted, 'and Lexie would not persevere in the Good Shepherd Sisters.' Further, he maintained, 'James Quinn would not be Bishop of Brisbane for long and would never interfere much with you...' That he was always wrong (he was 24 years out in his prediction of Mary's death) did not seem to bother him. As he himself said one time, 'God always spares me the pain of doubt.'

He also reported on 'conversations' he had had with Jesus' mother, Mary, and on 'visits' from the devil, during his sleep at night. '[One time] I was rudely awoke by a devil – the one which usually assaults me and whom I believe to be a fallen spirit of a very high order,' Mary read. 'He was like a hideous dog but walking erect with human limbs. He had a drawn sword of a very wide blade in his hand, a kind of sharp heavy scimitar... He gave me a blow on the left leg above the foot and nearly severed it,' Father Woods continued. 'I began to bleed as you may imagine and soon I was in a pool of blood. The bed and everything was saturated and I felt myself dying.' Eventually, however, Jesus' mother, Mary, came to rescue him. 'My guardian Angel removed everything from the bed that was saturated with blood and placed other things perfectly similar there. I am sure these blood-stained things will be found again some day.'

Father Woods' irrationality further alienated him from fellow priests, and reinforced their views that he was either a zealot, a crackpot, or both. His fellow priests' obvious contempt cut him to the quick. 'Some of the clergy will not notice me,' Father Woods wrote, wounded, 'and others speak against me openly and so that it will reach me. My authority is now merely a name. It is openly disregarded, and to crown all, there was a meeting last week to prepare a string of resolutions to have sent to the Bishop expressing dissatisfaction at the present educational system.' His strange behaviour could, in part, be put down to a combination of too much work, too much stress and a tendency towards hyperactivity, and the impact these had on his health, which had been weak since his days in training for the priesthood. Some even suspected that Father Woods was on the verge of total collapse.

Certainly, his own personal failings influenced his conduct. His vanity had led him to believe that he, and he alone, was chosen by God to perform important tasks, such as nurturing 'saints' like Ignatius, Angela and Mary Joseph. He believed he was guided by God in everything he did, and that he was therefore infallible. 'I own it troubles me to see the esteem in which I am held by the Sisters because I am sure I have [given] false impressions of myself by my vanity in word and action, which has caused me to do many things for the sake of being thought holy, or for applause and esteem.' These traits, coupled with an almost child-like faith in the goodness of other people, were his undoing. 'An old and sincere friend,' Mary related, 'said [Father Woods] was "too innocent, too much of the dove, and too little of the serpent in his composition". He could not believe that people with a fair appearance of piety were hypocrites. Unless he saw the evil done under his own eyes, he could not believe any wrong of those whom he trusted. This led to most painful results. It seemed very easy to deceive him; his wonderful share of "Charity, which thinketh no evil" left him at the mercy of impostors, who were not slow in taking advantage.'

With the animosity being stirred up by Father Woods' alarming behaviour, together with her continuing tensions with Dr Cani in Brisbane, Mary was overcome by a sense of hopelessness. In a letter to Father Woods, she revealed that beneath her seemingly endless reserve of good will, generosity and kindness were feelings of bitterness, anger and despair. 'Will you pray that, if it please God, I may have a little more confidence than I have got...in other fellow creatures around me? All seem false, and I am tempted to think everyone an enemy. But though these things prey on my mind, to my Sisters I speak the reverse of my thoughts, and whilst they think I am full of charity, my mind is full of poison, and everything, thank God, is a trouble and a cross.'

The 'mystics' debacle came to a head on 11 April 1870, with the disappearance of the Blessed Sacrament from the chapel of the Adelaide convent. The next day, bloodstains were found on the altar cloth, which left Father Woods convinced it was the work of God. About the same time, there was a series of unexplained fires in the convent, for which Father Woods blamed the devil. Fellow priests, however, had other ideas. They had a strong suspicion that Sisters Ignatius and Angela were involved. The Adelaide bishop's Vicar General, Father Smyth, a long-time supporter of Father Woods and the Sisters, said the disappearance of the Blessed Sacrament was a serious matter, and Church authorities in Rome would need to be advised. Father Smyth said that if this turned out to be a prank by some of the Sisters, Rome might well disband the Order altogether.

Sadly, Father Smyth died before the matter could be resolved. However, the reins were picked up by the Administrator of the diocese, Archdeacon Patrick Russell. He set up a Board of Inquiry, comprising nine priests, which found that the whole affair had indeed been orchestrated by Sister Angela. The report was sent to officials in Rome, who referred the matter to Adelaide's Bishop Sheil for his immediate attention on his return from Europe.

Several years later, in 1875, Sister Angela in fact admitted stealing the Blessed Sacrament, 'wilfully deceiving' Mary and Father Woods, and leading a life of hypocrisy in the convent. But even such hard evidence of her deceit failed to make any impression on Father Woods. In a letter to friend and adviser, Monsignor Tobias Kirby, head of the Irish College in Rome, Mary wrote, 'All that I used to think or say about them [the 'mystics'] was treated as a temptation by our poor Father, and even now that she confesses everything and that we have so many proofs she is sincere, he will not believe.' Interestingly, no confession was ever forthcoming from Sister Ignatius, who some believe may have had a mystical bent, and that Sister Angela only jumped on the bandwagon after she saw how much attention her colleague received.

In early 1871, Mary finally received word from Father Woods that she should leave Brisbane and return to Adelaide. However, the tone of his recent letters heightened her uneasiness about what had gone on there in her absence – for the first time she detected feelings of genuine despondency and resignation in him, to the point where Father Woods talked of stepping aside as Director of the Sisters. 'I wish most ardently that the [Order] was under some other priest. I long to die for the sake of letting my place be taken by someone else... I am unwise, but it is not that alone which troubles me. I am fearful of the trust and confidence the Sisters have in me which is surely a most fatal mistake and calculated to do so much harm to their work.'

Mary was relieved to be able to return to Adelaide at last, where she could survey for herself the trouble Father Woods was in. His worries were partly financial, she knew. He was weighed down by substantial debts, acquired in part to finance extensions to the Adelaide convent. He had proceeded with the work, convinced that God would never let him want for money, without considering for one moment the impact of high unemployment and a bad harvest year on contributions to church income. 'You won't be surprised to know I have no money,' he told Mary. 'I never indeed was so badly off. The diocese has none. I grieve to think of the state of things the Bishop will find before him. At present I am steering hopelessly into debt. Even the wisest and the most sanguine shake their heads doubtfully now.'

But Mary's instincts told her this was not the full extent of his troubles. These feelings were confirmed when Father Woods warned her, under the guise of another prophecy, that she would 'come into a nest of crosses'. This was no prediction. Father Woods knew that the months of tension and conflict in Adelaide were coming to a head, and that Mary was about to walk right into the centre of it.

CHAPTER 7

EXCOMMUNICATED!

MARY returned to Adelaide via Melbourne, Geelong and Portland, chiefly to visit some of the schools, but also to see her family. In Melbourne, she had received several cryptic messages from relative strangers about the trouble she would find in Adelaide. 'Strange things seem to have been said of the [Order] in Melbourne,' she told Father Woods. 'Indeed, it was dreadful to hear some of the things spoken of, and how they came to be known to those who spoke of them is a mystery to us. It is better not to enter into particulars on paper. We cannot be too careful in what we write. You may shake your head at my prudence or suspicions, but I really have less confidence in my fellow creatures than ever.'

At Duck Ponds, near Geelong, she was sorry to find her sister Maggie quite ill with rheumatic fever. Maggie's health had been weak since she was a child, and in December 1872, aged just 29, she passed away.

Mary arrived back in Adelaide in late April 1871, just two months after Bishop Sheil's return from his lengthy stay in Europe. Barely a day after his arrival, Bishop Sheil had been presented with a submission, signed by 10 Catholic priests out of the 32 in the diocese, listing detailed complaints against Father Woods and the Sisters. The priests claimed the Sisters were incompetent teachers, and took no advice or guidance from anyone but Father Woods, who, the priests claimed, was hardly suited to the task. Unless immediate action was taken, they said, the bishop would find himself supporting a group of ignorant and useless women.

While overseas, the bishop had heard that some priests were dissatisfied with the Sisters, but he was not prepared for the intensity of the opposition. He had been very ill while in Europe – hence his extended stay – and this shock on his return put him in bed for the next three days. Such a vicious attack on the Josephites was too much! They were his pride and joy: he had boasted of their achievements to his colleagues in Europe – 127 Sisters and 40 schools, solely devoted to giving a Catholic education to the poor. They were a neat solution to what had been a pressing problem in his diocese, and he was not about to throw them over for a handful of disgruntled priests.

Once recovered, Bishop Sheil met with Father Woods to assure him he was happy with both the Sisters and the Catholic school system. However, from that day, Father Woods claimed he detected a change in the bishop's treatment of him, a certain chilliness in his manner. He sadly confided to Mary that the bishop no longer paid him much attention which, for Father Woods, was the unkindest cut of all.

Before things got any worse between him and the bishop, Father Woods decided to reveal the grim state of his financial affairs. He had put off the meeting for as long as possible, as he was afraid of the consequences. However, Father Woods' debts for schools, convents, etc., had climbed to about 4000 pounds, one-third of the amount owed by the entire Adelaide diocese, and he was no longer able to meet even the interest repayments. The bishop listened, not unsympathetically, as Father Woods told his story, then gave him his verdict: he would not bail him out – he would neither accept responsibility for the debts nor help to pay them. Needless to say, it was not what the anxious priest wanted to hear.

By this time, Father Woods held his position as head of the Catholic education system in South Australia in name only, having reached a point where he could no longer cope. He was distraught and close to breaking point. Then, almost as if to convince himself that he was still in control, he began a round of rash decisions. In June 1871, he circulated a newsletter to the Sisters, saying he had appointed the 'mystics', Sisters Ignatius and Angela, as consultants to Mary.

To Mary's mind, it was nothing short of madness to put these two into such powerful positions, as they were sure to push their strange ideas onto the Sisters and harvest more trouble. She also knew that it would be an impossible arrangement for her, as she would certainly treat any advice they had to offer with great caution. But as Father Woods was still Director of the Order, and had already announced the appointments, she chose not to divide the Sisters' loyalties by openly challenging him.

In early August 1871, Father Woods left for Bathurst, about 200 km west of Sydney, where he had been invited to set up new Catholic schools. He was probably happy to go, as he was more than a little piqued at the treatment he was receiving at the hands of Bishop Sheil and the Adelaide clergy. However, with all her own worries, Mary had little time for his wounded pride. 'I have nothing more to write about, dear Father, except in imagination,' she told him. 'I am a perfect stranger to any of your present cares and anxieties.'

Finally, Mary had begun to emerge from the shadow of Father Woods. Her growing confidence and self-assurance meant she could no longer sit by silently while he made unwise decisions which threatened the Order. While she had a duty to obey Father Woods, as head Sister she also had a duty to provide wise and judicious leadership. 'Yes, I am changed, dear Father. I feel that at any cost I will say what I think to you in the future.'

Just as she learnt to stand on her own feet, however, she lost a valued ally in Bishop Sheil, for no apparent reason. Not long after Father Woods' departure to Bathurst, Bishop Sheil made it clear that the Sisters no longer had his support. The exact reason for his about-face remains sketchy, but there were a number of incidents that almost certainly played a part. While the bishop was away in Europe, the Administrator of the diocese, Archdeacon Russell, had filed a report with Church officials in Rome on the 'mystics', Sisters Angela and Ignatius, and their role in the disappearance of the Blessed Sacrament. On his return to Adelaide, Bishop Sheil received a letter chastising him over the guidance and training being given to the Josephites. Privately, Bishop Sheil was annoyed that Archdeacon Russell had sent the report to Rome without his approval, especially as it was critical of his much-loved Josephites.

Anxious to smooth things over, the Bishop advised Rome not to put too much faith in the report, saying it was inspired by pettiness, and was designed to undermine the Sisters. In an attempt to satisfy Rome's demands for action,

Bishop Sheil dismissed Archdeacon Russell as Administrator, claiming he had mismanaged the diocese in his absence. However, Rome considered this an inappropriate response, and reproached the Bishop for his actions. At this point, Bishop Sheil still stood firmly behind the Sisters. However, he resented the reprimand from Rome, and was also being worn down by almost daily accounts from Adelaide priests of how the Sisters' 'silly superstitions' were making a mockery of both him and the Church.

One of the bishop's most influential advisers during these months was Father Charles Horan. He was arguably the Sisters' most vicious enemy, due to their role in expelling his good friend, Father Keating, from the diocese, after claims that he had engaged in indecent behaviour with children. With his considerable power, Father Horan would have wasted no time in discrediting the Sisters at the ear of the bishop.

By September 1871, Father Horan's smear tactics had begun to pay off. On the first of the month, Bishop Sheil visited the Adelaide convent, which had become known as the 'Mother House', being the home base of the Sisters of St Joseph, from where all important decisions regarding the Order were made. At the time, Mary was in Kadina, about 145 km away. Bishop Sheil told the Sisters that he was in the process of reviewing the Order's Constitution, and that significant changes were soon to be made.

Knowing how sacred the Constitution was to Mary, the Sisters sent word that she should return to Adelaide immediately. One week later, Mary and another Sister met Bishop Sheil to discuss his complaints. The bishop labelled the Sisters at the Mother House as 'lazy' and those teaching at the schools as 'ignorant'. He proposed to change the

Constitution, to be more in keeping with the traditions of European Orders. He planned to split the Sisters into two 'classes', choir and lay, according to their merit and social status, and to put the convent under the control of the local priest. Each convent would be kept totally independent of all others, and there would be no movement between them. The teaching Sisters would be examined, to weed out the incompetent ones, and their schools would no longer accept students who could not afford to pay fees. The Josephite schools would turn out fine ladies, educated in the 'accomplishments' – music, languages, drawing, needlepoint and the like. Further, he said, the Adelaide convent would be handed over to another Order of nuns, the Dominican Sisters. Any Sister who did not agree to the new rules, he said, could leave. Bishop Sheil informed Mary the changes would be in place by the end of the year.

In the meantime, Bishop Sheil wanted Mary to return to Kadina and bring back one of the Sisters, Sister Ursula with whom, he claimed, the local priest had been having some difficulties. Mary raised her eyebrows at this – on her visit to Kadina only days ago, all had seemed well.

Mary was devastated by the Bishop's plans for the Order: they tore at the very heart of what the Sisters were all about. Placing each convent under the authority of the local priest meant that the Josephites would no longer be an Order for all Australians, as their work would be restricted by parish boundaries and subject to the politics of the local priest or bishop. The new rules would divide the Sisters into social classes, and force them to abandon the poor people whom they had vowed to serve, with no one to take their place. Mary knew that even though she owed obedience to the bishop, the future of the Order was at stake.

Mary consulted a number of priests for advice on what options were open to her. Their opinion was that because Bishop Sheil had initially approved their Constitution, he had every right to change it. However, the Sisters had taken vows to live by the original Constitution, and a new Constitution would require new vows from each Sister. Mary believed that Bishop Sheil was ill-advised in his move to change the Constitution, and that if she could only remind him of the inspiration for the Order, he would rethink his decision. With this in mind, Mary wrote the bishop a long letter in which she let him glimpse the effects of his actions. 'I know that you can withdraw your approbation from it [the Constitution],' she wrote, 'and if our good God so wills it, I am resigned. But oh pardon me my Lord if I say that I cannot in conscience see the [Constitution] altered and remain as a Sister... I feel that I must take the alternative you offered and leave the [Order]...'

The bishop was offended by the letter, and sharply reminded Mary of her vow of obedience. But Mary was not disobeying him, or even questioning his right to change their Constitution. She was simply saying that she might well accept the ultimatum he had offered all the Sisters at the outset. It seems incredible that after finally realising her dream to become a nun, and successfully setting up and leading an Australian Order of Sisters, Mary might throw it all away over the Constitution, which, after all, was just a piece of paper. But to Mary, the Constitution *was* the Order, and therefore was her dream. It captured the very essence of the Sisters of St Joseph – their spirit and identity, and their mission in Australia. Mary believed the Order's work was inspired by God, and as such, the Constitution should be considered sacrosanct.

Mary had begun her journey back to Kadina on 7 September 1871, unaware that Fathers Horan and Murphy had arrived at the Adelaide convent, ready to begin examining the teaching Sisters. The priests were selective in whom they interviewed – they invariably chose the youngest and least experienced of the nuns. Meanwhile, Mary arrived in Kadina to find Sister Ursula already gone, confirming her suspicions that her trip to Kadina had been a ploy to get her out of the way.

Mary returned to Adelaide a few days later with a sense of foreboding: she knew a storm was about to break, she just did not know how or when. She wrote to Father Woods almost weekly, keeping him informed of developments. To him, she indicated the extent she was prepared to go to defend the Constitution. 'I have nothing new to add to what I told you on Saturday. Many rumours reach us, but we know nothing certain as yet. Though quite in a state of suspense, and every moment dreading something new and terrible, yet thanks be to God, all are full of courage and resignation, prepared for any suffering rather than sacrifice our [Constitution],' Mary reported. 'The holy work of God has to be attended to, and if we are crushed and humbled to the very dust, as also laughing-stocks to all who know us, we must be faithful and look for rest and peace only in heaven...'

She searched for a way in which the conflict could be resolved quickly and quietly, but there seemed to be very few options. The likelihood of a backdown by Bishop Sheil was remote, particularly as his minders – those behind this whole business, she was sure – continually blocked her attempts to see him. She thought about moving the Sisters from Adelaide to a place where their Constitution would be accepted and respected, although where that might be she did not know. A showdown, she sadly realised, was inevitable.

On the morning of 21 September 1871, Mary received a telegram from Father Woods asking her to send some Sisters to the newly established school in Bathurst, New South Wales. This, she thought, would be a good excuse to see Bishop Sheil, and hopefully get some answers about his proposed changes to the Constitution. While Mary was moving about town that day, the bishop and Fathers Horan and Murphy visited the Adelaide convent and told the Sisters to assemble the following day for an important announcement. That night, Father Horan returned to the convent and told a nun there, Sister Teresa, to inform Mary that she was to go to St John's, about 80 km away, first thing in the morning. He then continued examining the Sisters. Sister Teresa passed on Father Horan's message, and also a strange comment he made about 'not worrying about the Constitution, as it would not be changed'. This was news to Mary, who thought she should see the bishop herself to clear up the confusion. With Sister Teresa in the room, Mary put her request to Father Horan. He told her he thought it was unlikely the bishop would see her, but that he would ask. 'I then said that my duty was to know about the changes in the [Constitution] that was proposed,' Mary wrote later to Father Woods, 'and that if the [Constitution] were really changed, I could not in conscience consent to it...

'I told him that I knew the Bishop had every right to do what he thought best in the matter,' Mary continued, 'but that as I had not only vowed to observe the original [Constitution] but had also been fully prepared for the greatest struggle in its defence, I really could not follow any other.' She also felt it was unfair that such significant changes were being made in Father Woods' absence, and asked that they be delayed until his return. Father Horan replied, somewhat acidly, that Father Woods was *not* the Bishop.

Father Horan then demanded an answer from Mary as to whether she would go to St John's the following day. Knowing that her words were sure to be used against her, she replied carefully: 'Father, how can I under those rules?' She later admitted that she was afraid of refusing to go, 'and yet dared not give my Sisters cause to think...I accepted the new [Constitution]'. Father Horan left abruptly, saying Bishop Sheil would see her in the morning.

Late that same night, Father Horan returned to the convent. Mary, drained and dispirited by the earlier confrontation, had gone to bed. He informed Sister Teresa that unless Sister Mary complied with the bishop's wishes, she would be excommunicated, that is, forbidden to enter a church or receive the sacraments. It is the harshest punishment that can be administered by the Church. Sister Teresa rushed the message up to Mary, and returned a short time later with her reply: 'I cannot act but as I have done.' Speaking on behalf of all the Sisters, Sister Teresa then told Father Horan that Mary had their full support, and that none were prepared to accept the new Constitution.

The Sisters woke to news of the extraordinary events of the previous night. They wandered about in a sort of daze, stunned and disbelieving, grappling with the news that Mary had been excommunicated. Unsure of their own status now, they did not go to the early-morning Mass as usual. At about 8am, they received a visit from Bishop Sheil and four other priests, demanding to know why they did not attend

Mass. On hearing their reason, Father Horan then told them that they had misunderstood. He did not say that Mary *was* excommunicated but that she *would* be if she did not obey the bishop.

Bishop Sheil then asked that Mary, who was sick in bed, be brought into the convent chapel. Minutes later, Mary, looking wan and drawn, approached the bishop, asking for his blessing. He refused it and announced to the assembled Sisters that Mary had been disobedient and rebellious, and that she was to be excommunicated. Instructing Mary to kneel before him, Bishop Sheil chastised her for her 'spiritual pride' and the 'evils' she had introduced to the convent. He then proceeded to read out the words which, to Mary's mind, were worse than a death sentence.

CHAPTER 8

'RESTORED TO OUR HABITS AND DUTIES'

DURING those few devastating moments on 22 September 1871, in which Bishop Sheil pronounced her excommunication, 29-year-old Mary 'simply felt like one in a dream'. As Mary knelt, dazed and silent, Bishop Sheil addressed the Sisters who had gathered around her, telling them that anyone who had dealings with Mary would also be excommunicated.

'An awful scene, one that I can never forget, followed,' Mary recalled. 'When I was ordered to leave the Church, my poor sisters followed, and some, particularly Sister Paula, seemed bereft of all reason. She shrieked like a mad being, and oh dear, I hope I shall never hear the like again... The poor things were for a while utterly unable to control themselves, and all this at the [chapel] door,' Mary said, shaking her head. 'But it did not last long. The Bishop called all back, and then one after another asked to be dispensed from their vows, saying they could not follow any but the [original Constitution]. At first he listened to a few, but seeing all of the same mind, ordered the rest back to their places, positively forbidding them to think of leaving without permission...'

Mary left the convent immediately, begging the Sisters not to tell anyone what had happened. For a short time, she lived with the family of Father Woods' brother, James, just a few doors away, but soon moved on to live quietly with a Protestant lady who was a friend. James Woods, a journalist, was outraged by the injustice Mary had suffered, and wanted to publicly clear her name. However, Mary made him promise that he 'would not write one word against the Bishop or priests as long as [I am] under his roof'. Mary felt very strongly about this, because she believed that priests and bishops were very special people, who spoke in the name of God. 'She would never allow any Sister to say a word against a priest or bishop,' a Sister noted some years later. 'She said she would prefer to have a dagger in her heart rather than a word be spoken against God's anointed.'

Up to this point, Mary believed that the reason she had been excommunicated was her stand against the new Constitution. However, she subsequently discovered that it was actually her 'refusal' to go to St John's. 'So far was I from wishing not to go to St John's,' Mary said, 'and so careful in my conversation with [Father Horan] as to the nature of my hesitation that it was not until some days [later] that I understood that it was on this plea...that the Bishop had passed the sentence.'

Within weeks of the excommunication, most of the Adelaide Sisters had been either expelled or dispensed from the Order, and the Adelaide convent passed to the Dominican Sisters who took over on 21 November. Country convents and the charities, such as the Orphanage, were not touched for the time being, although Bishop Sheil did order The Providence to shut its doors as soon as the lease on the building could be terminated.

Mary had made no attempt to influence the Sisters in their decision on whether to accept or reject the revision of the Constitution, but the fact that so many left the Order showed they were just as committed to the Josephite vision as she was. 'As soon as all the Sisters in town were dispensed,' she wrote to Father Woods, 'I from time to time went to see them, but as privately as possible to avoid scandal, when I found that so many were faithful to the [Constitution] and that they could support themselves by their work in town, I thought it but my duty to tell them to do so rather than to return to their homes in the world...'

Some of the Sisters took up jobs as servants or governesses, while a group of about 20 moved into a small house made available to them rent-free by a wealthy Jewish Member of Parliament, Emmanuel Solomon. They all wore lay clothes and, some say, even wigs, short hair being so unusual that they would otherwise have drawn attention to themselves. They did sewing, cleaning and embroidery to earn a bit of money to pay their way. Many of the women struggled with this new lifestyle. It was not the insecurity of it or the physical hardship which they found difficult – they were well-used to those things – it was the spiritual deprivations, such as not being able to attend the chapel for prayers each day. Some priests, unsympathetic to their predicament, delivered scathing sermons from the pulpit and refused to give Holy Communion to those who ventured out to Mass.

It is almost impossible to imagine Mary's anguish through all this, but for someone with such a keen sense of pride, the shame and humiliation of her excommunication would have struck at her very core. In today's terms, it would have been like the most senior and well-respected commanding officer of the armed forces receiving a dishonourable discharge, and yet being totally innocent of the allegations made against him.

Mary must have wanted to scream at the unfairness of it all – all she had ever wanted to do was to devote her life to God by helping people, and this is what she got for it. Priests outside the Horan circle, including her Jesuit friends, told her that the bishop had not followed proper procedure in handing down the excommunication and therefore it was technically invalid. Yet Mary carried on quietly, making no effort to have the sentence lifted or to clear her name. She believed this was a trial she and the Order were intended to endure and that it would reach its natural resolution. In the meantime, she tried to convince herself that she should feel privileged to be chosen to suffer for God's work.

Perhaps in her most private moments, Mary contemplated abandoning her life with the Sisters of St Joseph, and fulfilling her vocation some other way, or with some other Order. Yet there were many factors which prevented her doing this – namely, the loyal Sisters she would be deserting, and her belief that Australia needed the Sisters of St Joseph. Without them, who would teach the poor children; who would give food and shelter to the sick and homeless; who would provide care and comfort to those in distress? Mary believed that God intended the Sisters of St Joseph not only to survive but to prosper, to ensure underprivileged Australians, particularly those in isolated areas, would not be neglected again.

The true goodness of Mary's character shone through during these months, in that she never spoke a word against the bishop, in public or in private. How easy it would have been to denounce the bishop's actions to salvage her own name, or purge herself of the feelings that must have been raging inside her. But, in fact, Mary felt genuinely sorry for the bishop, who had always been such a loyal friend. She could see that those around him were manipulating him, using his deteriorating health to achieve their own ends. In a series of letters to her mother, she wrote: 'The poor Bishop has been our friend, and would be so still, but there are some about him whom God permits to be bitterly opposed to Father Woods and in a manner to myself... The holiest and best [of the priests] say I have only done my duty, and that our poor, dear old Bishop has made a terrible mistake. I tell you these things, dear Mamma, not that they may go further or that by mentioning them to other priests we may give them cause to think ill of some here,' Mary warned gently, 'but simply to ease your mind as my own loved mother...'

These sentiments of Mary did nothing to mollify Flora, who was outraged at the treatment her daughter had received. She decided to have her say anyway, and to no one less than the bishop. In an acrimonious letter to him, she wrote, '...Only notorious sinners could be so dealt with. That she, my ever good child, could be such, it would be hard for me...to believe... The great sin of her life, in my opinion, has been leaving me and putting herself under your Lordship's protection.'

Before long a report on the whole affair appeared in the Catholic newspaper, the *Irish Harp*. Mary said she felt like a criminal on the run, and was tempted to disappear altogether to some place where no one knew anything about her.

'[Once] all the disturbance in the papers commenced, had it not been for a kind few who encouraged me, I would have fled from the place altogether,' Mary revealed. 'I longed to go to the house of the Bishop and beg of him to remove the sentence from me, but feared... I did not fear the Bishop himself, but did some who were with him, and I only feared inasmuch that they might make me say or do something which would give them cause to say that the sentence was a just one...'

Mary's friends were unwavering in their support, and this buoyed her in her low moments. They made sure she always had a place to stay – it was their chance to repay her for all the times she had been there for them. Mary moved residence so often, her fellow Sisters found it difficult to keep up with her. With some amusement, Mary noted to Father Woods, 'My movements are well watched but as I have frequently to change my style of dress, the most absurd stories as to where I am living have gone about. Indeed the Sisters were on one occasion told by several that Sister Mary was dead and actually buried the previous Sunday.'

Other wild rumours also began to do the rounds, which showed there was no limit to some people's imagination. 'A very sympathetic priest called the other day at Government House,' Mary wrote to Father Woods, 'and Sir James Fergusson [then Governor of South Australia] in course of conversation made some remark in defence of what the Bishop had done to [me]. This led the priest to question him to his reason for so speaking, when to his great surprise Sir James told him that he had from the best authority, as he thought, heard that the Bishop's reason for so doing was that Sister Mary had actually spat in the face of the two priests he had sent to see her about convent matters.'

This sort of gossip incensed Mary's friends, who were more than ready to speak out and clear her name, if only she would let them. Charles Fox, the editor of the *Irish Harp*, published several editorials critical of Bishop Sheil, and a series of highly charged letters. If he thought he was doing Mary a favour, he only served to cause more of a fuss – exactly what she had been trying to avoid. 'That [letter] vindicates me,' Mary later told her mother, 'but oh at a terrible cost. It was written without my sanction and against my express wish... It is too painful. I am glad they did not know more to put in it... Dear old Bishop has made a terrible mistake... Be careful how you speak of any of these matters.'

During these eventful months, Father Woods was travelling throughout New South Wales and Queensland, conducting retreats, delivering sermons and visiting Josephite schools. For several weeks he was unaware of what had taken place in Adelaide, as Mary's letters took some time to catch up with him. A note from Bishop Sheil followed close behind, suggesting that Father Woods should stay in Sydney. In the few letters Father Woods sent to Mary in the aftermath of her excommunication, he told her the best thing she could do would be to somehow get past the bishop's inner circle of advisers and meet with the man himself. Mary replied that this would achieve little, as Bishop Sheil was 'not one who would admit that a woman has a right to differ from him in opinion'.

Towards the end of 1871, Mary and others noticed a further deterioration in Bishop Sheil's health. His fumbling confusion and inconsistency left those around him wondering what he would say and do next. 'The Bishop says one thing and is again contradicted by the priests,' Mary explained. 'Sometimes he says the [Constitution] is not altered and again he says it is. What he says to one Sister he contradicts to another. You may then imagine the confusion and perplexity of the Sisters. Latterly the Bishop has been much kinder in his manner to the Sisters. I really think he forgets one moment what he has just said a little before…'

Jesuit priest and long-time friend of Father Woods, Father Joseph Tappeiner, had reason to believe that Father Horan was giving the bishop significant amounts of alcohol, ostensibly to relieve his symptoms. The net result of this was that the bishop had become completely dependent on those around him, and was no longer capable of making a decision himself. If he attempted to address difficult topics, '[the bishop's] mind instantly became confused,' Father Tappeiner noted. 'He agreed with anything proposed, even what was repugnant to himself. His memory had been so weakened that after a few minutes he had forgotten what he had said before and proposed the opposite.'

Mary was under no illusions as to who was running the diocese, nor was she blind to the tactics being employed, although she found it difficult to believe that priests could stoop so low. 'Some of the priests have not been sincere. When they could they tried to mislead the Sisters…' Father Horan, she discovered, was telling blatant lies to cover his tracks. 'It was with a keen pang of sorrow and shame,' Mary informed Father Woods, 'that I heard from the Kapunda Sisters that he had positively denied the conversation we had [the night before my excommunication] and made it out to them that I had simply refused to obey the Bishop about going to [St John's, outside Kapunda]. Father, it is hard to think a priest could tell a lie and in such a grave manner.'

Her excommunication had now developed into such an ugly affair that, some days, Mary could not stop the flow of tears. That her desire to devote her life to helping others should come to this! Nor could she forget that Father Woods had a part to play in her troubles through his unwise direction of the Sisters while she was in Brisbane. 'Indeed, dear Father, your eyes will be opened after much misery has been done, to the danger of so implicitly trusting to the honesty of others... Oh I feel so sick, so weary of falsehoods and misery I see around me,' Mary told him. 'Were it not for the kindness of [some of the priests], I think I should have fled before this, for, as each week brought something fresh out in the *Harp*, I felt so tempted to go and never let you or anyone else know where I went.'

Finally, in mid-February, a light broke through. In the last days of his life, almost miraculously, the Bishop's mind seemed to clear, and he became aware of the duplicity of those around him. 'I am dying with a broken heart,' he said pitifully to a friend. 'Those whom I trusted contracted bad habits. At times I acted at their suggestions – I'm sorry. That is why I am so unhappy.'

On 23 February 1872, Bishop Sheil, who was staying at Willunga, received the Last Rites in preparation for death. That same day, he directed a trustworthy priest, Father Hughes, to find Mary and remove the sentence. Mary had recently left Adelaide for Willunga, about 50 km away. Father Hughes met her on the road and excitedly conveyed the bishop's decision. He then escorted her to the church in nearby Morphett Vale, where the excommunication was declared null and void.

Mary's mother was one of the first to be informed of the good news. 'The poor Bishop is indeed sorry for all now,' Mary wrote... 'Mine was but one part of much that the poor Bishop had to undo... Thanks be to God the poor Bishop had true priests near at a time when he much needed them...'

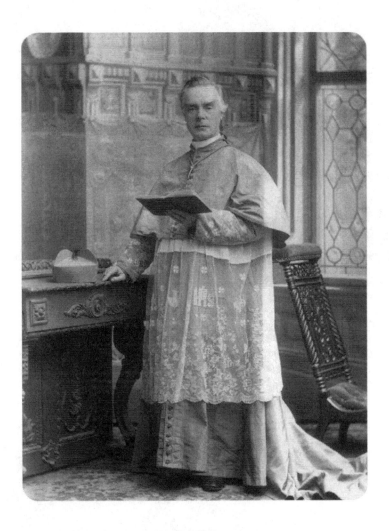

Christopher Reynolds, Bishop of Adelaide 1873–1893.
He was a friend turned foe.

Photo: Adelaide Catholic Archive.

James Quinn, Bishop of Brisbane 1859–1881. Mary described him as 'a terrible man', and yet 'charming' and 'most winning'.

Photo: Mary MacKillop Archive, North Sydney, NSW.

James' brother, Matthew Quinn, Bishop of Bathurst 1865–1885. He wanted the Sisters in his diocese, but on his own terms.

Photo: Mary MacKillop Archive, North Sydney, NSW.

Father John Smyth
(1824–1870). Closely associated
with Father Woods and Bishop
Sheil, he was Vicar General of
Adelaide 1865–1870.

Photo: Adelaide Catholic Archive.

Archdeacon Patrick Russell
(1829–1902), Vicar General of
Adelaide after Smyth and enemy of
Mary and the Sisters of St Joseph.

Photo: Adelaide Catholic Archive.

Laurence Bonaventure Sheil OSF (1815–1872), third Bishop of
Adelaide, 1866–1872. He 'sentenced' Mary to
excommunication.

Photo: Adelaide Catholic Archive.

Mrs Gertrude Abbott (1846–1934), formerly Sister Ignatius O'Brien, one of the 'mystics'. She joined the Sisters of St Joseph in 1868 and left in 1872. She was a close friend to Father Woods, who died in Gertrude's house with her associates around him. She also founded St Margaret's Hospital, Sydney, in 1894, leaving it to the Sisters of St Joseph after her death. This photo was taken in the 1920s.

Photo: St Margaret's Hospital Archives.

Father Charles Horan OFM (1837–1900). One of Bishop Sheil's most influential advisers.

Photo: Adelaide Catholic Archive.

Father Joseph Tappeiner SJ, who took over from Father Woods as Spiritual Director to the Sisters in 1872.

Photo: Adelaide Catholic Archive.

The Providence, West Terrace, Adelaide, in 1911. Run by the Sisters of St Joseph, it sheltered homeless children and the elderly at a time when social welfare was practically non-existent.

Photo: Mary MacKillop Archive, North Sydney, NSW.

The Refuge or House of Protection for Homeless and Penitent Women, Queen Street, Norwood, South Australia (1872–1901). It provided shelter to women in 'moral danger'.

Photo: Mary MacKillop Archive, North Sydney, NSW.

The Refuge, Fullarton, South Australia, 1902. It moved from Norwood in 1901 when the West Terrace premises became too small.

Photo: Mary MacKillop Archive, North Sydney, NSW.

Pope Pius IX. Mary, 'the Excommunicated one', met the Pope on two
occasions during her time in Rome.

Father William Kennedy, a member of Bishop Reynold's Apostolic Visitation of 1883.

Photo: Adelaide Catholic Archive.

Monsignor Frederick Byrne (1834–1915), Vicar General of Adelaide 1873–1882 and 1893–1912. A friend and classmate of Archbishop Reynolds.

Photo: Adelaide Catholic Archive.

Although Mary had been devastated by the actions of the bishop, she never blamed him, nor did she feel any real bitterness towards him. This great generosity of spirit came from Mary's extraordinary outlook on life. She believed that every person had a little bit of God in them, and against this, she could always overlook their faults and show them the respect and dignity they deserved as human beings. So while she could not control how other people behaved, she refused to think of herself as a victim.

Even with Bishop Sheil's advisers, Mary managed to be generous. This, despite knowing that they had manipulated the bishop at a time when he did not have the strength or clarity of mind to resist, and had misrepresented her actions to him as displays of stubbornness, disobedience and ambition. '...I believe that fault was found with my visiting the convents, it appearing to some of the priests that I did so for personal gratification, or from a love of authority, etc,' Mary later said. '[However] my simple opinion...is that in an [Order] such as ours...it becomes the bounden duty of someone from time to time to see and encourage them, and to endeavour to keep uniformity both in the schools and in the Sisters' minds.'

However, Mary could not deny that she and the Sisters were at least partly responsible for what had taken place. '...In our inexperience we were ourselves to blame in causing the ill feeling that reigned in the minds of some against us. I feel so grieved when I think of those poor priests who were so much opposed to us, and always dread saying anything which may make them seem too much in fault. It always seemed to me that they suffered even more than any of us did, for at first, through yielding to prejudice, they must have thought they [had] good reasons for all they did,'

Mary noted. 'They themselves were young and inexperienced in the ways of Australia, and one unreflecting word led to another, until, as I have cause to know, the most distressing statements were circulated about us.'

Mary emerged from the whole affair with her name and reputation completely intact. In fact, her irreproachable behaviour and judicious leadership during this time secured the future of the Order and elevated her to the status of a heroine in many people's eyes. If she had not kept the low profile she did, or if she had dared to criticise the bishop, her opponents would have had the ammunition they needed to bring a swift end to the Sisters of St Joseph.

In his last days, Bishop Sheil realised how he had played into the hands of Father Horan, and moved to lock him out as his successor. He ordered that, in the event of his death, Father Reynolds (a long-time supporter of the Josephites) should be appointed Administrator of the diocese of Adelaide. When the Bishop finally died on 1 March 1872, one of Father Reynolds' first acts as Administrator was to accept back into the Order all the Sisters who had been expelled or dispensed.

Bishop Sheil was always fondly remembered by Mary, who never forgot that for most of his time in Adelaide he was the Sisters' most steadfast supporter, without whom the Order may never have got off the ground. 'Our late and much loved Bishop was far too kind a Father to the children of the [Order] for any, much less myself, to forget his memory now. I think he thought too kindly of us, and when some who did not understand our struggles and intentions spoke, perhaps, too hastily of us, he believed what he heard and consequently felt bitterly disappointed in us…'

For Father Horan, the battle may have been lost, but he

still had some shots to fire. On 24 March 1872, he gave a sermon in honour of Bishop Sheil at two of his masses and had it published in the local papers. The sermon degenerated into a vicious attack on the Sisters. He described them as a 'confraternity of women who, for ignorance and fanaticism, have never, so far as my knowledge...had a parallel in the Church of God...' Father Reynolds promptly suspended Father Horan from his priestly duties, but the priest's words had their desired effect, and old tensions flared up again. In early April, two libellous letters were published in *The Protestant Advocate*, claiming that three of the Sisters had fallen pregnant, and that this was the 'real' reason Bishop Sheil had acted against them. The letters also accused the Sisters of drunkenness, prostitution and attempted murder. The publisher was successfully sued for defamation, and was fined and sentenced to six months' prison.

The Adelaide crisis of 1871 told on the lives of many, but none more so than Father Woods and Mary, who were never able to patch up the damage done to their friendship. Mary realised it was Father Woods' misguided leadership of the Sisters during her absence in Brisbane that had led to the escalation of tensions in Adelaide, culminating in the excommunication, and her confidence in him as Director of the Order was shattered.

Many of the decisions Father Woods had made in his last few months in Adelaide proved to Mary that they no longer shared a united vision for the Sisters of St Joseph. She strongly disagreed with his habit of sending untrained Sisters to schools, his changing of staff without consultation and his move to uproot the Sisters from Adelaide. Most particularly, she was unable to accept his continued support for the 'mystics', Sisters Ignatius and Angela. In March 1872, Sister Ignatius and others were readmitted to the Order. Angela's case, however, was still under consideration. Angela was living in the convent, on trial as it were, on the condition that she have no contact with Sister Ignatius. To have Angela and Ignatius anywhere near the convent was a major concession on Mary's part, as she believed neither was fit for life as a Sister. In frustration at this fascination with the 'mystical', Mary wrote, 'Much more mystery will I hope be spared me, for I have neither health of mind or body to bear it.'

In April 1872, Father Woods wrote to Sister Ignatius, deploring the fact that Angela had not been readmitted to the Order, and complaining in general about the treatment she and Angela had received. Annoyed, he took their case to Mary, and said it would be better for the pair to leave the [Order] altogether than to carry on as matters stood. Mary retorted, 'It certainly would be unless they obey their Superiors.'

Steaming, Father Woods pulled Ignatius and Angela out of the convent. Two other Sisters followed, and all four women settled for a time in Camden, south of Sydney, where they led a form of religious life under Father Woods' direction. Sister Ignatius later assumed the name Mrs Gertrude Abbott and became the leader of a group of religious women in Elizabeth Street, Sydney. Among other things, she founded St Margaret's Hospital in Sydney (which she left to the Sisters of St Joseph after her death).

This rash behaviour of Father Woods in moving the 'mystics' to New South Wales again drew him to the attention of Church officials, and he was summoned back to Adelaide. His position as Director of the Order had been under threat for some time, but with the recent events, the hierarchy decided to act, and his break with the Sisters came. 'We had not long been restored to our habits and duties,' Mary recalled, 'when more difficulties arose, the most painful differences of opinion between Father Woods and myself – when one day he told me that the Bishops advised him to give up the direction of the Sisters. I saw his hesitation, [and] I felt urged to write and tell him that it was better that he should do so for a time, and gave him my reasons for thinking so. This was a horrible task for me and caused me much suffering...'

Mary could not have forgotten Father Woods' words, from just a few years earlier – 'To think for one moment of letting another guide the [Order] would...be betraying my trust' – and was well aware of the impact that the decision would have on him. She nervously waited for his reaction to her letter.

She did not have to wait long. Father Woods was furious with Mary and with the bishops. He packed his bags and stormed out of Adelaide under orders not to return until the appointment of a new bishop. He refused to live in the colony again.

THE PATH TO ROME

THE recent troubles in Adelaide had been monitored with some concern by Church officials in Rome, who decided to instigate an inquiry. At the end of May 1872, the bishop of Hobart, Dr Daniel Murphy, and the bishop of Bathurst, Dr Matthew Quinn, arrived in Adelaide to begin proceedings. They were directed to look into the circumstances surrounding the excommunication, the alleged misuse of funds in the diocese, the activities of Father Horan and others, and Bishop Sheil's alleged drinking habits. Evidence was taken from Father Woods (during a fleeting return to Adelaide), Father Horan and other priests, Mary and some of the Sisters.

By late June 1872, the Commission of Inquiry had been completed. It ordered that Father Horan (who was found to have played a significant role in the events leading up to the excommunication) and two others be recalled to Ireland, and that a new bishop be appointed to Adelaide as soon as possible. The Commission found no evidence to support claims that Church funds had been misused, and said that the diocese's significant debt could largely be attributed to the financing of new churches and schools. The Commission confirmed that Father Woods should relinquish the directorship of the Sisters, and that his friend, Jesuit priest Father Joseph Tappeiner, should take his place.

Mary emerged from the inquiry unscathed. One of the Commissioners, Bishop Matthew Quinn, was quite glowing in his assessment of Mary, despite the stern reports on her he had no doubt received from his brother, Bishop James Quinn of Brisbane. '...From the way she acted during the most extraordinary troubles she had to undergo during the disturbances in Adelaide and from the spirit of her [Order], I believe her to be a very holy person.' Just months after this Commission of Inquiry, however, trouble was again brewing, this time in Bishop Matthew Quinn's own diocese of Bathurst.

In July 1872, three Sisters arrived in the agricultural and mining township of Bathurst, New South Wales, to open a school in Perthville, about 8 km out from town. Like his brother in Brisbane, Bishop Matthew Quinn wanted the Sisters in his diocese, but on his terms. He, too, disapproved of the central government provision in the Constitution, whereby a Sister, rather than a bishop, was given control of the Order, and he had several heated discussions with Mary over it.

By 1873, Bishop Matthew Quinn had begun protesting to Church officials in Rome about the form of the Constitution. To safeguard against changes being made, Father Woods – who still took a lively interest in the Order's affairs from distant Sydney – told Mary she should move quickly to have the Constitution approved. '...I don't see how this can be done without your going to Rome. My opinion certainly is that you should begin to make arrangements now... Depend upon it, we shall have trouble again if something is not done before long... It will be done better by you than by anyone else... Besides, I know that the Bishops were quietly making their representations to Rome and unless we have someone there before the end of the year, they will have got the [Constitution] approved without the central government.'

The Administrator of Adelaide, Father Reynolds, and the Sisters' new Director, Father Tappeiner, shared Father Woods' concerns. Without Rome's official endorsement, the Sisters were vulnerable: on a whim, a bishop could change the Constitution or abolish the Order altogether. On these grounds, they told Mary to make immediate plans to travel to Rome.

Mary was under no illusions as to the importance of the mission – the future of the Sisters depended on it being a success. In the short time she had, she sought advice from those who could help her break into Rome's closed circle. She was also keen to set up a meeting with Father Woods, as he had drawn up the Constitution and would have some suggestions about how it should be presented.

In February 1873, Father Reynolds sent a message to Father Woods to come to Adelaide, or else send a telegram if he thought he might be delayed so that Mary could postpone her trip. But Father Woods' letter in reply, which actually arrived on the steamer he himself was expected on, was that the Commission of Inquiry had forbidden him to set foot in Adelaide, and that Mary should visit him in Sydney in May. But it was too late – by this stage it was mid-March, and Mary was booked to leave for Rome in a fortnight.

'I am crushed to the earth with sorrow at having to leave as I do without seeing you, and this when you desired that I should...,' Mary left in a message for Father Woods. 'God knows that I suffer, but...I feel that this is God's holy Will and that...I am confident [God] will comfort you and teach you to regard it as such.'

But Mary had overestimated Father Woods' capacity for submission: 'I have had a good many trials about the [Order] but this was the worst,' he wrote to Sister Monica in Adelaide. 'I asked [Mary] to see me most earnestly and unless my name as Father is a mere name she should have come to me before she took other advice. Her position as [head of the Order] – which is not of my choice – did not require her to leave upon the advice of others, unless myself...'

When Mary discovered years later that he was telling Sisters, priests and anyone else who would listen that she had gone to Rome without his knowledge or permission, she sharply rebuked him. 'I only ask you as a priest to say what you have to say to me, or to those who should bring me to account, if I have wronged you or sought to exclude you from your former position...but do not talk to the Sisters against the Constitution or their superiors.'

Of course, what is most bewildering about Father Woods' attack on Mary is that in going to Rome, she was following a suggestion that he himself had initially put to her. The timing of the visit was never her decision, and the reason Mary left without seeing him was that he failed to send a telegram, as requested by the Administrator, Father Reynolds. At any rate, as Father Woods was no longer Director of the Sisters, it was not vital that he be consulted; his opinion was sought out of respect for his role in establishing the Order and in drawing up the Constitution.

In organising the trip to Rome, Mary did not have the luxury of time or money. There were only enough funds for the fare, and a one-way fare at that, so it was decided Mary should travel alone, despite the fact that this would be a most shocking faux pas in the eyes of the world – no woman travelled without a companion...and certainly not to Europe! However, Mary would not be daunted – it was not the first time she had redefined social boundaries, and it probably would not be the last.

Mary's advisers thought it best that she travel under a false name – Mrs MacDonald – and wear ordinary street clothes until she got to Europe. Such secrecy at first seems a little baffling, but there were several reasons for it. The political climate in Italy in the early 1870s was very unstable. Italy had recently been united, and control of the city of Rome had passed from France to Italy. This ended the sovereign rights enjoyed by Popes over the Papal States. To reassure the Catholic world, the Italian Parliament enacted the Law of Papal Guarantees, which gave the Pope special freedoms and privileges. However, Pope Pius IX, who wanted to be restored to his temporal sovereignty, refused to recognise the Act. This caused a further deterioration in the relationship between the Church and the Italian Government, and in May 1873 the government abolished the legal standing of religious Orders, turning them out of their homes, and taking control of their schools, hospitals and churches.

Mary's visit to Rome fell right in the middle of this political turmoil, and there is no doubt that if she had worn her habit and drawn attention to herself as a member of a religious Order, she would have had her activities severely restricted. As for the false name, there was no doubt that a woman travelling alone was vulnerable, and in calling herself Mrs MacDonald, she created the illusion that there was a Mr MacDonald, possibly on board with her. In fact, there was an amusing incident when the ship's purser asked her how many children she had. 'Oh, in fact, I have a great many,' she answered, smiling to herself at the poor man's obvious puzzlement.

But there was another reason for all the secrecy, one which years later gave rise to claims that Mary acted somewhat underhandedly, although it becomes clear that she was simply obeying directions. Mary's sole mission in going to Rome was to have the Josephite Constitution approved in its current form, and she was very much aware that at least one Australian bishop, Matthew Quinn of Bathurst, was equally determined to have the Constitution changed. Mary was advised to keep news of her trip quiet, as there was a very real possibility that Bishop Quinn would get his revisions endorsed in Rome before she had a chance to put her case.

How must Mary have felt setting out on this trip, knowing what was at stake? She would be a young woman alone, in a strange country, where she could not speak the language, and where she was sure to find herself at the centre of a political whirlpool. In these days of efficiently planned travel itineraries, it is hard to appreciate what a huge unknown this trip was. Mary carried letters of introduction from Adelaide priests, but there was no guarantee of accommodation or meals, and certainly no guarantee that she would be able to meet the men who counted in the Holy City. Contact with the Pope and his inner circle was reserved for the most distinguished persons – men preferably ranked somewhere upwards of a priest – so what hope for a mere colonial girl? And then there was the sheer magnitude of the trip itself – two and a half months at sea, in an era when if you ventured beyond the next township, you were considered well-travelled. The fact that Mary undertook this trip so willingly, and in such adversity, is testament to her courage and determination in ensuring the survival of the Sisters of St Joseph.

Mary left Port Adelaide on 28 March 1873, aboard the *Rangatira* – the only woman of its eight passengers – en route to Albany, Western Australia. Predictably, it was a turbulent trip across the Great Australian Bight, and for the most part Mary lay, green and limp, in her bunk. On arrival at Albany, she gladly took accommodation ashore, not in the hotel (which proved to be a popular choice with the male passengers) but in a tucked-away little cottage. It was here that she met her uncle, Alexander ('The King') Cameron, who, remarkably, she happened to spot walking past her window. Mary discovered, to her delight, that he and his second wife, Ellen, were also bound for Europe. Two days later, the threesome joined the mail-steamer, *Bangalore*, for their long ocean journey.

After the rough trip from Melbourne, Mary had little trouble adapting to the lurch and roll of the steamer, although one night – a night of violent thunderstorms – she must have wondered if she would ever see daylight again. The sea broke in through a large porthole, leaving Mary's berth awash. Looking beyond the damp bed and blankets, she perched herself on a nest of boxes and pillows, and simply admired the view. 'My berth is the top one and now I have got my desk leaning on it and am mounted on a lot of boxes and pillows to make it high enough to reach it, and thus I am able to write in comparative comfort with the beautiful blue sea rolling under my window.'

When the steamer docked for two days at Galle, Ceylon, Mary and the other passengers were put up in a plush hotel, complete with menservants: 'I had to sit down to a grand dinner, or rather "Tiffin", as they call it,' she wrote in one letter. 'I am sure there were 80 persons on it, all eating, laughing, and seeming to enjoy themselves – such a contrast to our dear quiet dinner. There were native servants running about in all directions,' Mary continued, 'and during the meal there were some stationed at various parts of the room pulling the "punker [sic] strings" and thus causing such a refreshing coolness. These punkahs are things used to fan the people and keep them cool. We had them aboard the Bangalore, and have also in this.'

Mary's heart went out to 'the poor natives', whose scanty clothing she took as evidence of their abject poverty: 'When we got into the harbour at Galle – even before we cast anchor – these poor naked creatures were to be seen climbing over the sides of the steamer, and then closely followed by others better clad, who came forward with various articles for sale, such as necklaces, fans, jewellery, etc. Those I saw were naked having only a handkerchief about their loins, but even under the scorching sun they have nothing on their heads.'

Several steamers later, Mary arrived at Brindisi, Italy, but, to her great dismay, she was not allowed through customs because she did not carry a passport. Inexperienced as she was at world travel, she had completely overlooked obtaining the document. She tried to explain to the customs officials, who spoke little English, how important it was she get to the Vatican City, but to no avail.

The crowd of passengers watching proceedings on the ship's deck included an old non-Catholic friend of Mary's, Mr Smythe, from her Sands and Kenny days. After a word in Mary's ear, he went ashore to the American Consul, where officials were able to pull a few strings and authorise her entry. Mr Smythe accompanied a very grateful Mary – who at this point parted company with her uncle and aunt – to the railway station and bought her a ticket to Rome.

Mary arrived in Rome on 11 May 1873, staying in a cheap hotel room which, it so happened, was opposite where her own father had studied for the priesthood. Wasting no time, she began on a round of visits, meeting the priests she had been advised to see. These included the Swiss Father Andeledy, who became her spiritual guide in Rome, the English Father Lambert and the Italian Cardinal Bilio, who was commissioned to look into the affairs of Adelaide on behalf of the Church. One of her most important contacts was Monsignor Tobias Kirby, Rector of the Irish College in Rome, who had direct access to the Pope. He organised for Mary to stay at a nearby convent with French nuns.

Despite Italy's unfavourable political climate, Mary's visit to Rome was actually quite timely, as officials were taking a close look at the Adelaide diocese and, importantly, were soon to appoint a new bishop (Father Reynolds).

One of Mary's first tasks was to prepare several documents in support of her quest to have the Josephite Constitution approved. Among these was a formal letter to the Pope, Pope Pius IX, in which she asked him to '...take into consideration the great distance at which we are removed from the Centre [Rome] we love so much...but without the protection of which we can do nothing'. Mary also included a short history of the Order, outlining its commitment to serving and educating the poor of Australia.

From her discussions – or rather, arguments – with Bishop Matthew Quinn, Mary knew there were three parts of the Constitution for which she would have to fight hard. The first was the Sisters' commitment to live a life of poverty. Mary wrote: '[The Sisters] shrink with positive terror from the idea of possessing property of their own'. Given the political upheavals in Italy, and lessons learnt from the past, Rome was very strongly in favour of independent means for religious orders. If an Order did not own its convents, schools, and Churches, then its members could potentially be turned out onto the streets at any time by the government of the day.

The second point was central government. Mary was very insistent on this, as she did not want the Order to be split across dioceses or colonies, or to be subject to the politics of the local priest or bishop. 'The work has not been intended by our good God for Bathurst or for Adelaide or for Queensland alone: it is for the poor of all Australia...' She then gave a guarantee that central government would not compromise any bishop's authority. 'I am as anxious for the rights of the Bishops as for our own – ours could be nothing and should be nothing without them... I would rather see the whole work fall to the ground than that the Sisters should not always try to be the dutiful children of the Bishop wherever they may be,' she asserted.

The third point was the teaching of instrumental music. In those days, musical instruments, such as the piano, were status symbols for well-placed, well-to-do families, and Mary believed such lessons were inappropriate for children who could not count on a hot meal at the end of the day, let alone a piano in the dining room. The Sisters' Director, Father Tappeiner, agreed whole-heartedly with Mary's position on this: 'Accomplishments, music for the service of God in the Church, all that is very good, but the poor, poor children, what will become of them? Go on with that sort of thing, give the Sisters a taste for accomplishments, music, etc. (others will follow likewise) and they will soon lose their interest in the dirty, ragged little girls and boys, they will soon forget what a precious soul there is under these rags.' However, Bishop Matthew Quinn insisted that Australians loved their music, and the Sisters' refusal to teach it was 'a very great drawback to their usefulness'.

Mary wrote reams of material in support of all three issues, hoping to convince the Pope and his officials of their worth. But, ever an advocate of fair-play, and putting paid to suggestions that she acted behind the bishop's back, she urged Monsignor Kirby 'to represent the Bishop's wishes more urgently to those in authority in Rome...' Mary did this because, in her mind, she had no doubt that she would succeed in having the Constitution approved. She believed it was God's wish that the Sisters of St Joseph should be given official sanction, so that they could survive, to carry out their much-needed work in Australia. '...I cannot say I have one anxiety as to the final result, indeed I sometimes wonder so much at my confidence upon this that I would think I was too sanguine or overpresumptuous were it not that in my heart I know that [those who trust in God] shall never be confounded.'

The Constitution and the accompanying paperwork Mary had prepared was sent to Rome's Father Raymund Bianchi for examination. She was initially a little wary of this choice, largely because she doubted whether Father Bianchi would be able to appreciate the need for an Order designed for peculiarly Australian conditions. She warmed to him, as it turned out, but her fears were not entirely unfounded. Father Bianchi frowned at the idea of Sisters moving about in twos and threes in far-flung areas, totally reliant on the charity of those they served. In her diary, she jotted: 'Found him kind, would not hear of the objection of the Bishops [to central government], but had some of his own, particularly about Poverty, which he thought would not be permitted in any case in the light we wanted it.'

At this point, negotiations on the Constitution were at a very sensitive stage, and Monsignor Kirby advised Mary to ensure that in her letters home, her business was kept confidential. 'For grave reasons, I do not want Monsignor Kirby's lively interest in us to go out of the colony for the present,' Mary wrote to the Sisters. 'We must not let the Bishops know too much, and Monsignor has particularly requested this of us.'

Although she was acting on the instructions of Monsignor Kirby in this matter, Mary herself had become much more politically astute over the years. She realised there were bishops and priests who would support the Sisters and their Constitution as long as they played by the rules, otherwise, they had better look out. '...Be very careful as to whom you share the contents of my letter with,' Mary warned her mother. 'I tell you for your own comfort things that I would not to everyone, even to many who call themselves my friends. I loved them and will always love them for their kindness to me, but I cannot feel that they have been the [Sisters'] friends... Be particularly reserved with the clergy...,' she wrote. 'In due time all will come out, but I would not like that my friends should be the ones to make these things known...'

In the weeks following her arrival in Rome in May 1873, Mary had met with many influential people, thanks to several letters of introduction she carried with her, and her own pluck and persistence. Some, who upheld their

European traditions proudly, were a little disconcerted by the fact that they were dealing with an Australian – 'There are some greatly surprised when they find it is an Australian and not a native of Britain or at least of Ireland who is speaking to them' – but most, to their surprise, were won over by Mary. They admired her for her gentle charms, her generosity and sincerity, and her enormous courage in surviving the political storms back in Australia. Where others may have been disposed of with a few kind, encouraging words and a piece or two of Vatican memorabilia, for Mary a path was cleared through to the Pope himself.

On 1 June 1873, just two weeks after her arrival in Rome, Mary had her first audience with Pope Pius IX.

TRAVELS IN EUROPE

F OR her papal audience, Mary decided that for the first time since her arrival in Italy, she would risk wearing her habit, so as to have it blessed by the Pope. There were many others present at the audience, including Monsignor Kirby, who acted as interpreter for the 81-year-old Pontiff. For Mary, it was a memorable day: 'He laid his hand so kindly on my head,' she told the Sisters, 'then gave his blessing, but he did not do so until [one of the officials] reminded him of Adelaide and our troubles. Before that he just gave me his ring to kiss as he did to all the rest...'

To her mother, Mary revealed the impact that the meeting had on her. 'What he said, and how he said it, when he knew that I was the Excommunicated one, are things too sacred to be spoken of,' she said. '...When he laid his loved hands upon my head, I felt more than I will attempt to say.' In her diary she wrote just these few words: 'A day never to be forgotten, a day worth years of suffering.'

Though her audience with Pope Pius IX, who had been Pope for 27 years, was a momentous occasion for Mary, it did nothing to hasten the passage of the Josephite Constitution through official channels. With time on her hands, Mary took numerous trips and tours, but not the traditional holiday variety – if it was not connected with the Catholic Church, she was not interested – rather, she visited churches, schools, saints' tombs, convents and monasteries.

However, as the summer heat intensified, Mary found herself ill most days with migraines, and struggling to get out of bed. 'Although I dearly loved Rome,' she wrote, 'Rome did not love me, for after the first month I was scarcely a day well in it.' Her friends and advisers recommended she leave the city as soon as possible. Initially, it was expected that Mary would return to Australia, but as her work was not yet completed, she got permission to go to London for what would essentially be a fundraising tour. She hoped to collect school supplies and money for her return fare, and to find new Sisters and priests for Adelaide. It was also suggested that she visit Scotland and Ireland but, despite the sentimental value of such a trip, she said she 'would not feel justified in going there unless there was aid to be obtained for our schools, and postulants, which we required very much'.

On 24 July 1873, about a week before she was due to depart for London, Mary had a second, much more intimate audience with the Pope. It was, she said, 'quiet and homely. It was not so to say, a State audience. There were only a few present.' Opportunity for conversation between Mary and the Pope was limited, as Monsignor Kirby was ill and unable to attend as her interpreter. However, she felt honoured to be in the Pope's company once more.

Mary left Rome for London on 1 August 1873. The 11-day trip took her through such places as Loreto, Germany and Belgium. It was a long, lonely journey for her – she spent many hours in railway waiting-rooms in the dead of night, watching nervously as rough-looking men drifted in and out, and in rail carriages, alongside strangers. It would have taken immense courage to set out on these long overland journeys alone, especially when it is remembered that Mary was unable to speak any of the Continental languages, had next to no money and was quite ill. However, she had great faith in her fellow human beings, and firmly believed they would help her along the way. She was not disappointed. Many times, porters and rail guards stoked a fire for her in the waiting room, gave her coffee or tea – one even offered her a bed at his family home!

By mid-August 1873, Mary was on a ferry for Dover. It was a wet and blustery day, and the vessel pitched and heaved, drenching those on deck in 'angry duckings'. She was made sick by 'the tricks the waves played', and was given a few spoonsful of brandy by one of the ship's aides to help settle her. Many hours later, when she heard cries that the White Cliffs of Dover had come into view, she roused herself to take a peek. While she had passed through other places of note 'without any desire to see things which should be nothing to a Sister of St Joseph', these 'oft heard of White Cliffs' captivated her. 'If I felt that for England's cliffs, what, you may imagine, must I not wish to see if I go near Scotland.'

But these warm feelings for England were short-lived. 'Well, I got to London, and oh, I did feel it a lonely and dreary place and myself so out of place there. No one met me and I felt more afraid in London where I could speak the language than I did amongst the Italians, Germans and French.' With some relief, she met her old friends, the MacDougall family (the Melbourne stationers for whom she once worked), who insisted she stay with them in their grand London mansion.

Mary was glad to have friends around her again, but she felt uncomfortable amongst all the finery and the bevy of servants. 'I thought...of what my dear simple Sisters would say if they saw me there.' She stayed with the family for one week, at which time they returned to Australia. Before parting, Mr MacDougall bought stationery and school supplies for her to take back to Australia.

During her time in Europe, Mary wrote regularly to the Sisters. She encouraged and guided them with beautiful, inspirational passages, and amused them with little anecdotes – such as that about the Protestant friend who was handed an anti-Catholic flyer in her presence, and who mischievously lit his cigar with it. Or the group of people who tried to guess her age (she was 31). 'One old woman took me to be about sixteen, but several others settled among themselves that I must be close on seventy. As in other places I have been spoken of as "that funny-looking old lady" or "that old lady dressed in black" etc. I think that my youthful appearance must be leaving me and I shall come back to you quite grave and staid...'

Just as the Sisters eagerly awaited Mary's letters, so did Mary theirs. This link to friends at home sustained her when she was feeling lonely and depressed. 'Ah, Sisters, Sisters, you little know how dear you are each to me, Queensland, Bathurst, Adelaide, all alike dear...'

Sometimes, it seems Mary almost felt guilty for being away, although she was hardly having a luxurious time of it. She told the Sisters earnestly, again and again, that she wished for nothing more but to be back home with them, helping them in their day-to-day work: 'One thing, my loved Sisters, you may rely upon – I shall come back convinced that for me, at any rate, there is no convent or home like my loved St Joseph's, the value of which is doubly dear since I have seen other places.' In spite of this, Mary knew that she should not return to Australia before Rome had approved the Constitution.

After a pilgrimage to Paray-le-Monial in France, Mary returned to London in September 1873. Almost immediately, the question was again raised – this time by some of the local priests – as to whether she should visit Scotland on her fundraising mission. Mary was concerned that if she agreed to go, it might be more for her own sentimental reasons than for the good of the Sisters of St Joseph. 'You, dearest Mamma, who know how my heart ever clinged to anything connected with Grandpapa and what he loved, to say nothing of yourself and Uncle, can imagine what a tempting invitation this is... If I can help our great work in any way then I know I can, but otherwise I may not think of it.'

In her efforts to resist the lure of a nostalgic journey, Mary came up with a totally inappropriate plan, suggesting that she write to the bishop of Glasgow with her requests for Sisters and funds for the Order. Knowing nothing would be achieved this way, her adviser in London, Father Christie, put her out of her misery and made the decision for her. He said that she herself must go, that 'God required it of her'. A friend of Father Christie's, Laura Vaughan, was also planning a trip to Scotland, to visit a Lady Gordon. She asked Mary to accompany her, generously offering to pay all costs. Mary accepted, and they left London for the Highlands in mid-October.

The Scottish property of their host, Lady Gordon, could only be accessed by water, and Mary and Laura were taken across by four Scots. The boatsmen nattered away in Gaelic, discussing the look of their passengers – one was a

'Sassenach' (an Englishwoman) they were sure, but the other they could not work out. Then, quite suddenly, there was silence, and the four men took up their rowing with renewed vigour. They had seen the hint of a smile at Mary's lips and crinkly eyes, and, much embarrassed, realised she had understood every word of their conversation. Observing their red faces and bowed heads, she tried hard not to laugh. A short time later, the pair arrived to a lavish reception at Drimnin House on Morvern, the home of Lady Gordon, who could barely contain her pride at having as her guest 'the first religious in that part since the time of the Protestant persecution'.

Scotland was, from the start, a second home to Mary – she felt as if, in some strange way, she had found a part of herself. She savoured the craggy mountainous beauty, the cold bracing air, the soft lapping of the sea: 'I am a changed being in appearance since I came here. Mrs Vaughan says I am getting quite rosy.'

Mary's sense of her Highland heritage was stronger than she could have ever imagined, and she yearned to discover more. She stayed with Lady Gordon for two weeks, then toured a large part of Scotland, including Edinburgh, Glasgow and the Highlands district of Brae Lochaber, from where both sides of her family had come. Here she met distant family and friends, many of whom remembered her parents. 'I met so many who knew my relatives on both sides,' she wrote to her mother, 'and all, even the MacKillops, declare that I am a regular McDonald… The moment I saw John Cranachan in Church, I felt that I was near one of our own, and strange to say it was more than I could bear unmoved… Won't it cheer you my own dear Mamma to know that your child sees the parts you have known and loved, and meets so many who have known and loved you.'

Despite the open-arms welcome that Mary received in Scotland, it was poor country, and her fundraising was more likely to turn up a hard-come-by pound of butter than much-needed cash. She also had no luck finding young men and women interested in leading a religious life in far-away Adelaide. These disappointments, together with the physical stresses of travel and sheer loneliness, left her homesick and miserable. 'Was so tired last night I fairly broke down before Mrs. Carmichael [her host] who got me some brandy... Became better but had a sad night. Cried myself to sleep. Was so weary of the struggle and felt so utterly alone...' At times like these, it was the support of her friends, her gutsy determination, and the knowledge that it was God's work she was doing that kept her going.

While in Europe, Mary had heard nothing from Father Woods, but plenty *about* him, and as far as she could tell, he was up to his old tricks. The Sister-in-charge in Brisbane, Sister Clare, wrote that despite the fact that Father Woods was no longer Director of the Order, he was still interfering. A letter from Father Tappeiner confirmed her worst fears: '...Things did not seem to go smoothly in Queensland. It appeared to me something like our state before the storm. Constant changing, sending novices and postulants away, priests complaining, and most of these things done without or even against Sister Clare...'

But Father Woods' interference was not confined to Queensland. He had secretly sent letters to two Adelaide Sisters, telling them that he needed them for a new Order he was setting up in Brisbane, to be headed by the former Sister Ignatius (the 'mystic'). To one, he wrote: 'I do not think it is advisable that you should remain longer in your present doubtful and unsatisfactory state. I always thought that Sister Mary ruled your mind...' These tactics of Father Woods shocked the Sisters' new Director, Father Tappeiner: 'I must say I do not find his way open or candid, as I thought it might be,' he informed Mary.

Father Tappeiner was also concerned about the state of affairs in Bathurst, and Bishop Matthew Quinn's continuing campaign against the Constitution: 'It is so necessary that something should be decided by [Rome],' he wrote to Mary. 'Perhaps it will come to schism in Bathurst yet. If the Bishop does not succeed,...he may take some of the new Sisters, form them to his own views and have them under his own command, and let the others go their own way. I must be very much mistaken if this is not his idea... It would cause some shock in the [Order], though it would be better than to have this everlasting drag on it.'

On 26 January 1874, Mary returned to Mrs Vaughan's home in London to wait for news from Rome on whether the Constitution was any closer to being approved. Mary never entertained the idea of leaving for Australia before this was achieved. If she did, it was likely that officials in Rome would put the matter on the back-burner, where it could stay for years. Alternatively, there was the risk that Bishop Matthew Quinn would slip in his dreaded amendments.

Mary used her time in London to write a pamphlet in support of the poverty provision of the Constitution, as she suspected that this point was in danger of being lost. By explaining the unique conditions and values which existed in Australia, she hoped Rome might reconsider its stand. '...What would seem much out of place in Europe is still the very reverse in most parts of Australia,' the pamphlet said.

'It is an Australian who writes this, one brought up in the midst of many of the evils she tries to describe... In the peculiar spirit of the Sisterhood, [bishops and priests] saw, at last, the answer to their frequent sighs and prayers.' A friend of Father Christie's, Lady Georgiana Fullerton, who was an author, admired Mary for what she was trying to achieve, and offered to edit the pamphlet. The pair spent hours with heads bent, poring over this word and that, becoming firm friends in the process.

Lady Fullerton was just one of many unlikely friends Mary made throughout her life – those closest to her were often people of rank and distinction, of different race, culture, religion and beliefs. There were the Protestant families who took her in after her excommunication, and the Jewish MP, Emmanuel Solomon, who provided free accommodation to the Sisters; her rich, non-Catholic colleagues at Sands and Kenny; Lady Gordon; Lady Fullerton; the Barr-Smiths (Robert and his wife Johanna were wealthy Protestants in Adelaide, who were friends to Mary and benefactors to the Sisters); and the non-Catholic Mr Smythe, who helped her through customs in Italy.

There were many reasons these people were drawn to Mary. They enjoyed her personality – her warmth, her humour, her openness – and admired the way in which she devoted her life to others. They also appreciated the fact that she was not a 'soap-box Catholic' – she did not preach to them or try to convert them, she lived by example. But, most importantly, these supporters were not subject to the politics and pettiness that had hold of some sections of the Church.

Those from within Mary's own Catholic circle, such as Bishop Sheil, Father Woods, and later, Bishop Reynolds (the new bishop of Adelaide), proved to be more fickle in their friendship. Interestingly, all were men, and Catholics. Like the colonial governments of the day, these men were quite territorial, and jealous of their power. Anybody who shifted the status-quo – and unfortunately, Mary fell squarely into this camp – was viewed as a threat.

In the end, these men felt intimidated by Mary's independent spirit and steely character, and moved to reassert their power and authority in destructive ways. They saw themselves as paternal figures, and Mary as a fragile, helpless woman who needed their guidance and protection – well-meant sentiments in what was, after all, unashamedly a patriarchal society – and could not cope when Mary began to think, and act, for herself.

'Well I don't know what to understand but I am quite sure it cannot be the will of God that a child should give up her Father,' Father Woods wrote after his dismissal as Director, 'and nothing will ever make me see anything but temptation in your impressions on this subject... I don't see how our counsels would differ if they both came from God.' In other words, Mary was misguided.

A similar line came from Bishop Matthew Quinn of Bathurst when he said he hoped officials in Rome would be guided by God's will in their decision on the Constitution. What he meant, of course, was that he hoped they would not be silly enough to take Mary's position over his. Years later, Mary wisely observed, 'It is terrible to think how easy it is for us to fancy we are doing God's will, when in reality we are doing our own.'

The wall of opposition encountered from within the Church frustrated and upset Mary, as quite clearly so much more could have been achieved if they all pulled in the same direction. 'Oh if the Church everywhere were only more united, not one Bishop against another, one religious Order or branch against another, one community so jealous of another, if the causes of these things were but removed, or some remedies applied, then God might get more...and a wicked world less.'

In December 1873, after months of waiting, Mary finally received the hoped-for letter from Rome. Monsignor Kirby wrote to say that the Constitution had been amended, and that it was ready for her to collect. Mary was troubled by the reference to 'amendments' and also by the fact that nothing had been said about the Constitution being approved, but she was optimistic nonetheless.

She arrived in Rome in March 1874, soon after receiving the letter, but it was actually three long weeks before Church officials handed her the new Constitution, as revised by Father Bianchi. The original Constitution was, he said, so confusing and illogical, he had needed to start from scratch (words which, needless to say, did not endear him to Father Woods!). He said the revised Constitution should be tried out for a number of years, and then be resubmitted to Rome for approval, with any suggested amendments. Until that time, it was to remain unchanged. While Mary was disappointed the Constitution had not received official approval, the fact that it could not be altered until it was again presented to Rome was significant. This effectively blocked any attempt by a bishop or priest – including Bishop Quinn – to change the Constitution, unless permission was first obtained from Rome.

In the new revised Constitution, Mary was pleased to find that central government had been retained. Other items specified that there was to be only one training house, or 'novitiate', for new Sisters and it was to be at the main convent in Adelaide. The music issue was not clearly addressed (music is outside the scope of a religious Rule), although Mary reported that 'all...were strongly opposed to having instrumental music taught by the Sisters'. While Rome agreed to allow the Sisters to live in small communities of twos and threes, it could not agree to their refusal to own property. In informing the Sisters that the poverty provision had been rejected, a disappointed Mary wrote: 'We were told that as long as we had no houses of our own, we could not possibly preserve unity, that in such cases we would be entirely dependent upon particular Bishops, that we would, at any moment, if we did not yield to all that they might see fit to require, be deprived of our Convents... We were also told that we could be very poor, and yet possess both property and funds for the [Order]... It is not always the poorest dressed and the poorest housed who are the poorest before the searching eyes of God.'

Mary was crushed by Rome's decision to allow the Sisters to own property, but she accepted it gracefully. Initially, she intended to again try to have the poverty provision included in the Constitution when it was resubmitted for approval in several years' time. However, she did not follow through with this, presumably because experience showed her that Rome's stand on the issue was a sensible one. Although she was quite passionate and single-minded in pursuit of her vision for the Sisters of St Joseph, this was tempered by a practical mind. She came to realise that property ownership offered the Sisters some protection against the whims of those in power, both inside and outside the Church.

The poverty issue aside, Mary felt that, overall, her mission in Rome had been a success. Although the Order was still without official sanction, Rome had presented her with a revised Constitution which was protected from further change. When she left Rome, she took with her signed papers to this effect.

With the formal business now completed, Mary looked to her next task – to try once again to secure new priests and Sisters for Adelaide. It was suggested that she should go to Ireland, which would also give her the opportunity of meeting with Bishop Matthew Quinn, who had recently arrived in Dublin, probably to see his family. Father Tappeiner suggested Mary 'break a lance with him', and settle their differences over the Constitution. On 20 April, she had her final meeting with the Pope before leaving Rome for the last time. Afterwards, she received a portrait of Pope Pius IX, together with a blessing carrying his signature.

Mary arrived in Dublin on 8 June 1874, for the first of three visits (one month, two months and two weeks, respectively). While there, she found eight girls willing to migrate to Australia to become Sisters, but very few priests. Three months later, she had her all-important meeting with Bishop Matthew Quinn in Dublin. As expected, he was 'annoyed' and 'sore' about Rome's decision to include central government in the Constitution. At a follow-up meeting a week later, Bishop Quinn told a dismayed Mary he planned to form his own Josephite Order in Bathurst, New South Wales, with the Sisters already working in his diocese. She pleaded with the bishop to at least give her and the Sisters a chance before taking such a drastic step, but his mind was set.

By this time, Mary had been away from Australia for just under two years, and the Sisters back home were beginning to wonder if she would ever return. 'We have made the sacrifice cheerfully,' Father Tappeiner wrote, 'but now we think we have had enough.' Mary, too, had had enough, and she gladly returned to London in October to make final travel arrangements. The group consisted of herself and 15 trainees or 'postulants', as well as three Dominican Sisters for Adelaide, three Good Shepherd Sisters for Melbourne, two priests for Bathurst (secured by Bishop Quinn), and one student for Adelaide. Sadly, Mary reported, 'There are no priests for poor Adelaide.'

On 31 October, the group boarded the *St Osyth* in London for the long voyage home. As the ship pulled out from the dock, Mary reflected a little sadly, 'I seem to have gone through ages since I left Australia.' They arrived in Melbourne almost two months later, on Christmas Day, 1874. However, the letter announcing their return was delayed, and so there was no welcome-home fanfare. In fact, the Good Shepherd Sisters had some trouble convincing those at their Melbourne convent of their identity. 'When they arrived,' one nun recalled, 'the Sisters thought it was a joke and [that] they were young ladies dressed up to give them a Christmas morning surprise.'

Meanwhile, after several days' delay, Mary and her group had boarded a boat for Port Adelaide, and then a train to the city. They reached there on 4 January. Bishop Reynolds met them at the station and escorted them to the new central convent ('Mother House') at Kensington, a suburb of Adelaide, where 100 Sisters were crowded outside the door to welcome Mary home.

Allowing herself just a few days to find her 'land legs' and recover from the long months at sea, Mary immediately set about carrying out Rome's instructions. She sent letters to all the Sisters, at that time numbering 196, explaining the new Constitution and announcing that a General Chapter, or general meeting of the Sisters, would be held. Delegates from Queensland, Bathurst and Adelaide, roughly one for every 10 or 15 Sisters, would attend. The General Chapter would vote in new head Sisters for the Order, and settle some 'vexed and tiresome questions' on the Constitution.

Bishop James Quinn of Brisbane, still attempting to gain control of the Sisters, 'granted permission' for the Sister-in-charge there, Sister Clare, to attend the General Chapter, though, of course, she did not actually require it. But in case Mary should mistake this gesture as one of support, the bishop told her he believed that any decisions regarding the Constitution would be better left to those who knew what they were doing. 'The formation of such a [Constitution] is hardly women's work,' he told Mary, 'and I cannot venture to hope that your Meeting of Sisters will accomplish it.'

Mary, on the other hand, had every confidence that the 'Meeting of Sisters' would achieve a great deal. As well as tidying up administrative matters, she hoped it would boost morale. The fact was, ever since Father Woods' departure as Director, she had detected feelings of resentment in some Sisters. She felt that out of love, respect and admiration for Father Woods, they were having difficulty coming to terms with his dismissal, and did not really understand the reasons for it. They felt they owed loyalty to both Father Woods *and* Mary, and this was causing friction in the Order.

For this reason, she asked Father Woods to join them for the meeting, or else send a letter to be read to the Sisters. Mary also saw it as a timely opportunity to gauge his reaction to events in Rome, and to determine how she currently stood with him. She found out soon enough. 'The very day I heard of your return [from Rome] I was taken ill and have been laid up ever since,' Father Woods wrote pitifully. Refusing to either attend the meeting or send a message, he said: 'It has been almost a death blow to me to see the poverty and simplicity of the [Sisters] of St Joseph destroyed...without my being able to say a word in its defence. I can never get used to that and it makes me sick with sorrow whenever I think of it.'

Father Woods was seething about a number of issues. First, that Mary had gone to Rome without meeting with him. '...Let me tell you that all hope left me when you went to Rome without seeing me as I asked... You know I suffered a great deal in my wanderings these years past, for I am not young now nor strong, so that whatever my delusions have been, I was still heart and soul in the cause and a good friend to the [Sisters]. No wonder then that I thought you tempted when you threw such a friend away.'

Second, that while she was in Rome, his carefully formulated Constitution had been criticised, and then totally rewritten. In his anger, he accused Mary of having the poverty rule deliberately changed – this, despite receiving a copy of the pamphlet she had written in defence of the poverty provision, and actually praising her for her efforts.

Third, that he had been dumped as Director of the Sisters. Mistakenly, he believed Mary had been behind it. '...You perhaps did not know how your having so completely thrown me aside placed me in a false position. Ever since I left Adelaide, I have been labouring for the [Order]... During that time, I have added more than 60 Sisters to its members. And now you write to me accusing me of deceit and want of charity, cruelty to you, turning against my best friends "that I have treated so badly", mistrust of you and Dr Reynolds [the Bishop of Adelaide], turning against the [Order] and trying to destroy it, and what is worse, disobedience to Rome. Well, my dear Sister, this is very hard language...'

Although Mary was responsible for none of these things, she was perhaps being overly optimistic in hoping to enlist Father Woods' co-operation for the Sisters' meeting, when he had been told so many times, and in no uncertain terms, that he was not wanted. For Father Woods, there was nothing worse than feeling unloved and unappreciated. However, he had a tendency to be overly sensitive, feeling slights where none were intended, and it was this that caused him to turn away from Mary. He was absolutely crushed by some of the actions taken against him – justified as they were – and saw them as a personal attack by a trusted friend.

While Father Woods clearly had his foibles, it is sometimes tempting to let these overshadow the fact that at heart he was a good man who wanted to serve God and help others in the best way he could. Admittedly, his vocation was spiked with a good dose of vanity and pride, and a desire for personal glorification, which he himself was the first to admit. 'My poor vulgar vanity, mean and silly, craving for notice, my falseness and hypocrisy – hard words, but God knows the truth.' However through it all, he was always working towards a worthy end.

The General Chapter meeting was held – minus Father Woods – on 19 March 1875, in a highly charged atmosphere. After much discussion, closely monitored by Father Tappeiner and Bishop Reynolds, the new Constitution was accepted and its finer details settled. The Sisters also formally elected Mary as the head of the Order, or Mother General.

When the Sisters emerged from the General Chapter one week later, having voted to make no concessions on any point of the Constitution, Bishop James Quinn of Brisbane was livid. He proclaimed there was no way this 'sentimental young lady' was going to decide the fate of his diocese, and promptly assumed control of the Queensland Sisters. He directed Sister Clare to cut all ties with Mary, or never set foot in Queensland again. Sister Clare chose the latter, and Bishop Quinn duly replaced her with Sister Collette, who he hoped would be more sympathetic to his views.

Bishop Quinn informed the Queensland Sisters that he was now in charge, and ordered them not to write to Mary or Sister Clare, or to open any of their letters. Any Sister who did not agree to the changes could leave – at a date of his choosing. In the meantime, they were to stay put, and do as they were told. In a withering letter to Mary, the bishop ordered her to 'cease to exercise any authority over the Sisters in Queensland and from sending them any communication which might tend to disturb or distract them in the discharge of their duties'.

CHAPTER 11

BATTLES WITH THE BISHOPS QUINN

M ARY had made a most dangerous enemy in James
Quinn. While outwardly charming, he could also be
quite calculating. He made it his business to know who
supported the Sisters and who did not, and was not above
using the latter to his advantage. In Father Woods, he found
a particularly useful instrument – he was well-loved by the
Sisters and had a lot of influence over them. The bishop
believed that if he could get him onside, there was a good
chance he would also win over some of the Queensland
Sisters.

On discovering what Bishop Quinn was up to, Mary
wrote to Monsignor Kirby in Rome, telling him of the
tactics being employed, and the trouble it was creating.
'[Bishop Quinn]…insisted to these poor Sisters that we had
treated Father Woods badly, saying he would get him over to
Queensland and make him their Superior again. I cannot tell
you, dear Monsignor, how much cause we have to deplore
such an unjust view of things by him. It is calculated to do
us an immensity of harm, and though it does seem
uncharitable to say it, I have no confidence in Dr James
Quinn's motives for so acting… He makes out to the Sisters

in Queensland that this has been my work,' Mary protested, 'and you can easily imagine the effect it is calculated to have upon the minds of poor young Sisters...'

She also asked Monsignor Kirby to keep a watchful eye on Father Woods, for although he 'would not intentionally injure even an enemy', she believed he was being led along a dangerous path. 'I have a deep conviction that some mischief is on foot... Altogether there is a painful want of straightforwardness in Father Woods' conduct which is a mystery to me in one so holy.'

Back in Brisbane, Bishop Quinn was making use of the Sisters' enforced break with Mary to coax them around to his way of thinking. Sister Catherine, who was wise to his ways, said he was 'as sweet as sugar to all of us', yet played mercilessly on their fears and insecurities. In one conversation with her, he advised: 'I am your Father now and you are my child. Mind, be obedient, for you don't know the minute God will call you to Himself as you are in delicate health, and [so] do whatever Sister Collette and myself order you to do...'

'I will tell you what I think of the Bishop,' Sister Catherine wrote icily. 'He thinks that if he gives us Father [Woods], we will do all he wants us to do, and then when he gets us under his thumb, he will send [him] away and do what he likes with us. That is truth. I feel sure that is why he is so sweet and kind...'

At the end of April 1875, with no sign that Bishop Quinn would allow the Sisters to adhere to the Constitution, Mary decided it was time to pay a visit to Brisbane. At the very least, she thought, she could offer support to those Sisters resisting pressure from the bishop who, she decided, was 'determined to oppose us in every way'. Mary's first meeting with the bishop was much as she anticipated, with lots of threats and insults. 'The poor Bishop disclaimed my authority over the Sisters, ordered me not to enter our own convent, insisted that I should stay with the Sisters of Mercy instead, and finally threatened to remove me by the police if I attempted to go to my own. Of course I did not mind his threats,' Mary said, 'but told him that I would do my duty and that, unless he agreed to the Sisters remaining faithful to the Mother House [in Adelaide] and observing the [Constitution], I would be compelled to withdraw them.'

With the meeting going nowhere, this was, in fact, what Mary decided to do. However, to be fair to the bishop, she said she would allow the Sisters to stay in Queensland one more year, until Bishop Quinn could find replacement teachers, provided there were no bans on her letters and that they were governed by a Sister appointed by her. 'His Lordship, however, insisted that they should be left entirely to himself, under the [Sister] he pleased, in no way connected with the Mother House, or allowed to communicate with it. He blamed me very much for not consenting to this, and said I was obstinate and ambitious, and that he would see I would not be in authority 12 months hence.'

James Quinn gave a disparaging report on his meeting with Mary to officials in Rome, telling them that the Adelaide Sisterhood was 'infected with fanaticism and insubordination to authority', and that Mary's sole aim was to 'subvert the whole system here'. Mary's calm resolution, even when threatened with the police, would have nettled the bishop. She appeared to be completely unflappable – nothing he said or did touched her. She pushed on relentlessly, determined not to be bullied into submission on something so important as the Sisters' right to live by their

Constitution. Underneath all the armour, however, Mary felt every blow. Although she denied her interviews with the bishop ever affected her, it would have been a harrowing experience to be verbally pummelled by such a powerful and imposing man.

Why did she put herself through it? Why did she not just give in, and save herself a lot of trouble? The reason was that if Mary conceded on the central government issue with Bishop Quinn, then she would be forced to concede it with every other bishop. By and large, the clergy of the day did not share her vision for a uniquely Australian Order of Sisters, and almost certainly, once they had the power, they would have worked at introducing the traditions of European-based Orders, completely dismantling the Sisters of St Joseph in the process.

Mary saw her role with the Sisters as something like that of the commanding officer of a regiment. With so many of the Sisters so loyally defending the spirit of the Order, she could not simply abandon them to the gunfire. In her heart, she was afraid for the outcome – whether the Sisters of St Joseph would survive the battle, and how many would be lost along the way – but she refused to wave a white flag.

There was also Mary's extraordinary belief in the will of God, which allowed her to forgive the seemingly unforgivable. She held that in undertaking this great work for the Australian people, God had intended for her to meet obstacles along the way. She had a remarkable attitude to adversity, in that somehow she was always able to look beyond her own sadness to the 'loving fatherly hand' of God. 'To me, the Will of God is a dear book which I am never tired of reading, which had always some new charm for me... I cannot tell you what a beautiful thing the Will of God seems to me.'

Mary referred to trials and injustices throughout her life, almost perversely, as 'presents from God'. She believed that through suffering, she was brought closer to God – and this was the ultimate reward. She viewed the people who caused her so much trouble not as enemies, but as 'instruments in the hand of God', and therefore counted them amongst her 'most powerful benefactors'. It would be a mistake, however, to think that Mary enjoyed this suffering. Although she was able to see most of the trials she endured in a positive light, she admitted that 'God's presents were often hard to understand' and that she was 'too often cowardly in accepting them'.

With Bishop Quinn, Mary's calm and tenacity finally yielded some good. Two months after their hostile meeting, in mid 1875, he called a truce. 'He has consented to receive [a head Sister] appointed by the Mother House, and to allow her the free exercise of [the Constitution] in every respect, "pending the decision of the Holy See",' she reported to Rome. 'He only did this at the last moment and when he found all the Sisters determined to return to their Mother House rather than remain with him separated from it...'

Mary agreed not to withdraw the Sisters from Queensland until Bishop Quinn found replacements for them. He told Mary he would begin searching for them immediately. Mary received little joy from this victory over her powerful opponent. The cynic in her told her he was probably only buying time to rethink his plans, but she did not have the energy to challenge him. The physical and mental stresses of recent years had left her exhausted and sick. 'I was for many weeks dangerously ill, so ill that I

nearly died... I was weary of the world and its crosses... The
mental conflict had been too much for me...'

Mary's doctors warned her that although the Sisters
needed her, they would not wish her to kill herself in the
process: 'My health is in a very uncertain state, and though
apparently strong enough, the Doctors say I may die very
suddenly, and that I have to try to keep as quiet as possible.'
Although she rightly suspected that constant anxiety was
the main cause of her ill health, the ceaseless travelling from
colony to colony, hundreds of miles at a stretch, did not help.
'I often feel inclined to envy my quiet country Sisters who
have the same daily routine and so much peace whilst I am
one day in a rough mail coach, again in a steamer, in rain
and storm, but worse than all, when I have to see Bishops
and Priests, and, in the cause of our loved work, have to hold
out against all their arguments and threats, I who would so
gladly obey the least amongst them.'

Despite the cease-fire with Bishop Quinn, Mary warned
the newly appointed Sister-in-charge in Queensland, Sister
Josephine, never to let down her guard, as it was all the
bishop needed to gain the advantage. 'Remember that your
least word may be twisted and turned every way by those
who do not understand us. Be guarded with the priests but
make friends with them. Be kind to the poor foreigners;
remember that I was a foreigner once and as such was never
laughed at, nor unkindly criticised... Do not be won over by
any of [the Bishop's] fine and most kind sayings – and do not
yield anything even in opinion to him – that is, concerning
the things in dispute,' Mary advised. 'But don't argue with
him, coax him rather by telling him how much the Sisters
really do love him and now more than ever since he is going
to work with [me] and not against [me]...'

With the problems in Queensland settled for the time being, Mary returned to Adelaide via Bathurst, New South Wales, where, if she could only have guessed, she was about to take her place in an almost identical battle with James' brother, Matthew. With Bishop Matthew Quinn still in Europe, his stand-in, Father McAuliffe, gathered together all the Sisters to give Mary a hearty welcome to Bathurst. Some of the Sisters took the opportunity to renew their vows, but Mary decided against allowing any new Sisters to make their vows, as it would have angered the absent bishop to find more nuns loyal to a Constitution that he, like his brother, refused to accept.

Mary had left Bathurst by the time Matthew Quinn returned in early December 1875. With him was a group of Irish women who wished to become Sisters. However, he was adamant they would join an Order of which he, and not Mary, had control. While in Europe, Bishop Quinn resolved to pursue plans to set up a new Josephite Order, with a Constitution of his own devising. The Irish women would be its first members, closely followed, he hoped, by Mary's Sisters in Bathurst. On Christmas Eve, at an assembly of all the Bathurst Sisters, he gave them an ultimatum – join his Order and stay at The Vale (the main Bathurst convent at Perthville, about 8 km out of town), or else be 'banished' to remote country convents. All but two packed their bags.

The bishop was perfectly entitled to form his own Order of Sisters. In fact, it was probably the best solution in what looked like becoming an unhappy situation for all. However, Mary was concerned that undue pressure was being placed on the Sisters to make the change-over, and that they were not being told the whole truth. She had discovered, for instance, that some of the priests were 'making the most

out-of-the-way statements, either to frighten [the Sisters]
into doing what was wanted or from some other motive best
known to themselves'. The bishop, meanwhile, was telling
the Sisters that if they quit Bathurst, Adelaide would not
take them back. Reluctantly, Mary prepared for another
sojourn in Bathurst.

On her arrival there in January 1876, Bishop Quinn
ordered Mary not to visit The Vale convent, but to stay with
the Sisters of Mercy, just as she had to do in Queensland.
While hardly expecting an open-arms welcome, this move
re-enforced her fears about Bishop Quinn's tactics. She
wanted no such games from the Sisters. 'I do not want to
influence them in any way. Tell them so,' she advised, in a
message smuggled to The Vale by one of the Sisters. 'If they
adhere to the [Constitution]...let them candidly tell the
Bishop so, but let there be no insincerity or double dealing
either with him or with me.'

Despite the bishop's orders, Mary was determined to pay
a visit to the Sisters who had been sent away from The Vale
for upholding their Constitution. 'I would gladly have
followed [the Bishop's orders] if my duty to my poor Sisters
allowed of it. As it was, I could not, and on arriving at
Trunkey [about 50 km out] how did I find these poor ones?
Their school closed, sickness raging in the town, Sister
Helena ill, Sister Mary Clare suffering from a dangerously
sore thumb, another Sister from something else, and no
Doctor near...'

There was another factor compounding Mary's souring
relations with the bishop. He was angry about her previous
visit to Bathurst, conducted while he was away. Desperate
not to become involved, the priest that had played host to
Mary, Father McAuliffe, was insisting, quite shamelessly,

that he had known nothing of the visit. 'He never gave me reason to suppose that he was anything but a sincere friend of mine...' Mary said, in explaining to Bishop Quinn the true circumstances of the visit. 'I did not believe it possible that he would allow you to remain under the impression that I had acted in any way without his full knowledge and consent... [I was told that] Father McAuliffe hoped I would not implicate him in any way, as to do so would cause him great trouble...'

This was one more problem Mary could do without, but even so, her thoughts were with Father McAuliffe. 'On my knees I implore you, my dear Lord, to forgive him if you really think he has deceived you. He must have meant well but was perhaps puzzled how to act.' This series of disputes with Matthew Quinn proved to Mary that they would never be able to work together as a team. To allow the Sisters to stay on in Bathurst, particularly in the shadow of a second Josephite Order which the bishop was still determined to establish, would be confusing and compromising to all. Mary had no alternative but to remove the Sisters from Bathurst, which she did in February 1876. Informing Cardinal Franchi in Rome, she wrote: 'The Sisters themselves implored me to take them away, saying they were so unhappy, that the priests were constantly urging them to give up their [Constitution], and turning into ridicule the actions of their Superiors. Some told me it was more than they could endure, and they feared getting into some trouble.'

Bishop Quinn was outraged by the withdrawal, and convinced himself that Mary, driven by spite and ambition, was trying to usurp his power. He told the Sisters 'he would not support the reign of [the bishop of Adelaide] Dr

Reynolds and Mother Mary, and not of them only but of any who would come after them'. Furthermore, he could not and would not allow a Sister from another diocese to 'upset mine and close my schools'. In vain, Mary tried to explain to the bishop that she was simply acting on the wishes of the Sisters. '...Nothing could induce [the Sisters] to remain at The Vale separated from us,' she told him. 'They said that, if it were true I would not receive them, they would go back to the world and earn their bread, and that, if their souls were lost I would be accountable, for they regarded me as their Mother, and now I was casting them off. I think your Lordship will soon see that as we could not work together as before, it was better to part at once. I have completely failed in my effort to save you from additional care and annoyance...'

But the bishop could not be placated – he was not used to being beaten, and especially not by a woman. '...Really how [Rome] could have allowed the essential portion of the rules of a community in my diocese without consulting me is a thing I cannot understand,' an indignant Matthew Quinn wrote angrily to Monsignor Kirby, 'and this too at the bidding of a woman who never spent one hour in religious training... Her claims to govern the Sisters of St Joseph in my diocese are mere pretensions...' She owed her position to merely being 'the first to present herself' to the Order.

Bishop Quinn's campaign against Mary had some impact. For many years afterwards, Mary was remembered in the Bathurst district not as a good and holy Sister, but as 'that woman who made her raid on us'. Even in Rome, her star shone a little less brightly. Monsignor Kirby told Bishop Quinn he thought Mary's decision to remove the Sisters from Bathurst was improper, ill-timed and imprudent. But

Mary was now wise to the politics of the Church, and could deduce the reason behind such a comment. 'Putting everything together, my opinion of the whole is this – [Rome] never anticipated so much resistance [to the Constitution], that if it had, it might not have given us so much power to act, but that having done so, it will uphold its work – only very carefully so as not to irritate any who are opposed to us...'

One thing Mary could not settle in her mind, however, was why Monsignor Kirby chose to be the confidant of both Bishop Quinn and herself. She wondered if it was simply to stay 'in the know', or whether there was another reason. 'I cannot help thinking how strange a post you have,' she told him. 'You are the one to whom above all others I look to advocate if necessary our earnest wishes on these matters, and with the same confidence this good Bishop looks to you for a like aid on his view of the whole.' After a time, Mary no longer felt comfortable with this arrangement with Monsignor Kirby, and decided it would be best to find another representative in Rome. This turned out to be a Scot, Dr Grant. Contrary to the comments of Monsignor Kirby, he reassured Mary that Rome approved of her decision to withdraw the Sisters from Bathurst, and that she had acted in line with the authority she had been given.

Upon the Sisters' departure from Bathurst, Matthew Quinn followed through with his plans to set up a diocesan Order of the Sisters of St Joseph, now known as the 'Black' Josephites (they wore a black habit) or the Australian–New Zealand Federation of Sisters of St Joseph. After Bathurst, they established themselves in Goulburn, New South Wales; Maitland, New South Wales; Tasmania; and New Zealand. Father Woods wrote their Constitution, adapting the

Adelaide Rule, restoring the poverty provision and removing all references to central government, so as to give the Bishop absolute control. For a time, he was also its spiritual director, until in 1882, after some difference of opinion, Bishop Quinn turned him out of Bathurst.

In April 1878, two years after the Sisters left Bathurst, Mary was again called to Queensland, where the uneasy armistice reached in 1875 with Bishop James Quinn was beginning to crumble. Despite his promise to find replacement teachers for the Sisters so that Mary could withdraw them from Queensland, the bishop had done absolutely nothing in this regard. Mary directed the Sister-in-charge there, Sister Josephine, not to open more schools 'to suit the convenience of a Bishop who is working against us, and who openly says he will only keep us as long as it suits him...'

But she had some trouble convincing Sister Josephine, who had been won over by the bishop's charm, that her hard line was warranted: 'I know...how hard you must find it to doubt the sincerity of so good a man as the Brisbane Bishop,' Mary told her. 'It grieves me so much that I cannot agree... I fear [that you], fancying all people good...may, now and then, be tempted to think the Mother General should give in a little more than she does, and that if so, all would end well... She must think of the [Order], its grand work and its future.'

The fact was, Mary had lost all patience with Bishop Quinn. She was battle-weary, worn down by the years of constant struggle, and found herself wondering, time and time again, when it would ever end. To one Sister, she revealed: 'I am ashamed to tell you that I have been tempted to fly from you all and from the eye of any mortal who would know me. I cannot tell you what I have suffered. I am not a moment sure of myself. Every way I turn there is deceit and falsehood. I see priests deceiving their Bishop, Religious deceiving their Superiors, I see myself tepid and cold and losing heart so dreadfully at times...'

On days like these, when her spirits were down, she often blamed herself for the Sisters' predicament. Without her, she thought, they may well be given the chance to live their lives in peace. Sometimes she felt so desperate that she actually prayed to God to end her life. 'I often think that rest will come to my dear Sisters when I am gone. Many prejudices are directed against myself, for Bishops and priests think me some extraordinary and bold woman. Sometimes it wearies me that they think this, and I have wished, as far as I dared without sin, that it might please God to take me away...' Adding to her misery was the fact that some of the Queensland Sisters were losing heart and thinking of quitting the Order. 'Believe me,' one Sister wrote harshly, 'it is a critical time and place to leave us young, untried Sisters who have had little experience of the world or of priests.'

To Dr Grant, her confidant in Rome, Mary revealed the Queensland situation was edging towards a crisis similar to that in Bathurst. '...Unless Dr Quinn will take more care of the Sisters in Queensland..., we can have no alternative but to recall such as we believe to be in danger. [I hope] to get this matter peaceably settled, but confess that my heart fails me sometimes, for I have very little confidence in Dr James Quinn.'

The likelihood of any 'peaceful settlement', however, was fast diminishing. Over recent months, the bishop had doubled his efforts to lure Father Woods to Queensland, as a sweetener for those Sisters who agreed to support him.

Mary could only hope Father Woods would not give in – although she had good reason to worry. A meeting she had with him in Penola in 1876 proved that Bishop Quinn was having some success in reshaping Father Woods' views. 'He told me that Dr Quinn wanted him to assist him in separating the Queensland Sisters from Adelaide, and to tell you the truth, I think he would do so if he were there – he would, I think, to gain his own ends. He would just look to the immediate result and not to the future of inevitable confusion that would follow... I pointed out to him...the injury he would do this [Order], his first work, by encouraging Sisters to leave it for another... He could not see anything wrong with it...'

More alarming were his ambitions to become Director of the Sisters in Queensland. 'He asked me...whether, if he were in Queensland, he could not direct the Sisters, that Bishop Reynolds [of Adelaide] would have nothing to do with that, that no one could interfere unless I did. Of course the question was a kind of indirect one, so painful to me that I avoided answering it, hoping his own sense would show that what Rome had ordered for the Sisters in one place applied to them in all places...'

Mary had gone to Penola with an offer in hand from Bishop Reynolds, who thought it better to accept Father Woods back into Adelaide than see him go to Queensland. But the conditions were harsh, and Father Woods bluntly refused the offer. 'But the morning we parted,' Mary reported, 'he promised me (unasked) that he would not go to Queensland... But he changes so – at one time doubting or not trusting Dr James, and at another seeming almost the opposite... Surely never was a work more tried than ours. If other works had enemies to contend with, they were outside;

we have our own dear Father both with us and against us. He is with us in affection and against us in opinion... Well, we parted – in friendship and affection,' she concluded, 'but in deep sorrow and disappointment on my part. I cannot describe the anguish I feel when thinking of him and his views. It is better not to dwell on this subject for it does me no good... He is too sensitive and tender-hearted to be a faithful guide of souls, poor dear Father.'

In Father Woods, once a good and true friend, Mary now saw another person out to deceive her. 'If I dared, I would complain, for my heart is literally crushed with sorrow. The stand-off coldness of [Father Woods], the inconsistency of his letters, at one time telling me that he cheerfully accepts the decisions of Rome, and at another writing in the reverse strain, misunderstanding me so grossly and avoiding me as he does. I tell you, Sister, these things have crushed me to the heart and I have even dared to envy the dead. I stand utterly alone... I trust no human being now...' This duplicity on Father Woods' part hurt and saddened Mary, but if she had recalled his words from 10 years before, she may have found some solace. 'You know that I was brought up in an atmosphere of vanity and untruthfulness, and I never can correct these two defects. I believe God will always leave me in them, and if [God] will accept such service as I give...well, then, I can go on tranquilly.'

As Mary had half-anticipated, Father Woods did finally agree to join forces with Bishop Quinn. In 1878, he made the move to Queensland. Instantly on guard, Mary instructed the Sisters to be 'dutiful and affectionate' to their former Director, but not to accept any guidance from him. Ominously, she warned that she believed many snares would be set for them. She was worried about the likely effects of

Father Woods' visit on the Sisters, and expressed her fears to Dr Grant in Rome. 'There is something too human, too like idolatry in the feelings I have heard some [Sisters] express towards him. He in his own pure-minded charity cannot see any danger in this. He is amiable, has a most winning manner, and great powers of persuasion...'

Once in Brisbane, Father Woods visited the Josephite convents, sounding out the Sisters to determine how much loyalty he still commanded. Pleading his case, he told the Sisters that Mary had treated him unjustly, and that she had caused him to be removed as Director. Not surprisingly, some of the Sisters began to wonder if perhaps what he said was true.

With this new danger presented by Father Woods, Mary, now 36, again set out for Brisbane, arriving in November 1878. 'The report here is that Father Woods was only feeling his way this time,' she noted, 'that he wanted to find out the Sisters most attached to him and most likely to yield to his ideas... He avoided me in the most marked manner, only calling at the last moment to say goodbye, and seeming on thorns until he got away. Seeing this partly opened [the Sisters'] eyes. He had not a good word to say of us in Adelaide, and even went so far as to tell Sister Josephine in the presence of others that now was a golden opportunity to separate from it [i.e. the Order].'

Mary was angry with Father Woods for his deceit, and his attempts to undermine her character, without ever having the courage to confront her with his accusations. In a letter to him several months later, she lashed out, 'You know how you hurried away from Brisbane last December, being there a whole day and night after you heard of my arrival and not granting me even five minutes conversation. You know how disobediently and deceitfully you had allowed some of the Sisters to act, how your remarks about me and Adelaide had prejudiced them against the Superior they were bound by their vows to obey; and you wonder that I felt called upon to ask the Archbishop [Vaughan of Sydney] to speak to you?

'But why,' she continued, 'if you had such charges to make against me, why did you remain over a week in Brisbane and not come to see me about them, and why did you rather say to the Sisters things so calculated to destroy their peace and to make them think ill of their superiors? Poor things,' Mary told Father Woods, 'they did not like to tell me, but they were unhappy, and fortunately for their peace they were candid with me. They told me you were sorry after you had told them, and I daresay you were; but was that enough to ease their minds or remove the unjust impression your words conveyed? ... If you think you have a grievance against me, tell it to myself, but not to the poor Sisters.'

Mary returned to Adelaide in January 1879, but was back in Queensland again in April, determined to force a resolution to the tensions. Before she left, she advised Dr Campbell in Rome (who replaced Dr Grant on his death) that matters were coming to a head: 'Our position is extremely painful in Queensland. The good Bishop there seems determined not to work with us and yet does not seem to wish any Sisters to return to the Mother House. As matters stand,' she said, 'we cannot help thinking that it would be much better to withdraw all our Sisters from a place where their vocations are greatly endangered and where their position seems to do more harm than good to Religion...'

This was, in fact, exactly what Mary did. In the last seven months of 1879, she recalled the Queensland Sisters and closed the remaining convents. The local community were outraged at losing their beloved Sisters and teachers, and entirely blamed the bishop. They wrote emotion-charged letters to the newspapers and presented a petition with more than 1000 names, pleading with the bishop to let the Sisters stay. This onslaught of publicity was the last thing Mary wanted, as it only served to provoke an already angry bishop. He accused Mary of being the ringleader, claiming she and her supporters had 'lied shamelessly' to the newspapers, when, in fact, she was making excuses for the bishop's actions, and begging the petitioners to end their campaign.

Shaken by these latest events, Mary escaped to Sydney, to take advice from her friend, Archbishop Vaughan. When Bishop Quinn discovered that she had retreated to the territory of Archbishop Vaughan (who, by virtue of being an Englishman, was necessarily an adversary of his), he believed he had unearthed a conspiracy. 'Whether she was in league with the Archbishop to remove the Sisters or not, is not clear,' Bishop Quinn wrote to Rome, 'but having created discontentment in Brisbane, she went off to Sydney for a few days, and returning from there took the Sisters holus bolus to Sydney...'

In a scathing letter to Bishop Reynolds in Adelaide, James Quinn denounced Mary as merely 'the daughter of a colonial seminarian', adding that it was 'impossible for me to accept the government of a woman or to have a community of nuns governed by a lady from Adelaide. I won't allow any woman to make a disturbance in my diocese.' But Mary would not be bullied. 'He defied me to be firm; I did what I believed to be my duty.' Accordingly, she completed the Sisters' withdrawal from Queensland in 1880.

CHAPTER 12

MOTHER MARY

IN dealing with the Queensland bishop with such conviction, Mary showed herself to be a woman of fortitude and tenacity, prepared to speak and act against those in power. For the era, she was quite remarkable.

In 19th century Australia, women mostly married and became mothers of large families – eight children was considered average – and, outside the cities, lived an isolated life. If women did paid work, it was usually in factories or other households, where they earned about a third as much as the men. In 1873, the Victorian Factory Act moved to improve the lot of women, by introducing eight-hour working days and better conditions.

Legally, women were considered an extension of their husbands – they were denied the vote, and were unable to acquire or dispose of property in their own right. (Interestingly, the first Australian colony to give women the vote was South Australia, where Mary was a leading figure. This legislation was passed in 1894.) Further disempowering women – especially working-class women in rural areas – was the fact that until the Sisters of St Joseph came along, many received little, or no, education.

A woman of Mary's power and strength was something of an enigma in a country founded on a spirit of mateship and grounded in chauvinism. In its own way, the Church embraced this ethos. The Church journal, *Austral Light*, commented that women 'need never stoop to that work which is better suited to the grosser nature of man' – speaking, in this instance, about women's right to vote, although it could equally have applied to their stand on any number of issues.

In challenging powerful Church figures like the Bishops Quinn, Mary helped redefine the role of women, not only in the Church, but in society. She believed she was called by God to perform a task, and if she offended the sensibilities of some powerful men, then so be it.

In resolving the crises in Bathurst and Brisbane, Mary successfully piloted the Sisters of St Joseph through some of their most turbulent years. However, the troubles were not without impact. Between 1875 and 1880, only 48 Sisters joined the Order, while an unusually high 37 left it. Compare this with the two-year period, 1873 to 1874, where 78 Sisters joined and only four left, and the extent of damage becomes clear. The late 1870s were an oppressive time for the Sisters – not only politically, but financially as well. Money had always been in short supply, but with the building of the Mother House convent in Kensington, Adelaide, the Sisters began to know the nagging worry of monthly mortgage payments and burgeoning debt. To cope, the Sisters often did without basic household items, such as candles and kerosene, and went begging door-to-door for small parcels of food, which were always carefully rationed. However, they could always rely on Mary's concern for their welfare.

Photograph taken at the Bishop's House, Adelaide, when Reynolds became
Archbishop, September 1887.
Front row: Bishops John Dunne, Wilcannia; James Moore, Ballarat;
Daniel Murphy, Hobart; Archbishop Thomas Joseph Carr, Melbourne;
Cardinal Patrick Moran, Sydney; Archbishop Christopher Reynolds, Adelaide;
Patrick Moran, Dunedin New Zealand; Martin Gibney, Perth; James Corbett, Sale.

Second row: Fathers Patrick Hurley, Peder Jorgenson, Philip Landy;
Dean Michael J. Ryan; Dr D. F. O'Hagan, Sydney; Archdeacon Patrick Russell;
Mosignor Frederick Byrne; Father Thomas Lee.

Back row: Father William McEvoy; Dean Daniel Beechinor, Launceston;
Father James Byrne, John J. Power, Edmund O'Brien and Michael O'Brien.

Photo: Adelaide Catholic Archive.

Mary, in the year of her excommunication, at the age of 29.

Photo: Mary MacKillop Archive, North Sydney, NSW.

Sister Bernard Walsh in around 1883. She took over from Mary as Mother General of the Sisters of St Joseph – amid some controversy – in 1888, and died in that role ten years later.

Photo: Mary MacKillop Archive, North Sydney, NSW.

Annie, Mary and Donald
MacKillop around 1898.

Photo: Mary MacKillop Archive,
North Sydney, NSW.

Annie MacKillop, who, as a teenager,
loved to pull pranks on her older
sister, Mary.

Photo: Mary MacKillop Crypt, Kensington, SA.

Mary's brother, Donald MacKillop, aged
about 30. He was a Jesuit priest.

Photo: Mary MacKillop Archive, North Sydney, NSW.

Sister Monica Phillips, Mary's loyal and dependable deputy in Adelaide during the battle with Bishop Reynolds in 1885.

Photo: Mary MacKillop Archive, North Sydney, NSW.

Mary and Sister Josephine McMullen (kneeling). In 1867 she became the first Adelaide resident to join the Sisters of St Joseph.

Photo: Mary MacKillop Archive, North Sydney, NSW.

Sister Mechtilde Woods, daughter of Catherine Griffin and James Woods, elder brother of Julian Tenison Woods. A close and loyal friend to Mary, she joined the Sisters in 1869.

Photo: Mary MacKillop Archive, North Sydney, NSW.

Mary and Sister Annette Henschke, her lifelong friend and confidante, in the mid-1880s.

Photo: Mary MacKillop Archive, North Sydney, NSW.

Sister Annette Henschke and her niece.

Photo: Mary MacKillop Archive, North Sydney, NSW.

Elzear Torreggiani (1830–1904), Bishop of Armidale, New South Wales, 1879–1904. Mary often turned to him for advice.

Photo: Mary MacKillop Archive, North Sydney, NSW.

Roger Bede Vaughan (1834–1883), one of the few senior churchmen who was constant in his support for the Sisters. He was Archbishop of Sydney 1877–1883.

Photo: Mary MacKillop Archive, North Sydney, NSW.

St Joseph's Convent, Kensington, South Australia, in
the late 1870s. It became the 'Mother House'. Due to
a lack of funds, the building was not completed for
another 30-odd years.

Photo: Mary MacKillop Archive, North Sydney, NSW.

Opening of the newly
completed Kensington
Convent, South Australia, on
24 June 1906.

*Photo: Mary MacKillop Archive, North
Sydney, NSW.*

Emmanuel Solomon, a Jewish merchant and Member of Parliament, who provided a row of cottages rent-free on several occasions to accommodate Mary and the Sisters during the troubled beginnings of the Order in Adelaide and following her excommunication.

Photo: Mortlock Library, State Library of South Australia, SSL: M: B2767.

Johanna Barr-Smith. She and her husband Robert, both Protestants, were generous benefactors to the Sisters.

Photo: Mortlock Library, State Library of South Australia, SSL: M: B2767.

'On one occasion,' Sister Mary Placid remembered, 'when I was a young professed Sister, another young Sister and I were sent to the country. The train left about 7pm and we would not reach our destination until about 11pm. We left Mount Street [convent in Sydney] without tea; somehow Mother found out.

'A few minutes before the train left,' Sister Mary Placid said, 'Mother Mary arrived almost breathless with some lunch in a paper bag, and some fruit. When she saw our distress at her coming, she smiled gaily and said she could not have her children without anything to eat until after 11 o'clock.'

Another time, Mary travelled almost 300 km to be with a dying Sister at Port Augusta: '[The Sister] was putting out a crude kerosene lamp in the church after evening devotions,' Sister Patricia related. 'The lamp burst and in a moment the Sister was engulfed in flames. She lingered for some days in great agony and each day kept asking for Mother Mary.' On hearing of the tragedy, Mary set out from Adelaide immediately, taking a private coach as no other transport was available at that time of day. When she reached Mount Remarkable, about 60 km from Port Augusta, she could not find a coach-driver willing to drive her the rest of the way, as it was dark, and a rough and dangerous trip. Mary walked into the local hotel, convinced she would find some able men there. '…Mother said, "Gentlemen, my Sister at Port Augusta is dying, and is constantly asking for me. If one of you will lend me a horse, I will ride there."

'Chivalry was not quite dead in those Celtic hearts,' Sister Patricia said. 'Two or three jumped up, got a pair of spanking horses and a buggy, and drove her on that afternoon, where she was in time to console the dying Sister.'

The expense of this constant travel, as well as food and clothing for an ever-growing number of Sisters, saw the Sisters relying more and more on the good will of friends and supporters. Sometimes they gave money – Mary's friend, Mrs Johanna Barr-Smith, the non-Catholic wife of a high-profile businessman, donated 2000 pounds towards the new Mother House – other times, they gave their services.

One of their benefactors was Adelaide doctor, Doctor Benson, a Protestant, who always called on the Sisters without charge. When, after years of his dedicated care, the doctor died, Mary promised to do all she could for his near-destitute family: 'Oh! Sister I feel this death more than words can express... Poor dear Doctor, he is universally loved and regretted. He left very little provision for his wife and children. His too generous heart never allowed him to save. We have offered to educate for the present Lottie and the younger boys. Poor Mrs Benson is so grateful. When I made the offer she cried and embracing me said, "He told me you would be kind!"' So that the doctor would never be forgotten, Mary arranged for the Josephites to give land for a monument to be built in his honour.

While debts and lack of money remained a problem for many years, one thing the Sisters never ran short of was support – they were loved and appreciated by nearly all wherever they went. One of their many champions was Stanley James, known as 'Vagabond', who regularly wrote stories on social injustice for Australian newspapers. Several times, he wrote about the Sisters of St Joseph, in articles which were poignant and rich in their praise.

'A sight familiar to all in the streets of Adelaide, in the tram cars, and more particularly in what back slums this beautiful city possesses – and there are vile dens and haunts as bad as any in Australia – is that of two female figures, clad in coarse brown and black alpaca garments,' he wrote in *The Victorian Review* journal. 'Their bandaged features and the rosary slung from the waist show that they are nuns... These are the Sisters of St Joseph, who are ever to be seen busy in the cause of their Master... The proof that they are esteemed by all classes is the liberal support that they receive from Protestants, as well as those of their own Creed. Many leading Protestant citizens of South Australia they refer to as being their "best friends"...' With piercing insight, he added, 'Not only have the Sisters of St Joseph been unchecked by Protestant criticism, but they have been warmly supported by Protestants... Indeed, the only troubles they had were with the officials of their own faith.'

One of the things that most endeared the Sisters to the community was their willingness, in the spirit of Jesus, to help the down-and-outs that no one else would touch. Mary passed on to the Sisters this egalitarian spirit, where every person, regardless of their social standing, religious beliefs, race or education, was valued and respected as an individual. Sister Annette saw this spirit in action at the Refuge in Adelaide, a home for 'fallen' girls. 'Her great idea was to save the poor unfortunate girls. She did, indeed, show great anxiety to keep the work going. She instructed me to be very kind to them, not to treat them as slaves or servants... Many of the girls would not have stayed except for Mother's influence. We had bad characters who came from the gaols, streets and everywhere. She said they were to have every comfort...'

Sister Annette said the one thing Mary could not bear was for a child to feel they were somehow less important because they were born into a poor family. If it was at all possible, she would act to remedy the situation, even if it meant crossing high-ranking members of the clergy, in this instance, Archdeacon Russell. 'The Archdeacon had a school at Glenelg [10 km from Adelaide] in which there was a partition separating the high school from the poor school,' Sister Annette told. '...When Mother went there, she had the partition taken down because she wanted there to be no distinction.'

Sister Annette also recalled a visit Mary made to an Adelaide gaol, to offer comfort to a man, Fagan, sentenced to death for murder, and reputedly one of the worst criminals the colony had seen. Dr Reynolds and the priests went to see him but he was like a lion and had to be chained down. 'He was just like a wild animal. Mother Mary and Sister Felicitas went to see him. The warders told them not to go in. They went in and prayed, and Mother was so affected that the tears poured down her face. This so moved him that he knelt and prayed with them. At the beginning he was abrupt with Mother but he calmed down and became as gentle as a lamb.' Mary persuaded Fagan to allow a priest to hear his confession and give him Holy Communion. On the day he was to be hanged, she asked to be allowed to climb the scaffold with him, but the authorities refused.

Many years later, Sister Mary Bridget – 'a little insignificant Sister' – recalled the tender loving care she received at Mary's hands, which probably saved her life. 'I was very ill when I was a young professed Sister and was supposed to be dying. Mother Mary put me in her own room and looked after me for nine days and would not let anyone but herself mind me, waiting on me hand and foot. When I was getting better, she said I was to eat meat on Friday and take stimulants ordered by the doctor... When I had recovered sufficiently to travel, she sent me to Camden [south of Sydney],' Sister Mary Bridget said. 'I got worse there. The night I was anointed, Mother arrived in Camden at 12 o'clock at night. She came to Camden for three weeks until I was sufficiently well to return to North Shore [Sydney]. I owe her a lifelong gratitude. Fancy her doing so much for a little insignificant Sister like me.'

Mary's acute social conscience was never more evident than in her position as Mother General. She was always even-handed and fair with the Sisters, and never considered herself as anything other than one of the workers. 'She would do what other Sisters would not do,' Sister Annette noted. 'In those days there was no water drainage, and she would clean those places out. Other Sisters refused to do this, saying a man should be employed.' Her bedroom in the Mother House convent in Kensington, Adelaide, was small and modest, even by Josephite standards, and despite all the paperwork she had to sort through, she had no office – she used the common room, or sometimes the cellar. This humble existence ensured that Mary did not lose touch with the people she and the Sisters were working to serve.

But Mary's generous and caring nature was not always appreciated by the Sisters – on one particular occasion, it cost two of them a long walk and a good deal of sweat: 'Another Sister and I were travelling with Mother Mary in Cobb & Co's coach which had its full complement of passengers,' one nun recounted. 'When we came to a very steep hill, Mother thought it was too much for the horses. She got out of the coach, and we also, much against our will as the hill was very long as well as steep, and to make matters worse, Mother asked us to join her in saying [prayers] for the driver of the coach. (He was a most disagreeable man who was swearing at his horses much of the time.) Mother walked to the top of the hill in the best of spirits and provided the driver with some refreshments as the day was very hot.'

Mary herself could little afford such selfless gestures – her health had been shaky for a number of years, made worse by long days spent in rickety traps or hot, airless coaches. She had heart trouble from time to time, but by far the most persistent and debilitating problem was dysmenorrhoea (painful periods) – something which many women, even today, know all about. However, Mary's attacks seemed particularly severe, often accompanied by migraines, dizzy spells, fever and nausea, and occurring not monthly but fortnightly.

It was not something she could talk about openly – 'women's problems' were taboo in all but the most intimate conversations with another woman, usually a close female relative, and even then, one never went into details. To her mother, Mary wrote: 'The illnesses you know of try me terribly. Doctor orders quiet and freedom from care... I have determined when the next is coming to go away for a few days where no one can see me or bother me, and try what effect that can have.' She refused to give in to the pain if she possibly could, but sometimes it was unbearable. 'The least mental exertion brings on the wild throbbing of my temples, and as you see my hand is far from steady...'

One of her close friends, Sister Mechtilde, who was also Father Woods' niece, noted: 'With these headaches [Mary] could not lift her head sometimes, and could not touch any food while she had them. Yet I never heard her utter an impatient word. She used to fight against them. She tried to keep at her duties until she could not last out any longer...

These headaches sometimes lasted two or three days, and she used to get them very often...' The only thing that seemed to help was one or two spoonsful of brandy, which was a common home-remedy for such conditions. Mary was aware that some in the Church regarded those who touched spirits, whatever the circumstances, in the same light as murderers and thieves. However, she was grounded in a sound Scottish heritage, where a nip of spirits was about as scandalous as a glass of red wine over dinner would be today. It was therefore impossible for her to view a medicinal dose of brandy – prescribed by a doctor, and the only thing that could keep her on her feet – with any sort of horror. However, Mary was well aware of the fine line between use and abuse. She recognised the risk of becoming alcohol-dependent, so as a precaution – and to safeguard against anyone ever misconstruing the facts – she always had an assigned Sister carefully measure out the dose, and then lock away the bottle.

In the early 1880s, a decade of expansion and change in Australia, Mary and the Sisters found themselves in relatively calm waters – the stresses created by the Quinn brothers had been removed, and one of Mary's most ardent supporters, Archbishop Vaughan of Sydney, had provided a warm welcome for the Sisters exiting Queensland. 'The Archbishop...gives [us] full play – treats me with trusting kindness that goes to my heart after the past in Queensland.'

In 1880, the Sisters opened their first Sydney school in Penrith, in the western suburbs. Later came The Providence in the inner-city area of The Rocks – a dismal, squalid place in those days – and schools in Sydney's Kent Street and High Street.

In early 1881, Mary began planning for the second General Chapter meeting in which a new Mother General was due to be elected. She did not consider herself eligible for re-election, as she had already served in the position for more than the maximum 12 years set down in the Constitution. She admitted to her closest friends that she was looking forward to passing on the reins of what had been a demanding and stressful job. 'Before I came into Religion,' Mary confided, 'I used to long for it as a state of rest to mind, if not to body. I used to think that then I would have no care…' Although she had since tossed away the rose-coloured glasses, she certainly hoped that by stepping down as Mother General, she would be able to enjoy a more peaceful and spiritually fulfilling life. In what she expected to be her last letter as Mother General to the Sisters, Mary asked for forgiveness for the times she had let them down, and offered support for her successor.

Another issue that was to be settled at the General Chapter was whether Archbishop Vaughan of Sydney should be given the go-ahead to open a novitiate to train new Sisters. What made this a particularly ticklish question was that the Quinn brothers had each requested a novitiate, but had been refused on the grounds that Rome would not allow a second novitiate (there was one already in Adelaide) until the Order was more established.

The reason the bishops were so keen to have a novitiate in their diocese was that it would give them some influence over the training received by new Sisters, and hence some control over the future direction of the Order. Mary had always intended opening a second novitiate, and spoke about it as early as 1874. 'I do not want to confine the novitiate to Adelaide save for a few years, and that if God spares us and he generously co-operates with us, a second one will surely have to follow.' It was a matter of timing, and finding a trustworthy manager, such as Archbishop Vaughan.

However, even with him, she guarded against any trouble in the future: 'The members of my Council...naturally enough want to know how it [the novitiate] will be supported, whether the Archdiocese will give us a house for it, and a guarantee that no future Archbishop will take it from us or interfere with the Constitution.'

Mary wrote to Rome for permission for the second novitiate in Sydney, which she received on 24 March 1881. But a majority vote from the Sisters at the General Chapter was also required – and they, it seemed, would take a little more convincing. Bishop Reynolds was against the idea – probably because of the power and kudos he stood to lose by the establishment of a second novitiate – as was the Sisters' Director, Father Tappeiner. One Sister who attended the General Chapter meeting recalled that Bishop Reynolds told them 'that Rome did not wish a second novitiate, that Mother General could and possibly would be censured, and that he himself ought to have been consulted before it was asked for...'

Fortunately, Archbishop Vaughan was allowing matters to run their course, despite having in hand Rome's permission for the Sydney novitiate (arguably all the authority he needed). 'I leave all to you and your advisers whether you begin the work soon or put it off for a time,' he told Mary, 'for naturally you ought to know your own interests, though you cannot love them better than myself...'

The week-long General Chapter meeting began on 19 July 1881, at the Mother House, Kensington. The big surprise of the meeting was that Mary was nominated for the position of Mother General. Understandably distressed, she explained to the Sisters that she could not hold office again, as it would be going against the Constitution. However, she was overruled by both Bishop Reynolds and Father Tappeiner. 'Dr Reynolds...said that her election as Mother General only dated from our first Chapter [six years previous] when the Constitution was adopted and put in force,' remembered one Sister. 'On that distinct understanding, the Sisters almost unanimously re-elected her – by a majority of 23 against four.' Mary accepted her re-election with, as she herself put it, 'very bad grace'.

Her disappointment at being thwarted in her attempt to retreat to a quieter but more productive life can be gauged in her letters in the following months. To Dr Campbell in Rome, she wrote: 'The [Order] has gone through a great deal during the last few years. It has had troubles without and troubles in itself from some of its members. I was hoping that under a new Mother General many of these troubles would cease, and I must confess that I was longing for rest myself. But God knows what is best...' And to the Sisters in Sydney: 'I had so yearned for rest, and hoped that another Mother General would be given to you. I did not and do not feel able for another six years of office – the prospect frightens me, so pray hard for me...'

A year later, with a batch of fresh worries, she wrote: 'I often do feel so tempted (is it temptation?) to send my resignation to Rome and to implore [them] to appoint some other [Sister] for a time. I feel this, particularly when I am ill, and see myself so unable for the important duties of my position.' Another disappointment for Mary was the Chapter's decision to reject plans for the Sydney novitiate (17 votes to 10), although it gave the Mother General and her Council the power to open it in 18 months' time, if they so desired. Mary felt that this decision was a slap in the face for their good friend, Archbishop Vaughan: 'I regret the delay exceedingly,' she told him in a letter, 'the more so as I did not expect it, and fear it may cause annoyance to you who have been so kind to us...'

If his patience was tried, the archbishop certainly did not show it. '...He generously did not press for it when he understood our difficulties at the time,' Mary reported to Dr Campbell in Rome. 'On the contrary, both by letters to myself and by gentle advice to the Sisters here, he recommended patience, saying that he knew we would comply with the permission as soon as possible, and almost his last words to me when leaving Sydney were a blessing, and thanking me for the comfort and boon the Sisters were to him in the Archdiocese...'

Some of the Sisters and priests accused Mary of 'playing soft' with Dr Vaughan, in attempting to give him what she had refused the Bishops Quinn. However, Bishop Torreggiani of Armidale laughed at the suggestion: 'He told me...he had the word of Bishop Quinn himself that nothing short of absolute control would satisfy [him and his brother], that the granting or not granting of a second novitiate had nothing to do with it,' Mary told Sister Mechtilde. 'Please tell those Sisters who have been led to think otherwise how much they have wronged their Mother in thinking that she weakly gave in to one what she had refused another. At best this is a weak, if not silly argument raised by some friend of the views of the Bishops Quinn, but I regret that it should have been imposed upon our own Bishop, who at least should have known its falseness.'

Although Archbishop Vaughan was denied the novitiate for some years, he was rewarded for his patience in the resounding success of the Sisters in New South Wales – just two years after arriving in Sydney, the Sisters had set up 11 schools in the colony.

However, the pool of Sisters available to staff these new schools was running dry. Mary now had the competing demands of Sydney and Adelaide to contend with, and the increasing petulance of Bishop Reynolds. While at first he supported the expansion of the Order into New South Wales, when he discovered how it impacted on his own diocese's teaching force, his resentment was clear. Almost certainly, it drove his efforts to halt the new Sydney novitiate, as he believed it was evidence that Adelaide was about to be supplanted as home-base for the Sisters of St Joseph.

Tending the needs of both Sydney and Adelaide became a very delicate balancing act, with fragile egos on both sides, and the strain of it soon began to tell on Mary. When a Sydney Sister put in a request for more teaching nuns, she issued a brisk response: 'You ask me to send more Sisters – I cannot. I cannot meet the wants here, and already there is great dissatisfaction amongst the priests who have accused me of sending Sisters to New South Wales who were required here. I grieve to say that I can scarcely keep my patience with some of them – they are so selfish, so unlike the priests you meet in New South Wales...'

Mary was also conscious of the fact that she was pushing the limits of Bishop Reynolds' generosity and friendship. 'So far Dr Reynolds is truly friendly to us and was willing for the good of the [Order] to let some of his schools suffer..., but we must not try him too far.' Bishop Reynolds saw in Archbishop Vaughan a threat to his position with the Sisters, although as Mary pointed out, he really was the last person he should fear. 'I like the Archbishop for his kindness to us,' she told Bishop Reynolds earnestly, 'and because I believe him to be your friend, and I fear you have not many that I can call true friends...'

In early 1882, just six months after the second General Chapter meeting, the Sisters of St Joseph suffered a great loss – their much-loved Director, Father Tappeiner, took ill and died. In a touching letter, Mary wrote: 'We have lost a treasured friend and Father, one whose like we need not hope to meet again.' Father Tappeiner was replaced as Director of the Sisters and adviser to Bishop Reynolds by Father Joseph Polk.

On top of this came the death of Archbishop Vaughan, aged 49. But barely had he been laid to rest when the Irish bishops in Australia began insisting he be replaced by one of their own countrymen, and *not* 'another foreigner'. As one of the Sisters noted somewhat wryly, 'Soon it will not suffice to be a Catholic, it will be necessary to be Irish also.'

Around this time, another two of Mary's siblings also passed away. Her youngest brother, Peter, only 20 and engaged to be married, died in 1878 of heart disease. Just a few years later, in December 1882, Lexie, aged 32, died after a short illness. Mary sadly noted to her only surviving brother, Donald, 'There are only three now left out of eight.'

BANISHED FROM ADELAIDE

URING the trials in Queensland and Bathurst in the late 1870s, the firm foundations of Adelaide provided the Sisters of St Joseph with a modicum of stability without which they may never have survived. Bishop Reynolds worked hard to maintain this secure environment for the Sisters, and yet, as Mary knew only too well, he was not without his foibles. He was more than a little possessive of the Josephites, and was given to petty jealousies.

These sprang largely from fears that others thought him unfit for the job. Bishop Reynolds was conscious of the fact that, unlike the Vaughans and the Quinns, his education was not extensive, and he had very little spiritual or ecclesiastic training. He was, as Mary delicately put it, 'a good, holy hardworking Bishop, but not what many would call a clever man'. To disguise these shortfalls, the bishop ensured he enjoyed all the trappings of his position, so that on a superficial level at least, he would always stand up to comparison. This was particularly evident on his 27-month trip to Europe between 1879 and 1881, when an embarrassing lack of funds saw him travelling second-class. With some disgust, he wrote to his then Vicar General,

Father Frederick Byrne, 'I have to relinquish every personal comfort to meet the wants of a thoughtless if not ungrateful flock, for had they done their duty by me I need not be in such straits for means.'

Anything that detracted from his image as the consummate Church dignitary, Bishop Reynolds learned to dread. One issue on which he became particularly sensitive was alcohol abuse among the clergy, following a humiliating incident in which his judgement was called into question. While in Ireland, he had sent two priests, Fathers Sheridan and Guinane, to Adelaide to begin work there. Much to the horror of all, they proceeded to drink the colony dry.

'They went to a hotel and began to drink and were found by the police drunk on the sandhills...,' Father Byrne reported. 'Sheridan came to the Terrace between 6 and 7 o'clock on Saturday evening in a half-muddled state, dirty and disgusting, and returned...to bring up Guinane, but he could not succeed and both continued to carry on their spree during Saturday night and Sunday to the great scandal of everyone who saw them. In fact they were the talk of the place, everyone saying, "Did you see the two drunken priests who came by the steamer?"'

Still smarting over the whole affair, Father Byrne closed his letter with some sharp words for the bishop: 'Behold the first fruits of your labours, at which everyone is astonished knowing how bitterly you inveighed against Dr Sheil's judgement in selecting priests... I don't think of anything more to say, only don't take any more priests like Guinane and Sheridan.'

Bishop Reynolds, a teetotaller, was riled by the suggestion that he had known all along of Sheridan and Guinane's boozing ways, and reproached Father Byrne for his 'bitter taunts'. But the scandal was slow to die and, once home, he was forced to defend himself against charges that he had neglected his duties and had somehow been in collusion with the two priests. With his good character at stake, the bishop promptly issued orders that all alcohol, other than wine, be banned from his house, and that all Adelaide priests be forbidden to drink alcohol before dinner.

The bishop's enemies – and he had many – used these incidents to compromise his credibility in the eyes of Church officials. Some years earlier, a number of Adelaide priests had sent a 13-page document to Rome claiming that Bishop Reynolds was unfit to hold office, alleging he was reckless with money, 'dishonest', 'cruel', and a 'downright priest-hater'. The bishop was exasperated by this lack of support from his fellow priests. 'Bathurst says I am led by the nose by Jesuits! Jesuits say I am haughty and the mitre has turned my head...,' he complained in a letter to Mary. 'I have not a friend – not one – even amongst those who owe all they have to me...'

Mary sympathised with the bishop, and often pleaded his case with those in Rome: 'I think it must be almost impossible for you to realise the trouble he had with some of his priests,' she wrote one time to Monsignor Kirby. 'I hear things from time to time which make me shudder, the more so as I see how unsuspecting he is. Whatever his enemies may say of him, dear Monsignor, he is really a holy man, but not clever enough for some he has to deal with.'

While he was alive, Father Tappeiner had fostered good relations between the Sisters and the bishop, but this was a role the Sisters' new Director, Father Polk, seemed unable – or unwilling – to take on. Father Polk was a hard, strict man, who did not endear himself to the Sisters. Some disliked him so much, they refused to tell him their sins in Confession.

'Sister Francis Xavier and Father Polk had a great row a few weeks ago,' Mary read in a letter from one of the Sisters. 'He frightened her. He put his face up into her face and said she was an impudent bold woman and that she ought to be ashamed of her Protestant name [Blanche Amsinck] and her Protestant face. He told her that all the priests disliked her and that the Vicar did not like her...'

Even Mary's brother Donald was acquainted with the reputation of their new Director: 'My poor Mary, how you must have suffered. Do you remember the warning I left you about Father Polk? I know him well, know him to have some strange fancies and to be very headstrong where he can. I did not fear much [for] you – you would be more than enough for 50 Father Polks...' Donald was right – while Father Polk presented a problem, it was nothing Mary could not handle, as she was well used to dealing with forceful personalities. No, it was another person who was causing her the most anxiety. She had detected a change in Bishop Reynolds; an iciness in his manner, indifference almost, in place of his usual warmth and compassion.

The bishop had had words with Mary about the Order's mounting debts. In 1880 they owed 3000 pounds in all, a sum which rose to 10,000 pounds in 1883, and formed a substantial proportion of the liability of the entire Adelaide diocese. However, as the bishop himself had often pointed out, this was not as bad as it seemed, given the number of schools the Sisters had opened and the meagre financial assistance they received. More recently, though, he had begun to claim that the Sisters were mismanaging their affairs and being financially irresponsible.

This new, unsympathetic attitude in Bishop Reynolds surprised Mary – she could only put it down to resentment over the successful expansion of the Order into Sydney: 'Dr Reynolds was once a true kind friend. He was so until the work began to prosper in Sydney. From that time, step by step, he began to change.'

There was also the influence of Bishop Reynolds' Vicar General, Archdeacon Russell, who had been an enemy of the Sisters since he was dismissed by Bishop Sheil for filing a report with Rome on 'the mystics' in 1870. Contempt could best describe the feelings Archdeacon Russell held for the Sisters, Mary in particular. On one occasion, he even tried to have her put in jail over an unpaid account of 50 pounds with a local Adelaide bootmaker, Mr Birmingham. Archdeacon Russell had directed Mr Birmingham to send the police after Mary with a court summons. As one of the Sisters later explained, a friend, Father Lee, caught up with her to let her know of the plot. 'He put Mother on her guard and told her the police were on her track and advised her to cross the Victorian border as soon as possible. At thattime there was no Federal Government and one colony could not interfere with another. Mother got over the border very narrowly and I think even the police were pleased.'

Mary began to suspect that perhaps Archdeacon Russell was imposing his views on the bishop, thus accounting for the bishop's sudden change in behaviour towards the Sisters. Her fears were reinforced when, in April 1883, Bishop Reynolds announced that he had received a letter from Rome ordering him to conduct a special inquiry into the affairs of all the Orders in Adelaide, starting with the Josephites. The inquiry, known as an Apostolic Visitation, would be carried out by a Commission comprising Bishop Reynolds, Archdeacon Russell and four other priests.

Mary was told the Visitation would begin at the Mother House, Kensington, in July 1883. In accordance with the bishop's orders from Rome, the Sisters were told to have all diaries, accounts and bank books ready for inspection. Although Mary was somewhat startled at the suddenness of it all, she had expected an Apostolic Visitation at some stage. It was an ideal opportunity, she thought, for the Sisters to get their grievances out into the open, and hopefully, for some solutions to be formulated.

Most of the Sisters shared Mary's view that they would emerge from the Visitation a stronger, more united force. 'I felt myself bound in conscience to mention anything blameworthy that had ever come under my knowledge,' one Sister wrote. 'As a body we had our faults and were prepared to submit to reproof and correction. If we had exactly obeyed our Mother and followed her instructions we should not have required proof...'

Not long after the Visitation began, serious doubts were raised as to the way in which it was being conducted. Over its three-month duration, less than half the Adelaide Sisters were interviewed, mostly the youngest and least experienced. The six members of the Commission rarely sat in at interviews – often it was Archdeacon Russell alone. Transcripts of evidence, where they existed, were scanty, detailing the answers only, and were not given to the Sisters to read or sign (they were told that if required, they could correct their evidence at a later date, but those that tried were turned away).

Another unusual element of the Visitation was that the Sisters were put under a life-long oath never to reveal a single detail of their interview with the Commission. 'Each Sister being put upon oath all remained a great mystery,' Mary noted some months later to Dr Campbell in Rome. 'That some of the Sisters went through painful ordeals was evident, some being ill for days after, and requiring the greatest encouragement to keep them from imagining that another great trouble or upset as they called it was coming upon the [Order]. I was kept in complete darkness about everything.'

Some of the Sisters became suspicious of the motives of the Commission, and resolved not to volunteer any information: 'When the Visitation commenced, I thought of course it was a very good thing, there were a good many things that needed correcting, and my first intention was that if I thought of anything that was not as it should be I would mention it,' Sister Mary Borgia Fay recalled. 'I was going to be something of a reformer, I suppose, though in a small way. I daresay a good many of the Sisters thought about it in the same way... However, I changed my mind, resolved merely to answer whatever questions would be put to me the best way I could. I mean, of course, truthfully...'

The Sisters were quizzed on Mary's doings, and were actively encouraged to speak out against her. The Commission concentrated on her use of medicinal brandy, and asked the Sisters whether they thought this was really necessary, and whether Mary took any on the quiet. Most were horrified by the suggestion, and told them so, but three or four ran with the bait. They claimed that cartons of liquor were emptied in a fortnight, that they had seen Mary 'drunk and vomiting brandy'.

Recalling her interview, Sister Mary Borgia Fay said Mary's 'drinking problem' was put to her as a fact: 'Now, conscientiously, do you not consider it a scandal that the Mother General should be addicted to drink?', the Commissioners asked.

'I do not look on it in that light at all, she only takes it as a medicine,' Sister Mary Borgia Fay replied.

'What would you say to the fact that it was contrary to the doctor's orders that Mother General took the drink?'

Sister Mary Borgia Fay told the Commission that with all her years at the Mother House convent, if there had been any evidence Mary was an alcoholic, she would have known. As it was, she said, the claims were completely untrue. For her trouble, she was dismissed by the Commissioners as a 'flatterer' who 'pampered' Mary.

It is difficult to reconcile the fact that Bishop Reynolds, one-time friend of the Sisters, was a key member of this seemingly biased Commission. However, it would be a mistake to think that the bishop was actively seeking to bring Mary down. It appeared that for one reason or another, he honestly believed she was an alcoholic and, with his fingers burnt once before on the alcohol issue, he was determined to get to the truth. The question is, who had convinced him? Archdeacon Russell would certainly be a prime suspect. He had been openly hostile towards Mary and the Sisters, and no doubt encouraged the bishop to believe the worst of the rumours that reached his ear.

Discontented Sisters and town gossips were also spreading rumours. James McLaughlin, the same man who wrote letters to a Protestant journal in the early 1870s claiming the Sisters were prostitutes, drunkards and attempted murderers (the publisher was successfully sued for defamation), had also, in 1873, written a letter to Rome containing the allegations: 'My mother-in-law, Mrs O'Sullivan...most solemnly assures me...that she helped to carry in Sister Mary...to her convent when she fell of [sic] a vehicle hopelessly drunk. She is ready to appear before her

God on the truthfulness of this statement, that she had gone into the [convent] twice and that Sister Mary and others of the Sisterhood were so drunk that they neither knew what they did or said.'

Another local, a Mrs McDonald, had a story which she took straight to Bishop Reynolds. However, a senior Adelaide nun, Sister Annette, insisted there was no truth to it. '[Mary] was watching the children who came to meet her. She slipped down a step. Mrs McDonald went to the Bishop, Dr Reynolds, reporting that Mother Mary was drunk. I could take my oath she did not take anything that day. I was with her all the time.'

There was also a troublemaker from within the Sisters' own ranks – Sister Clare, who had since left the Order after Mary 'demoted' her. 'We all felt that Sister Clare was instrumental in causing this enquiry...' Sister Annette revealed. 'She was ambitious and jealous, and Mother Mary felt it her duty to remove her from office. She found fault with Mother Mary's ruling when what was arranged did not please her, and bitterly resented Mother Mary's actions in her regard. She became unsettled and spoke disparagingly of Mother Mary to some of the Sisters, to outsiders and to some of the Church authorities...' Sister Annette said Sister Clare 'told everything' to Archdeacon Russell and Father Polk, who promised they would hold an investigation.

Due to the oath of secrecy given by those appearing before the Commission, Mary was unaware of the case the Commission was building against her. She believed them to be simply investigating the Order's financial affairs and other day-to-day business. In fact, when it was her turn to be interviewed, these were exactly the topics discussed.

It was a calm, friendly interview, in which her so-called 'drinking problem' was not even raised. However, before her interview, Dr Reynolds made vague reference to some of the claims that had been made. 'In a private interview,' Mary later said, 'the Bishop had in the kindest manner warned me that some whom I little suspected had made remarks about my having had to use stimulants in my illnesses, and to be on my guard with them, at the same time encouraging me to mind what was said, but not to trust those who were sometimes about me...'

The other serious charge that the Commission made was that Mary had used the Order's money to buy gifts of furniture and clothes for her family and friends, and had kept incomplete accounts to prevent the payments being traced.

Mary was the first to admit the standard of book-keeping was poor, and that she was not a good financial manager, but the suggestion that she had defrauded the Order was ludicrous. However, as the Commission had taken possession of all the account-keeping books, she had no way of proving her innocence.

'...The Vicar General brought me a...command in writing forbidding me under any pretext to borrow money,' Mary wrote afterwards in a letter to Dr Campbell in Rome. 'Later the same day, the Bishop bitterly upbraided me with having borrowed money, and kept the place in debt... I...showed him a book in which he had himself authorised me to do the very thing for which he now blamed me. He asked me for the book, and I gave it to him much to the annoyance of the Sisters who said that with that book I had given up the only proof I had that the Bishop had authorised me to do what he was now condemning me for.'

In a report prepared for Archbishop Moran in Sydney some months later, Mary spoke out against the unfair treatment she and the Sisters had received at the hands of the Commission: 'I cannot write upon this subject without expressing what I feel, and that is that we were very unjustly dealt with about our books. We might at least have been allowed to go over them and to clear ourselves if we could. But at the time of my examination I had not a suspicion that they were going to blame us as they did later, nor had I the most remote idea of their questioning my own honesty. All that was to come later.'

When the Visitation wound up in September 1883, Bishop Reynolds reported to Mary that 'we had much to thank God for, that...no grave evils or – I think he used the word scandals – had been met with, that there were many things to be remedied, but nothing grave, and that he had been able to send a most consoling report to Rome.' Seemingly, a satisfactory result all round.

But within the space of just two months, all that changed. The bishop and Archdeacon Russell arrived at the Kensington convent, waving about a 'Memorial of Directions', issued, they said, under authority from Rome. It ordered changes to senior appointments within the Order, as well as modifications to the Sisters' daily routine.

Mary had not been consulted at any stage about these changes, and when she ventured to point out some problems they may not have considered, the bishop took it for opposition. He promptly served her with a letter in which, after a vicious personal attack, he ordered her to leave Adelaide immediately, claiming, once again, to be acting on instructions from Church officials in Rome. 'You have done your best to keep me in the dark, to conceal the scandalous habits of some, notwithstanding your promises of "being open and candid with your dear Father in Christ"...

'You – from whom I expected every assistance – did your best and still continue to do your best to your own ends to frustrate all my best efforts and intentions,' Bishop Reynolds raged. 'You govern by party spirit and by clique. Hoodwink the Bishop – that is your motto. I am but too well aware of how you have violated religious poverty, how you have squandered (I will refrain from a stronger term) the means of the Diocese...

'I therefore notify your Maternity to prepare at once to leave for Sydney, as you have no longer the confidence of the Sisterhood...'

CHAPTER 14

A HAVEN IN SYDNEY

MARY realised it was pointless to try to reason with Bishop Reynolds in his current frame of mind, and so she quietly packed her bags for Sydney: 'The instructions in your last letter surprised me but I submit. All is, I hope, for the best – at least, I know you so intend it.'

While Mary held up a brave face to the bishop and moved to Sydney without any fuss, those closest to her knew she was ashamed and humiliated by what he had said in his letter. 'Our good friends of the Visitation have done their best one way or the other to ruin my reputation, but God's will be done,' she wrote unhappily to long-time friend, Sister Mechtilde. The bishop's stinging words haunted Mary's every thought, so that she could not even find peace in sleep. 'I am so sorry for [Bishop Reynolds] but night or day cannot forget his cruel writings to me,' she told Sister Mechtilde. 'It is strange but last night is the first time that I did not wake up dreaming of some thing or other that he wrote.'

In a letter to Dr Campbell soon after her expulsion from Adelaide, she speaks bitterly about the unfairness of it all: 'I felt that I was blamed for the debt that was upon our convents, and though I might have shielded myself by showing that the Bishop had even in writing authorised much that I was myself (as I say, indirectly) blamed for, I thought it better to be silent... I feel for the Bishop and the position in which he is placed,' Mary wrote, trying to be kind, 'but I think he has acted (as far as I can see) weakly. I think he has allowed himself to exaggerate our pecuniary difficulties without remembering that he had known of their existence before, and forgetting that the whole Catholic education of the poorer class had been carried on by us in his diocese...'

She then revealed that she could never see herself returning to Adelaide, as her confidence had been shattered. '...I think I am getting cowardly for I have a positive horror of Adelaide and some who are there – I mean of dealing with them again,' she admitted. 'But I do not mean with the Bishop. I esteem him as much as ever and do not wish any blame to be attached to him.'

Although Mary still did not know the worst of what had been said before the Commission, due to the oath of secrecy the Sisters were under, the bishop's startling allegations led her to suspect there had been some double-dealing going on. 'Our Bishop has been very hard on me, but I do not blame him,' she wrote to the Adelaide Sisters one month after her banishment to Sydney. 'Some amongst the children who have professed love and affection for me must have been insincere, and he has had to act upon what he has heard from these. If it is true that I no longer possess your confidence,' Mary wrote, 'and you believe me to be what I am represented, a squanderer of the means of the [Order], and I will not say all the other hard things, but you will hear them later, if, I say, you believe these things to be true – say so honestly, but if not, let our poor Bishop know the truth. I do not enter into any explanations – I simply deny the charges made against me. Appearances in some instances gave a colouring to some charges, but surely those who know me so well, who were constantly with me or in my confidence, ah, surely they could tell a different tale...'

In some ways, Mary's banishment to Sydney in late 1883 was a blessing in disguise. Once there, she found a haven of sorts, where she could lay aside the worries and anxieties that, at times, had threatened to overcome her. Now 41, and a veteran of more battles than she wished to count, she hoped she might yet taste a little of the quiet life. 'I wish I could settle down quietly in a little nook and get charge of the novices. Perhaps this one boon may yet be granted to me.'

A magnanimous gesture of an old priest, Dean Kenny, who was a friend of Mary's father, saw the Sydney Sisters take up residence in Mount Street, North Sydney, a prime position on the North Shore. The surroundings were idyllic: 'The place is beautifully retired, though near one of the chief streets, it is as quiet as if miles away from other people,' Mary wrote. 'We have no noise, bustle or excitement, have a nice little garden and paddock with high fences, and little birds singing around us. Their singing and the ticking of the clocks being the only sounds... [Dean Kenny] says this little nest must be the garden for rearing real saints, that nothing else will satisfy him.'

In these peaceful surrounds, Mary got her 'boon' and took charge of the trainee Sisters, musing that she had found 'a little heaven almost'. One of the novices, Sister Isabelle Colvin, remembered how everybody loved Mary, that her genuine charm and the warmth of her personality drew people to her. 'She had only to smile and a gentleman would run for a chair, a lady would offer her a rug or a book, children would come to her knee, and in a few moments she would be at home with everyone...' She ruled the novices with a firm hand, but somehow her reprimands never seemed too terrible – she softened them with kind words or gestures, or called on a little humour to ease the tears.

'As a novice,' Sister Isabelle said, 'I had charge of the [chapel] and Mother gave me charge of supplying a vase of flowers for the Dean's table. You see, we had this garden and in his new home next door he had no flowers. On Christmas Eve, flowers were very scarce in our garden and the weather was very hot. I could scarcely scrape up enough flowers for our little altar. In fact I had to pick the red flowers of the Crown of Thorns bush to brighten it up. Mother had left us that week for Annandale [a suburb of Sydney] to visit a Sister who was thought to be dying. We had nearly given up hope of seeing her when we heard the rattle of a cab and Mother's joyful face appeared. She made her way to visit [the chapel] and came out to us with a radiant face. She kissed me and said my altar was lovely.

'In the morning we were waiting for the Dean to say Mass,' Sister Isabelle told. 'As he suffered from hip trouble, I had to help him with his vestments. While I was waiting, Mother asked me if I had given him his flowers. Of course I hadn't. I told her I had so few for our Lord. With a stern face she ordered me to take one of the vases from beside the [altar] and take it to the Dean's table. I protested that it would destroy the whole look of the altar, but that didn't appeal to Mother. I hadn't carried out her orders. With many tears I had to obey,' Sister Isabelle said. 'The Dean had left something behind and he left orders that I should bring it to him, so with red eyes I had to face him and he wanted to know where I was that I was not there to help him with his vestments. Of course I had to tell him whereupon he said Mother was a nasty old Scotchwoman and he made me hold up my habit and he filled it with the most delicious fruit.

'I knew then that Mother had told him of the incident and I found her waiting for me at the front door and smiling. "Well, what did the Dean say to you?" I told her he called her a nasty old Scotchwoman. She laughed heartily. I then showed her the fruit he had given me, and we had a very happy Christmas.'

Another young nun, Sister Helena McCarthy, recalled that Mary was always quick with an apology if she thought she had been at all abrupt or inconsiderate with the Sisters. 'I never knew Mother to give a correction in anger, nor would she ever reprimand in an impatient or overbearing manner. I distinctly remember her sending for me one day. "Do you want me, Mother?" I asked.

'"Yes, dear," she answered. "I want to beg your pardon for the impatient way I spoke to you when you came to me this morning. I feared I had given you pain, and I am sorry for having done so." Mother Mary may have felt irritable and thought she had betrayed it in her words or manner, but I had no knowledge of it and I told her so for she had been most gentle and kind to me.'

Once the Sisters were established in the Mount Street convent in North Sydney, it became clear that they would soon need to extend to cater for the increasing number of Sisters. 'In the early days at Mount Street,' Sister Helena McCarthy said, 'we had only a wooden structure of two rooms and the old stone building behind. We had no space and when the paddock at the back was to be sold, Mother Mary set everyone praying that she might secure it. We knew she had no cash at all and we had not her simple faith, so I thought our prayers useless as regards the land.

'On the morning of the sale,' Sister Helena told, 'she called a young novice and said, "Sister, I want you to go to [the owner of the paddock], tell him how badly off we are and how much we need that land and ask him not to let them run the price up too high." Needless to say, the novice did not like her task, but of course obeyed. The gentleman saw she was confused; he was very nice, listened attentively and then sat back and roared laughing. He said, "What beautiful simplicity", and asked what countrywoman Mother was. On learning that she was of Scottish descent, he told the Sister that so was he and said, "I hope Mother Mary gets the land." And she did. She reproved us then for our want of faith and trust. I was the novice concerned so I can vouch for this.'

During these first few months in Sydney, Mary had not forgotten those horrible events which had seen her depart Adelaide in such haste. In the aftermath of the Visitation, she had begun writing to Rome for advice, but she little suspected the effect her letters were having. As Bishop Reynolds had assured her he was acting on the authority of Rome – in conducting the Visitation, putting the Sisters under a life-long oath of secrecy, issuing the Memorial of Directions and dismissing Mary from Adelaide – she spoke openly about these matters in her letters. However, the truth was, Rome had not issued any such instructions, and knew nothing of what had been going on.

In February 1884, Dr Campbell informed Mary that Bishop Reynolds had exceeded his powers in turning her out of Adelaide, and Rome would see that justice was done. Mary was utterly bewildered by the disclosure. 'God's ways are most mysterious,' she told the Adelaide Sisters. 'What can the poor Bishop have been thinking of?' However, she could not accept that the bishop had lied to her. In reply to Dr Campbell, she wrote: 'I had not for a moment allowed myself to doubt that the Bishop had received some power from Rome ere he would have acted as he did. The whole affair is a mystery to me... I cannot understand the Bishop's upbraiding and command in the face of all he knew unless some untruths had been told to him and that he had in some way been deceived. My opinion is that Archdeacon Russell, now Vicar General, has had much to do with the Bishop's change of views, and that he saw harm in what the poor Bishop did not... I have every reason to believe that the Vicar General, Archdeacon Russell, is not, and has not for years been my friend, nor can I think that in many ways he has been the Bishop's...'

In September 1884, the new archbishop of Sydney, Patrick Moran – an Irishman – arrived in Sydney to take up office. Mary had hoped that he may have been asked by Rome to look into the Adelaide affair, but the archbishop said he had not been, and what was more, was not looking to be either. Before coming to Sydney, Archbishop Moran had spent considerable time in Rome, and had heard quite a bit about Mary from his contact with Australian bishops. 'Dr Reynolds has tried to prejudice him against me, laying the debt and drink at my door,' Mary wrote to Sister Monica, now the Sister-in-charge in Adelaide. 'Imagine my feelings when the Archbishop told me this. I did not think he would dare to go as far as the latter... Dr Reynolds now wants to crush me.'

With all the secrecy surrounding the Adelaide Visitation, and Mary's quick exit from the diocese, rumours about what exactly had gone on in mid-1883 were flowing thick and fast. 'One who has been in the Bathurst diocese...tells me that he [heard the] most absurd things about Adelaide,' Mary wrote to Sister Monica, 'how there was a regular break-up there, how the Mother General had to leave, or was sent away, the debts, and though he was too nice to pain me by the rest, I suppose the grand other name given to me... God knows I had the shame and humiliation of often taking stimulants and of knowing that I was kept up by such when I should otherwise have sunk and not been able for any duty, but far better to have yielded then and given up than have this shame and sorrow brought upon me...'

She then disclosed how close she had come to simply walking away from it all. 'Dearest Sister, forgive me if I seem to speak bitterly. I am wounded to the heart, and not being well or able for this constant struggle, am so tempted to give up and seek a rest that up to this I have never got... Your unswerving fidelity and that of a few more like you is about the only thing that makes me keep up. For very shame I cannot desert those who are so faithful in this dark hour...

'Things have gone too far to be silent longer if you all wish to retain me as your Mother General,' Mary noted sadly to one Adelaide Sister. 'From what has been told to Dr Moran, I can judge of what has been told to others. The character of your Mother General is at stake. She is guilty or not guilty. If guilty in the eyes of the Sisters, let them say so,' Mary pleaded, 'if not, let them clear her or she must cease to be their Mother General... How well [Archdeacon Russell] has succeeded in his plot, but the end has not come, and before it does I think he will be sorry enough...'

Back in Adelaide, the Sisters were having a tough time coping with Bishop Reynolds' vehement hostility. He openly accused them of being liars, and served up some 'choice' adjectives that, according to one Sister, were the 'most disgusting she'd ever heard'.

Another pleaded with Mary to save her from the awful mess: 'Is it possible we will be driven to destruction after our long years in religion through the bad members that are in our [Order] running with their dreadful lies and tales? Must we all perish through them?... I beg of you to take me to you and send me to New Zealand or any place out of this. I am really sick thinking of the state of affairs here.'

There were also reports that Sisters who had given 'years of hard labour' were being denied respect even in death. One of the Adelaide nuns had complained to Archdeacon Russell that Sisters were being buried with as little sympathy from the clergy as if they had been 'ducks that had died at the bottom of the yard'.

Finally, in October 1884, Mary received an important piece of news that she hoped would shed some light on the treatment she had received in Adelaide. Archbishop Moran had been informed that the Pope had absolved the Sisters from the oath of silence they had taken during the Visitation. Not surprisingly, Bishop Reynolds was livid. Fearing what the Sisters may now reveal, he tried to convince them that the dispensation was invalid, and that they were still bound by oath.

'As this document was obtained under a mistaken plea,' Bishop Reynolds told the Adelaide Sister-in-charge, Sister Monica, 'it is of no effect, pending further letters from Rome. Mother Mary of the Cross should have notified me of her sending you such. She has not done so. To prevent further scandal bring in that document to me, as I wish to satisfy myself of its genuineness.'

One month later, in November 1884, Archbishop Moran received instructions from Rome to look into the 'misunderstandings' that arose in Adelaide. Mary and the Sisters were asked to send him their accounts of what had taken place. Mary was pleased to at last have the opportunity of vindicating herself, but not, as she warned the Sisters, at the expense of the bishop: 'Mind, my solemn charge to you. Excuse the Bishop in what you write.'

Bishop Reynolds was understandably nervous about the investigation that was about to be launched, and began to mount his case. A timely warning came from a friend in northern New South Wales, Bishop Murray of Maitland, on the importance of being absolutely honest in this: 'If she and her party have written to Rome against you, you will then have to tell the truth, the whole truth I mean, and of course nothing but the truth.' Bishop Reynolds prepared a brief report on the Visitation for Roman officials, and sent them the transcripts of the Sisters' evidence. He had never intended for Rome to see these, or indeed anything to do with the Visitation, but he realised that too much had been revealed for him to remain silent.

He also prepared letters for Archbishop Moran, and Cardinal Simeoni and Monsignor Kirby in Rome, defending his actions. In them, he made a number of serious allegations against Mary, saying that since the early 1870s she had been an alcoholic. He alleged that a group of Sisters, sometimes even school children, brought in cases of drink as often as every fortnight, and in return, Mary allowed them to flout the Constitution. He was told about the problem, he said, by some of the Sisters and two of Mary's doctors.

Bishop Reynold's letters also accused Mary of 'reckless expenditure' and being 'uncontrollable'. The reason he put the Sisters on oath, he said, was to prevent gossiping and to unearth the truth about what exactly had been going on in the Order. Mary, too, wrote a letter to Archbishop Moran, answering the charges Bishop Reynolds had laid against her upon her dismissal from Adelaide, albeit somewhat reluctantly. 'It has cost me a great deal to write it, for I would rather suffer any blame than reflect in the least on the Bishop of Adelaide.

'I am confident that he meant everything for the best,' Mary wrote generously, 'and that most extraordinary evidence must have been given against me ere he could write to me as he did... I plainly see the work of a few discontented and troublesome Sisters in it all... I did not know how cruelly one at least of the Commission tried to make me out – that dreadful thing that I cannot bear to name or even think of...'

Within days, letters from the Sisters proclaiming Mary's innocence landed on the archbishop's desk. From Sister Monica: 'He [Bishop Reynolds] accused her of the abuse of stimulants of which she was innocent. I have lived in the house with her for years and very seldom a night passed when she was here that I did not see her last thing and get her blessing, and never saw a sign of what she was accused of.'

From Sister Philippa: 'I have been informed that wicked calumnies have been circulated about our Mother General such as I blush to name, accusing her of intemperance. I for one declare that to be a falsehood. During all the years that I have known her and been in her company night and day,' she wrote, 'I never saw anything that could give the slightest foundation to such a malicious statement... I was her infirmarian... It seems strange to me that when the Commissioners accused Mother of such a gross thing they did not take the evidence of all the Sisters and of those who are the longest in the [Order]...'

From Sister Mary Borgia: '...Though I lived for nearly six years at the Mother House, I had never heard or seen anything that could cause the slightest suspicion of such a thing... She never helped herself [to brandy], but took it always from the hands of another, and not without assuring herself that it was a moderate quantity, and mixed with water...'

Most of the Adelaide Sisters also signed a petition, in which the charges against Mary were denounced as a 'scandalous falsehood', a 'gross calumny on the fair name of an innocent person', a 'malicious report' and 'a base fabrication'.

Archbishop Moran presented his report on the Adelaide crisis to Cardinal Simeoni in Rome in March 1885, the thrust of it being that there was fault on both sides. On the Adelaide Visitation, he concluded that Bishop Reynolds had made a serious mistake in claiming he was acting on orders from Rome and in putting the Sisters under an oath of secrecy. In fact, Archbishop Moran judged the matter to be so grave, he advised that his report be kept confidential. Accordingly, the report was hidden away in Rome. Ultimately, this led to the Beatification process being interrupted in 1931, as there appeared to be no official documentation which cleared Mary of being an alcoholic and embezzler. The process was resumed when Archbishop Moran's report was discovered some 20 years later.

In his report, Archbishop Moran agreed with the bishop that the Sisters' account-keeping was haphazard, but said there was no evidence that Mary had defrauded the Order and spent its money on friends and relatives. Archbishop Moran also dismissed the charge that Mary was an alcoholic. He said she was directed to take brandy by her doctors, but sometimes it was of such a poor quality that it made her sick. This, he said, explained why some of the Sisters thought she was drunk and 'vomiting brandy'. He also noted that Mary had never tried to cover up the fact that she took a small dose of brandy when ill, but that she, and almost all the Sisters, emphatically denied she drank to excess.

As for that ongoing issue of contention – whether the Josephites should be controlled by bishops or centrally governed – Archbishop Moran referred to an upcoming meeting of Australasian bishops.

In its response to the archbishop's report, Rome made two significant points. First, it reiterated that the Sisters of St Joseph were a centrally-governed Order, and as such, their rights were to be respected. Secondly, it had 'become aware' that Mary's re-appointment as Mother General at the last General Chapter had been illegal, as she had held the position for longer than the stipulated 12 years (Mary did point this out at the time of her election, but she was 'overruled' by Bishop Reynolds and Father Tappeiner). Rome ordered that a new Mother General be elected at the next General Chapter meeting in 1889 – in the meantime, Cardinal Moran (he was made Australia's first cardinal in 1885) was to appoint a temporary replacement. He chose Sister Bernard, who took up the position – with some misgivings – in November 1885. Mary was later made her

Assistant. Despite her self-doubts, the Irish-born Sister Bernard was, in fact, a wise choice, politically at least. 'She is popular with the Bishops for more reasons than one, and I am not,' Mary noted, relieved to finally be able to step aside. 'I firmly believe that those who have been against us hitherto will now unite.'

One who was not prepared to 'unite', however, was Bishop Reynolds, who was cynical of the reasons cited for Mary being stood down as Mother General. 'She and her party are loud in their cry of victory...' he told Monsignor Kirby. 'It is certainly less painful to all to say "that she was set aside through an informality in her election" than to say she was deposed for drunkness [sic] and misappropriation of funds.' He went on to describe her as an 'unfortunate woman' who was 'humbled but not amended'.

Meanwhile, in Adelaide, Bishop Reynolds was aggressively campaigning to have central government written out of the Sisters' Constitution. During several visits to the Mother House convent in Kensington in early 1885, he had demanded that the Sisters submit to diocesan control. He was 'absolute Superior', he said, and if they did not like it, they could leave. Bishop Reynolds gave the Sisters one day to make up their minds...but just in case they had thoughts of fleeing to Sydney, he told them to forget them, as Cardinal Moran would not be 'hoodwinked'. (In fact, Cardinal Moran had written to Bishop Reynolds' office saying specifically that he *would* take Adelaide Sisters into his archdiocese.)

Almost unbelievably, Bishop Reynolds again claimed to be acting on instructions from Rome in insisting on diocesan control. 'I, as Bishop of Adelaide, received letters from Rome...and it has been decided that the [Order of the Sisters of St Joseph] is to be divided into Diocesan Communities, and the Bishop in each case to be Superior in his own Diocese. Mother Mary's authority here has ceased and she shall never under any circumstances whatever return to this Diocese.'

THE SHADOW OF DEATH

BISHOP Reynolds' courage to claim Roman authority for bringing the Order under diocesan control may have come, in part, from a letter he received the previous year from Monsignor Kirby, in which Monsignor Kirby stated that the Josephite Constitution 'had not an atom of Papal...authority'. He told Bishop Reynolds to feel free to exercise his full episcopal powers. This was quite a surprising statement, given that the Constitution Mary brought home with her from Rome, signed by Monsignor Kirby's colleagues, specified that central government should remain in place, at least until the Constitution was again presented for endorsement.

At any rate, the Sisters were determined this time to see the bishop's 'letter of authority' from Rome. 'Sister M. de Sales respectfully asked his Lordship would he not read the Roman document. He replied, "No, am I so untruthful that I cannot be believed?" Sister M. de Sales rejoined, "Oh no, my Lord, but it will be more satisfactory to the Sisters." His Lordship replied, "My word is sufficient and they will get nothing else."'

Sister Michael sent a note to Cardinal Moran, asking if he

knew anything about this letter from Rome the bishop claimed to have. '...I do not wish to doubt or disobey [Bishop Reynolds],' she wrote, 'but I do wish to do what is right. If His Lordship has been instructed to make these changes, I am quite willing to submit, but if he insists on the Sisters submitting without producing his authority, I am certain it will end in public scandal.'

However, no one, it seemed, was entirely certain of the facts. Accordingly, Mary decided to go straight to the source. From Sydney, she wrote three letters to Rome – to Father Bianchi, Cardinal Simeoni and Dr Campbell. The first, to Father Bianchi, was quite cleverly worded in that it highlighted not the shortcomings of Bishop Reynolds or the suffering of the Sisters, but the way in which his actions were compromising the Church's authority. This would prompt some action, if nothing else would.

'The Bishop of Adelaide is openly setting them [the Constitutions] aside – saying that they are of no value – were bits of paper – and that he, and he alone, is to be Superior in Adelaide...,' Mary wrote. 'The arguments some Bishops use is that the Constitutions have no force – that they were drawn up by someone who knew nothing of what was required in Australia, and that they are not in any way binding either on Bishops or Sisters...'

In her letter to Cardinal Simeoni, Mary begged for protection from bishops who insisted on 'terrifying and abusing' the Sisters. Her final letter, to Dr Campbell, spelled out the frustration of having to continually fight forces from within the Church. '[Bishop Reynolds] simply wants separation from all authority beyond his own, and he tried to make them believe that they would have to agree to this or go away and that they would not be received elsewhere.

What terrified some of the Sisters was his saying that he had authority for what he was doing... Why, when it is acknowledged that they do their work well, cannot the Bishops who desire their services work with them in peace according to their Constitutions or do without them if they are not willing to do this?' Mary asked in exasperation.

Other than writing these few letters, she kept a low profile in this new crisis. She felt for the Adelaide Sisters, but it was a battle they would have to fight for themselves. She urged them not to be intimidated by Bishop Reynolds, nor to take the easy way out. 'Anyone who says, "Go with the stronger party; there is no use in struggling more for Central Government", is not, in my opinion, a true Sister of St Joseph.' Mary assured the Sister-in-charge in Adelaide, Sister Monica, that Bishop Reynolds was again acting outside his powers, and that if the Sisters stood firmly behind their Constitution, Rome would do the rest: 'I mention no names and give no authority, but what I say is true. The Bishop has no authority for what he has done. He is sure to be censured. ...Rome is very jealous of its authority, and the manner in which it has been set aside in Adelaide will not help the Bishop's cause.'

After this, Mary did not write to the Adelaide Sisters for some months. She – and others – needed to know that the Sisters of St Joseph were a lot more than Mary MacKillop, that they were not mere puppets on a string. It was time for them to emerge from her shadow, just as she had emerged from Father Woods' all those years ago, and prove that they were committed to the Constitution and all that it embraced.

There was also the undeniable fact that Mary's health could not have withstood another bout with Bishop

Reynolds – physically or emotionally. She spoke candidly with a few of the Sisters about the way in which constant stress and worry had affected her, admitting she was close to a breakdown: 'I now feel the effects of years of care and anxiety. It seemed only to require this quarrel with a Bishop I loved to make me almost completely break down. I say *almost* for I am trying hard for my Sisters' sake to keep up, but there are times when the effort is too much for me and I break down and am quite helpless...'

With Bishop Reynolds' rash actions in taking control of the Josephite convents in Adelaide, it was timely that just months later, in November 1885, the Australian bishops met in Sydney to decide, among other things, whether the Order should remain centrally governed and under the control of the Mother General. The issue was debated vigorously, but the motion for central government was defeated, 14 votes to three.

It is interesting to note the way in which politics influenced the result of this vote. Most of the bishops then in Australia were Irish-born; those that were not were very much on the outer. Two distinct camps formed, and rarely did a bishop ever 'cross the floor'. Unfortunately, Mary, being of Scottish heritage, had the support of the small, non-Irish camp, and so the vote on central government was lost. It was a long 16 months before Rome finally considered the outcome of the bishops' vote, and when it did, it found it unsatisfactory. It said it could find 'no known reason' for their rejection of central government, and overruled the decision.

In 1888, Cardinal Moran returned to Sydney from Rome with news that settled the issue once and for all. The Sisters of St Joseph were confirmed as an Order, and their

Constitution had been endorsed *with* central government. The Constitution was now untouchable. This was a major victory for Mary. Fourteen years after she left Rome with the 'experimental' Constitution in hand, Rome had finally given it its stamp of approval. It was, Mary said, a privilege she 'didn't think she'd live to see', and was more than ample reward for all those long, hard years spent in conflict with angry bishops.

The documents from Rome also ordered the Mother House to be moved to Sydney, and decreed that Mother Bernard was to remain as Mother General for another 10 years. This decision on Mother Bernard disappointed Mary, as it meant that the Sisters would not have the opportunity of electing a Mother General of their choice at the General Chapter meeting in 1889, as they had expected. However, Mary was too overwhelmed by Rome's unexpected decision to approve the Order and its Constitution to focus too long on this.

The good news came at a time when Australia was celebrating the centenary of white settlement in the continent. Each colony organised special events in honour of the day – picnics, parades, carnivals, balls, banquets and fireworks displays. School children in some colonies were given half-day holidays, as well as commemorative medals. In Sydney, 50,000 people came together in Hyde Park for the unveiling of a statue of Queen Victoria. Two days later, the landmark Centennial Park was opened. Melbourne held an International Exhibition of Arts and Industries at the Exhibition Hall in Carlton, which ran for eight months.

In this general spirit of good will and celebration, Mary wrote to Bishop Reynolds, saying she hoped they could patch up their friendship, and undo the damage of their 'cruel and mischievous enemies'. However, Bishop Reynolds, feeling sorely defeated over the Constitution, was in no mood for a reconciliation, and dismissed the letter as 'insolent'. The fact was, Rome's decision on the Constitution placed Bishop Reynolds in a difficult position – if he insisted on control of the Sisters, he would lose them, together with the only means of providing a Catholic education for the bulk of his diocese. Then again, if he gave in, he would be sacrificing his pride. After many months of badgering by Cardinal Moran for a decision one way or the other, Bishop Reynolds finally relented, and accepted the Sisters on their own terms.

Rome's decision to ratify the Sisters of St Joseph closed a turbulent chapter of Mary's life, not only politically, but personally as well. While Mary was in the thick of her trouble with Bishop Reynolds, she was also coping with the deaths of her closest friends and relatives. It is testament to Mary's single-mindedness and strength of character that despite these losses, she was able to remain focussed on guiding and protecting the Order, so that it could continue with its vital work.

One of those who passed away was Mary's favourite uncle, Donald MacDonald, 'a dear harmless old man whom everyone loves to watch and shield from danger'. He became very ill in 1884 after a series of strokes which left his mind so foggy, he forgot family, friends and even his religion. Concerned that he would not have the consolation of prayer in what looked to be his last days, Mary led her uncle through them as she would a child.

Shortly after, Uncle MacDonald began making an impressive recovery, recalling names and faces, and most happily for Mary, 'those matters relating to his soul'. When he died three years later, such was the regard in which he was held that Father Woods, who had not spoken with Mary for years, took the time to write a letter of condolence, saying Donald MacDonald was the kindest heart he had ever met.

Not long before this, in September 1885, Mary heard the wonderful news that her only surviving brother, Donald, had been made a priest. 'What a fine cry you will have over this,' read his letter from Wales. She noted to Annie, with a good deal of sisterly pride and admiration, 'Fancy our dear brother being now Father Donald.' Mary's mother, Flora, had missed her young son during his many years in training for the priesthood with the Jesuits in Austria and North Wales, and looked forward to his return to Australia. Sadly, though, she would not be there to welcome him.

In early 1886, Mary had taken charge of a fundraising venture for one of the orphanages, and hoped to convince her 69-year-old mother, whom she had not seen for some time, to make the trip to Sydney to help out: 'You took no notice of my hope that you might come over some time this year. I should like it above all things,' Mary wrote.

Flora found it hard to resist this appeal from her eldest daughter and so set out for Sydney on board the ship, the *Ly-ee-moon*. Tragically, on 30 May 1886, the *Ly-ee-moon* struck a reef at Green Cape, off the New South Wales South Coast, in treacherous conditions. All 76 passengers died. 'When [Mary] heard of her mother's death,' Mother Laurence recalled, 'she went to the [chapel] and spent two hours on her knees. During her life she kept in touch with her mother by letters and visits. Her mother, at the beginning, felt that it was hard of Mary going to be a nun, but Mother Mary won her around by the kindness she showed her.'

Notifying Donald of the horrible accident, Mary wrote '...I cannot now attempt to describe the dismay with which

I heard the sad news. It was too terrible to be true, but its truth was too soon proved... Hers was the only body picked up by the pilot boat, and the only body found anywhere without being injured by either the rocks or the sharks... She looked as if she were asleep.'

As all too many of us know, losing a mother is like losing the very foundations of your life, and the loneliness, fear and desperation that often rises from this can be overwhelming. Add to this the horrible guilt that Mary surely felt for organising her mother's trip, and we can begin to imagine the emotions that would have been twisting inside her. But Mary refused to allow herself to be consumed by these feelings. Instead, she looked to the freedom granted to her mother through death. 'Oh Annie,' Mary wrote, 'I had so yearned to see her again and all the Sisters were planning to make her visit a bright and happy one. Poor, dear, long-suffering Mamma. I am sure she has gone to a well-deserved rest and will no longer have to feel her dependent position...'

Another friend Mary lost to death around this time was Father Woods, on 7 October 1889, aged 56. Since their falling out, Father Woods had largely ignored her, dodging both her and her letters. He never referred to her by name, merely as 'the Sister who went to Rome' or 'the teacher' or one of 'the first assistants God sent me'.

Most of Father Woods' time had been spent conducting missionary work just about everywhere in Australia except Adelaide, of which he had stayed well clear since his troubles there in the early 1870s. He spent a lot of time in Northern Queensland, and also visited countries to the north of Australia, including Japan, Hong Kong and Malaysia, after being commissioned to undertake scientific observation on behalf of the British government. (Father Woods was a talented natural scientist, who wrote many scientific papers throughout his life, including one on Australian fisheries.)

The extent of the ageing priest's travels amazed his friends, but it was a form of escapism, as Father Woods explained in one letter. 'I dare say my dear old friend that you say to yourself, I wonder what can have taken Father Julian to those outlandish perilous and unhealthy regions at his time of life?' he wrote to William Archer. 'Well love of science has something to do with it and love of travelling and adventure sure, but these are not exactly things for a middle aged priest to be influenced by. I dare say too I had grown rather weary of trying to do good in another way in the face of so much unkindness, hard usage, and is it too much to say envy and bitterness.'

Father Woods returned to Australia in mid-1886 in weak health, stopping off in the Northern Territory (then under the control of South Australia) to report on mineral districts, and later Brisbane, before finally settling in Sydney. By this stage, he was largely immobile, suffering partial paralysis of the arms and legs, and was cared for by a band of ex-Josephite Sisters, notably Mrs Abbott (formerly Sister Ignatius, 'the mystic').

On hearing of his illness, Mary made efforts to see him, but he insisted that she, and the other Sisters, stay away. This was difficult for Mary, as she wanted to put matters right with him before he died. But Father Woods' position was understandable – he was hurt by the snubs he had received over the years, and wanted to hold onto at least a little pride in these last, fragile days.

'Mother Mary was kind enough to ask permission to come and see me,' Father Woods wrote politely to Sister Monica, 'but I was obliged to decline. Under no circumstances could I consent to renew my relations with your [Order], and I think that visits from the other Sisters under present circumstances would only cause confusion. She wrote to me saying that they still cling to me as their Father, an expression which shewed [sic] me what misunderstanding would arise from any renewal of intercourse.'

But Mary's persistence, and a disinclination on Father Woods' part to take his grudge against Mary to the grave, finally won through. In August 1887, he wrote: 'I hear that you are still anxious to see me and wish to come and pay me a visit, notwithstanding my declining it for the present. Well, my dear Mother Mary, if you insist upon this, I must defer to your wishes, but I must ask you to bear in mind that I utterly decline to renew any relations with your [Order]... If you write and say when you will call, I will take care to be at home for you...'

While Father Woods' heart may have mellowed, those of his minders certainly had not. They let Mary know, in no uncertain terms, that she was not wanted. 'When Mrs Abbott and the other ex-nuns clubbed together to look after Father Woods, Mother Mary used to go to visit him but she was refused admittance,' a Sister wrote years later. 'The woman who came to the door banged the door in her face. Mother Mary when she met this girl embraced and kissed her...'

Despite this opposition, Mary saw Father Woods several times during his illness, which turned out to be long and painful. 'Instead of the early death, the quick transit to the unseen world so often alluded to in his writing of former days, he had to endure nearly three years of slow torture, with no hope of sufficient recovery to complete his unfinished work; or to arrange the abundant material gathered with unsparing labour and energy during his travels – sufficient for several volumes.'

Mary actually went to see Father Woods on the day of his death, but arrived fifteen minutes too late. '...I had no idea that he was dying when I started to see him – of course, he had been so to say, dying so often and got better. I saw him about a fortnight before and then he said, "It looks like the end but it's not." It was so painful to see him and be of no use that after that I used to send and enquire but did not care to go too often myself. They tell me he used to like a few strawberries. I tried now and then to send him some.'

Father Woods was buried at Waverley, a suburb of Sydney, after a requiem Mass in St Mary's Cathedral in the city. He was remembered as a kind, lovable and passionate man and, not least, as founder of the Sisters of St Joseph. Unfortunately, many also remembered his very public breach with the Sisters. To guard against this eclipsing all else, Mary wrote a book on Father Woods' life, focussing on his wide and varied achievements in religion and natural science.

Many years later, Mary submitted her manuscript to Cardinal Moran for approval for publishing. This was refused. As far as the Church was concerned, Father Woods was not one of its more illustrious figures, having led an unconventional life and been a thorn in the side of many. No doubt, Cardinal Moran wanted Father Woods to rest in peace, in more ways than one.

However, his legacy, in the form of the Sisters of St Joseph, lived on. By the late 1880s, the Sisters of St Joseph had schools or charitable homes in most of Australia and New Zealand. In late 1889, Mary went to Victoria to set up the

Sisters' first convent there – in Numurkah, about 200 km north of Melbourne. In March 1890, the Sisters opened their first school in the colony in Bacchus Marsh, about 40 km out of Melbourne, followed by a Children's Home, Providence and school for homeless children in different parts of the city of Melbourne.

The school for homeless children was a two-room cottage with about 60 children, many of Syrian and Chinese background. Often, the Sisters would take the children back to the convent to ensure they had at least one good meal a day. The Providence was located in one of the worst areas of the city, marked out by prostitution, street violence and homelessness. '[It] was a dreadfully noisy place,' Mary's sister Annie recalled. 'Women screaming at night used to be so awful I thought it was murder; also cattle used to be driven past going to market; they and the dogs with them made great noise...' With surprising success, Mary would enter the brothels and hotels, coaxing the men and women there into attending Mass.

These foundation years in Victoria were tough – the Children's Home proved to be an expensive exercise, and the Sisters had very little in the way of financial backing. Mary organised fundraising tours, but they never really took off because of a pressing shortage of Sisters, and the fact that the whole of the country was in the midst of a depression. The Sisters at the Children's Home were overworked, with just three of them tending more than 30 children. Those who went out collecting donations during the day had to do heavy housework on their return, leaving them run-down and sick.

What frustrated Mary most of all, however, was the lack of support shown to the Victorian Sisters by their new

Mother General, Mother Bernard, in Sydney. No money or clothes were sent, and Mary's requests for more Sisters did not even draw a response. In fact, Mary received so few letters from the Mother General that she believed she was being deliberately shut out. Mother Bernard often did not see fit to seek her advice on important changes, even when these directly affected Mary's work in Victoria or, more importantly, the spirit of the Order.

'[The Sydney sisters] painfully disregard my wishes on some important matters – making themselves teachers as it were of opinions different to those first taught by their founders...' Mary noted with some concern. On one occasion, when Mother Bernard proposed an unwise swap in staff, Mary all but lost her temper: 'You cannot change Sisters here without doing harm and bringing trouble on yourself, and I have good reason to put you on your guard. Besides, what is the use of being your Assistant if you do not let me advise you – I who am on the spot should be better able to advise than those who are not and who perhaps may not be free from prejudice.'

Another time, when Mother Bernard announced she was sending one nun, Sister Emelda, to help another, Sister Mary Gonzaga, with fundraising, Mary spoke out with the same firmness: 'Now, my dear Mother, I told you that I thought [Sister] Emelda would do nicely for the begging provided you let her understand from the first that there would be a lot of walking. But as for Sister [Mary] Gonzaga having the begging in turn with her, I certainly say NO to that. Sister [Mary] Gonzaga must attend to the house and correspondence...'

In this letter particularly, Mary seems patronising, almost bossy, in her manner, and certainly some have raised the criticism that she knew how to give orders but not how to take them. There was probably an element of truth in this – Mary was a born leader, who had nurtured the Order from its inception. While she had been glad to be relieved of office, it would have been difficult to adjust to being second-in-command, especially to someone she assessed as not being up to the job.

Mary was very strong, focussed, unwavering and uncompromising in her vision for the Sisters of St Joseph, but she was not driven by ambition or power. Rather, by a determination to adhere to the spirit and values enshrined in the Constitution, as she believed these best equipped the Sisters for serving the Australian people. When the Order showed signs of going off the tracks under Mother Bernard, Mary believed she had the right to speak up, both as founding member and in her role as Assistant to the Mother General.

With Mother Bernard not a particularly strong letter-writer, Mary felt it important for the unity of the Order that she herself spend time with as many of the Sisters as possible. In October 1891, Mary paid a short visit to South Australia, touring all the convents in the northern half of the colony. However, while she was there, her health began to fail. She wrote to Mother Bernard warning against overloading her with duties, lest it bring on a serious illness. '...I have had a very heavy strain on me and am now feeling the effects of it,' she said. 'Was very seriously ill in Adelaide, and just one week after I was better, got very bad again – so bad that I had to keep as quiet as possible, in pain and misery for another week. Owing to your fears – and wicked minds – I could not take the remedy that would have done me good, so that I lost a week of valuable time.'

On her return to Melbourne late in 1891, the illness she had been dreading finally hit – a serious attack of bronchitis, from which complications developed. Confined to bed, Mary showed no signs of improvement, despite the best medical attention. Doctors claimed she was beyond their help, and Archbishop Carr was called in to administer the Last Rites in preparation for her expected death.

WITH THE SISTERS IN
NEW ZEALAND

A GAINST the prognosis of her doctors, Mary eventually recovered from her illness, with the help of her sister Annie, who was called in to help nurse her. Although Mary remained conscious during the fever, later she could remember very little about it. 'For three days and nights, they tell me, I was cold as ice all over – just like a corpse. Though I never quite lost my senses, everything now seems so like a dream. When I thought I was dying and His Grace [Archbishop Carr] was preparing me, I felt quite happy to die, but oh, so lonely at the thought of leaving my dear children...

'My legs continue to give me much pain,' Mary reported, 'and I am not allowed to walk without support, and even with that I suffer intensely after the least exertion. My heart's action is much calmer and I can now speak without the terrible difficulty I had. For weeks I lived on a little milk daily mixed with lime water, but now am able to take proper nourishment in small quantities at a time... I have every care and attention, much more rest and freedom from care than I have had for years.'

During her recovery throughout 1892, Mary was moved, in the comfort of Archbishop Carr's own carriage, to a convalescent home in the coastal town of Sandringham, just outside Melbourne. In March, she wrote: 'I am still at Sandringham. The Doctor wants me to stay as long as possible and hopes I can soon be able to walk to the seaside. As yet I cannot put a boot on and have to wear big slippers.'

Surprisingly, just two weeks later, Mary had not only left the convalescent home, but was hundreds of kilometres away in Bungendore, in central New South Wales. She herself admitted she was not fit to travel, and that the doctors had advised against it, but it seemed Mother Bernard was determined she should leave Melbourne: 'Mother Bernard did not rest until she got me away from Melbourne. I am sorry she persisted in it against the Doctor's wish... One of the things he feared has taken place, and I am obliged to stay here until I get better again.'

It is clear that, by this stage, Mary and Mother Bernard were not on very good terms. Even after her serious illness, Mary found herself stranded at points around the country, relying on scanty donations to cover her travelling costs. These contributions were harder to come by than usual, because in the early 1890s, the country had been hit by its worst depression since white settlement. The Providence and other welfare houses of the Sisters of St Joseph were under unprecedented pressure.

Sister Annette in Adelaide was one of the few who provided some much-needed money for Mary. 'I wish more of my Sisters would follow your example and send me some help,' Mary implored. 'You are the only one... May God bless you, but you might perhaps give some more a hint that I am not here without being under expense and that help from them would be welcome. Mother General has not given me one shilling. She does not think of it.'

Not long after Mary's recovery from illness, news came through that Archbishop Reynolds (he was made archbishop after a reorganisation of dioceses and archdioceses in 1885) was very sick and not expected to live long. Mary's thoughts were immediately with him, with not one look to their bitter past. 'I have had a lot of Masses said for him and you may be sure many prayers and Holy Communions offered. Sometimes I have thought of writing to him, but fear I might do more harm than good by doing so.' Archbishop Reynolds remained seriously ill until his death on 12 June 1893, aged 59. His funeral was held the following day in St Francis Xavier's Cathedral, but Mary decided it would be best if she did not attend.

About six months after Archbishop Reynolds' death, Mary made her first trip to New Zealand, 11 years after the Sisters first established themselves there, in Temuka on the South Island. It was 1894, a year after New Zealand women gained the vote, and the year in which the same right was extended to South Australian women. Mary was marvelling at the beauty of the country in which she now found herself. 'This is lovely,' she commented, surveying New Zealand's island-dotted ocean and the craggy, smoking volcano she spied from the convent window at Matata. The cooler climate also suited her: 'While you in Australia have such melting heat, we have wet, cold and stormy weather. But you may be sure I won't complain of the cold. To me it is simply delightful.'

New Zealand became a firm favourite of Mary's – the place was thick with MacDonalds, many of whom she knew to be relatives of her mother; and her own brother John was buried there. What is more, it was a welcome escape from Sydney, a place she now preferred to avoid: 'I like New

Zealand very much and have been so well here. I believe that another year in Sydney with its cares and annoyances would have nearly killed me. Now that, as I suppose, Mother General is back there, she will have many a difficulty to face and will learn to understand much that I have hitherto saved her from.' New Zealand was also free from many of the 'misunderstandings' Mary had encountered with Australian priests, as she had learned to get signatures to agreements on how things would operate *before* she committed any of the Sisters to their schools.

During her year-long stay in New Zealand, Mary visited each of the Josephite convents, at Auckland, Matata, Meeanee, Temuka, Waimate, Kerrytown and Rangiora. Her sister Annie, who happened to be in New Zealand on a short stay, accompanied Mary to Matata, and wrote a vibrant account of it in her diary. 'The Matata Sisters sent a man with a light wagon to meet us [at Tauranga]. There was only one seat. Mary sat on it, also the driver. A board was fastened across the back for Sister Teresa and me. The back was also filled up with all sorts of necessaries for people at Matata – I had a saddle up to my knees. We started on our fifty-six mile [89 km] drive and got to our first stage eighteen miles [29 km] away at about 3pm,' Annie wrote. 'The driver expected to stay there for that night, but Mary and Sister begged of him to get them to the Convent that night, not knowing how dreadful the road was. They did realise it a little when they saw how horrified the landlord looked when he found that we were going on. We again got nothing to eat but dry scones and black tea...

'As we drove along that afternoon,' Annie noted, 'many Maoris passed us; many of them came up and spoke to the Sisters, welcoming them, but never looked at me. I asked the driver why it was so, and he said that they knew the Sisters' habit, and looked on the Sisters as belonging to them, but that I was a pakeha, "white stranger"... It was a dreadful road, up and down hills, with the road just wide enough for one trap. Here and there on the hillside were cut recesses for one trap to wait in till the other meeting it would pass. Just as we began to go down a steep hill, our driver noticed a buggy at the far end, so he popped into the recess and waited; so did the other man, but he came on when our man coo-eed for him. Then we went on. It was very dark, neither moon nor stars showing, but our eyes got used to it. I kept fancying that I saw shadowy figures flitting about, and at last whispered my fancy to Sister, of whom I stood rather in awe in those days. To my great surprise, she whispered back that she had been fancying the same thing!...'

On their arrival, Mary was shocked to see the way in which the Sisters were living – the convent was a breezy, rat-ridden two-storey barn with not a single fireplace. 'In fine weather it is all right, but when rain and wind come, the first pours in in all directions and the second causes the whole place to shake and the fire to smoke. Indeed, at such times, to keep the fire alight and do any necessary cooking, Sister Genevieve has to stand in water – and for the purpose wears strong leather boots... The balcony has no roof,' Mary reported, 'and the only thing to keep one from falling off is that, since I represented the danger of it to Father Madan, he came up one day and tied some long rails to a few uprights. Of course no one dare lean on these – or go near them – but their presence saves one from getting giddy...'

Food was in short supply, and the Sisters relied on the local Maoris to supply them with some of the basics. 'Meat was hard to get,' Annie wrote. 'I think that generally a butcher called once a week. There were only a very few white people among the Maoris, [and the Maoris] were good to the Sisters and sent them fish, etc, when they caught them. The curate went out on Saturday to try to shoot something for Sunday's dinner and only got a water-bird. It had to be skinned before cooking. The priests lived in a whare – Maori house – the Sisters cooked for them, so gave them the bird for dinner.

'I don't know what else they got or what we all lived on,' Annie admitted. 'My last meal was dry bread and a tomato. The Sisters could not keep poultry then because they were surrounded by Maoris who had maize plantations and they had no wire-netting or other way of keeping them from the Maori's places. There was neither butter nor dripping. Before she left New Zealand, Mary sent them kegs of butter, dripping, necessaries, and wire netting she begged while travelling about...'

Mary stayed in New Zealand for fourteen months, returning to Australia in March 1895. However, during the ocean journey, she received some startling information from the ship's captain that left her feeling as if her 'heart had ceased to beat'. He told her that during her absence, two 'select' schools had been set up in Australia by Mother Bernard. The captain, though surprised that Mary knew nothing of these new schools, believed he was imparting good news, and told her that the select secondary school in Adelaide would 'do wonders'. Mary, in fact, was livid at this departure from the Constitution, which specified that the Sisters were to teach only at local primary schools for poor children, where fees would not be charged.

Mary had had differences with Mother Bernard before over the direction in which she was taking the Josephites, but this was the most serious. These select schools, Mary vowed, would 'never have my sanction', as they 'directly opposed Father Director's and my own first ideas'. (The bulk of the Sisters obviously shared Mary's views, as the two select schools closed just months later, after a vote was taken by the Sisters at the 1896 General Chapter meeting.)

Back in Australia, 53-year-old Mary spent most of her time travelling to convents and schools in outlying areas, and maintaining her reputation as an avid letter-writer. 'You have no idea how busy I am,' she told one Sister. 'From five in the morning until late at night, but thank God, I am in better health than I have ever been... I cannot understand myself, and sometimes think a miracle has been worked in my regard...' It is likely that this 'miracle' was none other than menopause, which would have brought to a thankful conclusion the distressing bouts of dysmenorrhoea that Mary suffered throughout her life. Although she now struggled against 'crippling rheumatism', she considered this a fair trade for the condition she had learned to dread: 'What the Doctors said has come true of me – those terrible past attacks have ceased, and the Doctors have all said that if I could survive them, I would be healthier than I ever was, and so it is. Oh, how I used to dread every fortnight as it would come around. Now there is no trouble and I don't know what it is to get a headache...'

During her travels, Mary spent time in some of Australia's most rugged and inhospitable regions, although advances in transport now afforded her the relative luxury of rail over the jolt and thrust of Cobb & Co coaches. Between 1896 and 1897, she paid a long-awaited visit to South Australia, now under the control of Archbishop O'Reily. In the few short years of his reign, a whole new mood had enveloped the place. He was friendly and supportive, and the Sisters were once again a happy, united crowd. 'No contentions, strife or jealousies here...and this is how it should be,' Mary observed with satisfaction.

Around this time, a proposal was raised to send another contingent of Sisters to New Zealand's South Island. Nominated for the job (and no doubt thrilled at the prospect) were Mary and three other Sisters. In October 1897, Mary and the three Sisters set sail from Melbourne for the Bluff in southern-most New Zealand. They arrived at the Bluff on 22 October 1897, from where they planned to make their way to Port Chalmers, about 250 km away, on the eastern coast of the South Island. But quite unexpectedly, they were met by a Father Keenan (pastor of Arrowtown, an isolated township near Queenstown), who ushered them to a waiting carriage. Bewildered, Mary listened as he told them he had arranged overnight accommodation for them in Invercargill, and would take them to Arrowtown the following day. Mary explained to Father Keenan that she was terribly sorry, but there had been a mix-up – they were in fact headed for Port Chalmers, and they did not have enough Sisters to send to Arrowtown this time around.

But Father Keenan was quite determined, saying his bishop had promised him Sisters for Arrowtown, and that he had a house ready for them. He then spoke of the desperate plight of the Arrowtown children (unwittingly sealing the success of his mission). 'So well did he plead for his little wayback children,' Sister Margaret Mary recalled, 'that...consequently he carried off the whole company in triumph to the Cold Lake District in Central Otago.' Luckily for Mary, the priest at Port Chalmers was understanding,

and said that as long as he had Sisters for the new school
year, he would not complain.

After a six-hour train trip to Kingston and three hours by
steamer to Lake Wakatipu, the group arrived in Queenstown.
Throughout the journey, Father Keenan followed them
like a shadow, nervous that another, equally zealous priest
might whisk them away. 'At Queenstown,' Sister Margaret
Mary said, 'the saintly Father O'Donnell met Mother and
her Sisters for the first time and as he knew nothing of the
work of the Order, he thought it foolish to expect two or
three Sisters to live in such an out-of-the-way place as
Arrowtown. But later on, when he took charge of the parish,
he became one of the greatest friends and admirers of
Mother Mary and her Order, the members of which were
prepared to labour away in the lonely mountains for the sake
of a few children, even though deprived of the help and
consolation of daily Mass... When, through shortage of
Sisters and the small number of Catholic children in the
school, there was a question of withdrawing the Sisters, he
wrote begging of Mother to leave [the Sisters], offering to
support the community at his own personal expense if
necessary...'

Back in Queenstown, Mary and the Sisters were making
preparations for the last leg of their journey to Arrowtown,
which they began on 25 October 1897. Once there, they were
escorted into town by an exuberant crowd who, for all their
enthusiasm, could have been welcoming the Queen herself.
Mary recounts, 'When about six miles [10 km] from here, a
number of men and women on horseback met us; and nearer
again, several in buggies. They cheered and cheered again.
Such an entry as we made into the pretty town!... Father
Keenan was a proud man that day. For ourselves, we were

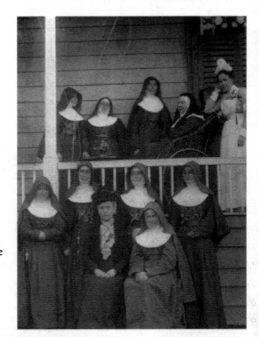

Mary on her last visit to New Zealand in 1902, in which she received medical treatment at the Rotorua Springs. She is pictured here with a group of Sisters, Nurse Glasheen, and her sister Annie at Remuera.

Photo: Mary MacKillop Archive, North Sydney, NSW.

Mary with a group of Sisters at Temuka, New Zealand, during her first visit there in 1894–1895.

Photo: Mary MacKillop Archive, North Sydney, NSW.

St Joseph's Convent, Mount Street, North Sydney in 1904. It was here that Mary spent her last days.

Photo: Mary MacKillop Archive, North Sydney, NSW.

Memorial Chapel and Convent, Mount Street, North Sydney, as it is today. The chapel holds Mary's tomb.

Photo: Mary MacKillop Archive, North Sydney, NSW.

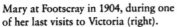

Mary at Footscray in 1904, during one
of her last visits to Victoria (right).

*Photo: Mary MacKillop Archive,
North Sydney, NSW.*

Mary MacKillop after a stroke in New
Zealand in 1902 (left).

Photo: Mary MacKillop Archive, North Sydney, NSW.

Sixty-five year-old Mary in 1907, confined to a wheelchair as a result
of a stroke five years earlier.

Photo: Mary MacKillop Archive, North Sydney, NSW.

Mary, her sister Annie and brother Donald, just one year before her death.

Photo: Mary MacKillop Archive, North Sydney, NSW.

Pope John Paul II officiates at the Beatification ceremony
Randwick Racecourse, Sydney, in January 1995.
Photo: Mary MacKillop Archieve, North Sydney, NSW.

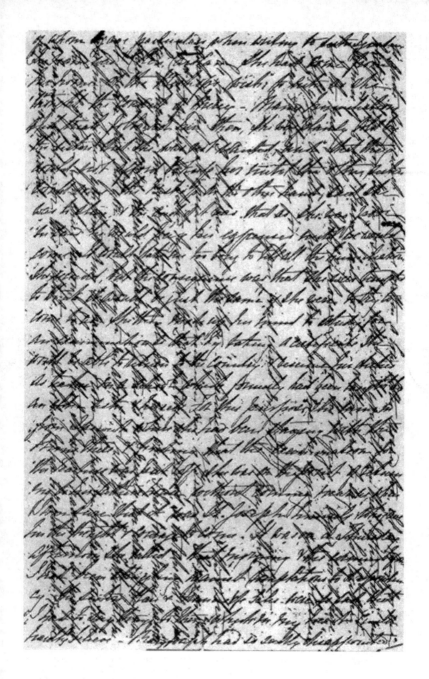

An example of Mary's handwriting. She wrote across
the page and then down the page to save paper. This is
a letter to Father Woods, dated 8 February 1870.

Mary had to write using her rheumatic left hand when a stroke left her right hand paralysed. This is a letter to her brother Donald, dated 15 June 1903, expressing her happiness that her *Life of Father Woods* has been completed.

Photo: Mary MacKillop Archive, North Sydney, NSW.

Mary's tomb in the Memorial Chapel at Mount Street, North Sydney.
The inscription reads:

Mother Mary of the Cross
[MacKillop]
Foundress of the congregation of the
Sisters of St Joseph of the Sacred Heart.
Founded in South Australia 1866.
Died in Sydney, August 8th 1909.
Requiescat in Pace.
Amen.

———

glad when all was over, and we could sit down to a quiet meal in our own nice little convent…'

Mary stayed at Arrowtown for about a month, returning there after a short trip to Port Chalmers, Dunedin and Rangiora. Her hasty return to Arrowtown was due to her uneasiness about the set-up there – the Sisters were secluded, and their living quarters were inadequate, even by Mary's humble standards. Cold, damp and breezy, the house offered no protection against the weather, and with heavy snowfalls expected in the winter, Mary insisted alternative accommodation be found. Father Keenan, for all his early eagerness, was slow to act on her requests for a weather-tight convent, so much so that she found herself threatening to withdraw the Sisters unless something was done. 'Father Keenan is full of good intentions,' she noted, 'but terribly slow. However, after many annoying delays, the [new convent] is nearly ready and will be very comfortable.'

As there were now only two Sisters at Arrowtown, one having gone to Port Chalmers, Mary decided to stay on for a time as 'Little Sister' (the Sister in charge of the convent). The Sisters were understandably nervous at having this luminary in their midst, but Mary quickly put them at ease, scrubbing their floors and cooking their meals. '…As both Sisters were engaged in the school,' Sister Margaret Mary recalled, 'the "Little Sister" willingly and cheerfully undertook the cooking and the general housework. It was her delight to have a comfortable lunch ready when they came in from school. But in order to have the meals up to her standard, she sometimes had to ask the lady next door for advice and assistance, especially when the flounder she was cooking fell to pieces. Her distress was so great that the lady came in and gave her a lesson in frying flounder, with the result that it was beautifully cooked. Mother was as proud of her success as if she were cooking for the queen instead of for two humble little professed novices.

'Mother was very particular about the washing of the gimps and bands,' Sister Margaret Mary noted, 'and more than once she rose early and had them washed before she gave the morning call, lest in the hurry to school they might not be so well done as she would like. She also took her share of washing up the dishes and sweeping, dusting or gardening – in fact, she lent a helping hand in anything that was to be done... When the time came for Mother to begin the visitation of the other houses, she feared her little 'Arrow' community would be very lonely so far away from all the other convents, so before leaving them, she impressed on them the necessity of creating a bright, cheerful atmosphere in their little isolated convent, saying that she would rather see Sisters who had to live in small communities in out-of-the-way places bright and cheerful than strictly observing the rule of silence...'

It had been an arduous few months for Mary, but it served to reinforce in her mind that it was in places like Arrowtown – remote, poor and overlooked – that the Josephites belonged. With an increasing trend towards city foundations, she made the point to Mother Bernard: '[Our] real work lies more in the scattered country parts – and I hope we shall never forget this...'

After Arrowtown, Mary toured quite extensively through New Zealand, visiting convents in Temuka, Kerrytown, Waimate and Rangiora.

While in New Zealand, her health improved significantly. The cooler weather invested her with a strength and stamina that, at a less-than-sprightly 55, frankly amazed her: 'I am so much stronger that really you would wonder to see how I can climb the hills without puffing,' she wrote to Sister Annette. 'I believe that freed from worry, and in this lovely climate, the heart has got strong.' To her sister Annie, Mary wrote: 'Would you believe that I am the most active Sister in this house? All say I am getting young again – certainly this climate has a wonderful effect on me...' But general aches and pains brought on by rheumatism showed no signs of letting up – her thumb was so sore with arthritis that she could barely hold a pen – and it was with real disappointment that she was forced to leave many of the letters she received unanswered.

Just two months after her arrival in New Zealand, on 8 December 1897, Mary received word from Cardinal Moran that Rome had given him permission to retain Mother Bernard as Mother General until the General Chapter in 1902. 'Personally I am not disappointed or pained,' Mary told her long-time confidante, Sister Annette, 'but I am sorry for the disappointment of my dear good Sisters and oh, I am sorry for Mother Bernard herself.'

CHAPTER 17

HAVING FOUGHT
SO HARD

D ESPITE her assurances to the contrary, Mary was disappointed and pained by the decision to extend Mother Bernard's term of office. On receiving the news, Mary wrote her a short note, saying she would not congratulate her as she knew what the decision meant for her. 'As for myself, I will do all I can to help you – but I implore you not to bring me back to Sydney, for some time at least. I am happier away, and you can do your work better without me.'

Clarifying her position, Mary added, 'Much as I wish to help you dear Mother General, I do not feel that our views are the same with regard to some important matters... I have a horror of any contentions and of again being placed in a false position – so grant me, I beg of you, the favour I ask. Let me stay here as long as possible...' Mary then consoled Mother Bernard on the lukewarm reaction she had received on her reappointment: 'Do not blame any Sisters who feel hurt at not having an election. Naturally they cannot understand why the Constitutions are made so little of in so important a matter...'

Mary could not hide her sympathy for the Sisters because,

yet again, they were being denied the opportunity to elect their own Mother General. Mother Bernard had been foisted onto the Sisters for what would be a long 17-year term – five years more than the maximum allowed under the Constitution, the very ruling on which she herself had been stood down. Mary could not appeal against this breach of the Constitution because Rome itself had endorsed it.

Why, when there were so many misgivings about Mother Bernard's performance, was Cardinal Moran so determined to keep her in office? Many believed it was because he did not want Mary back as Mother General. Exactly why this should worry him is not clear – Mary thought it was because he disliked her, but there is no real evidence of this. In fact, in the future, he was to show himself to be a solid, reliable friend. The reason probably had more to do with Mary's poor track record with Irish bishops, and the fact that the Order needed to prove it could survive without her.

Mary was not resentful of having to relinquish leadership of the Sisters – in fact, nothing would have made her happier than to sit back and watch the Order flourish under someone else's careful guiding hand. But she was convinced this hand did not belong to Mother Bernard. On a personal level, she had the greatest respect for Mother Bernard – she was kind, thoughtful and a good Sister – but as Mother General, she left much to be desired. She procrastinated when firm decisions were required, shunned advice, lacked the necessary fire and spirit, and had trouble maintaining discipline.

Some have argued that the real problem was that Mary could not accept a leadership style that differed from her own, and that no one could ever have met the standards she herself set while in office. In part, this may have been true, but the real issue was one of far more import. She objected to the fact that Mother Bernard was leading the Sisters away from the founding concept of who and what the Josephites should be.

Over the years, Mary had quite a few disagreements with Mother Bernard over this very matter. In 1879, while Mary was fighting a do-or-die battle with Bishop Quinn in Queensland, the then Sister Bernard was enjoying herself in Adelaide at a fancy-dress ball. 'John Hewitt will take Sister Mary Matthew, character Bonaparte and Josephine, but Sister Mary Matthew says she will not go with John Hewitt, so we must get someone else for her,' Sister Bernard wrote. Evidently, Mary must have let Sister Bernard know she was not overly impressed by these 'good time had by all' tales, as Sister Bernard's follow-up note carried a tone of great indignation: 'I have never received such a letter from you as this. I do not wish to excuse myself in the least. I feel I am not guilty of what you have accused me of... When we wrote we had no harm in it only to cheer you up... I feel too keenly what you say. Many a time I have longed to go to you when you are here but [with] your cold way, I cannot go...'

A decade later, by which time Sister Bernard had assumed office as Mother General, these squabbles had become more serious. One time in 1888, when Mary made a change to staff in her absence, Mother Bernard gave voice to her true feelings: 'I never thought you would do such a foolish thing,' Mother Bernard wrote. 'Why disturb a school like Villa Maria at the wrong time to please others?... When I go back I will make the change again... I see now why you wanted me to go to Western Australia or not to be in a hurry home,' Mother Bernard wrote pointedly. 'I received a telegram last week from you in which you said His Eminence [Cardinal

Moran] agreed or some such word, but I think the word was put into his mouth. If I wished to speak I would tell you more than I would here. I have heard plenty but always hid it but will no longer...'

However, when matters became too hot to handle, Mary was always the one everybody expected to take control. One such case occurred in Adelaide after Archbishop Reynolds was forced to accept the Sisters as a centrally-governed Order. In his rage, he banned all fundraising by the Adelaide Sisters – the only way in which they could find the money to meet loan repayments. By 1890, the mortgagees were threatening to foreclose on the Kensington convent. Mary advised Mother Bernard to send over Sister Veronica, a financial whiz, to negotiate a solution. However, Mother Bernard wavered, no doubt reluctant to engage the hostile archbishop.

This indecisiveness placed Mary in a quandary. She could see that firm, fast action was required, but it was obviously not going to come from Mother Bernard. If Mary intervened, she could be accused of 'forgetting her position, and interfering in what is her Superior's business'. Mary explained her misgivings to Cardinal Moran, quite effectively as it turned out, because soon after, Sister Veronica was on her way to Adelaide. She sent back details to Mother Bernard on the best course of action, by which a settlement was eventually reached.

Another repercussion of Mother Bernard's timidity was that some of the Sisters had become unruly and rebellious. On one occasion, in 1891, one nun, Sister Mary Borgia, refused an order by her Superior, Sister Calasanctius, to transfer to another convent. She subsequently appealed to Mother Bernard, demanding to stay where she was. Bishop

O'Reily, then bishop of Port Augusta, felt bound to step in, saying that Sister Borgia's obedience 'must be insisted on'. Alerting Mother Bernard to the dangers of taking a soft line, he wrote: 'I am afraid your timidity will incline to milder counsels than those I give. I pray God to give you courage therefore, for milder counsels in the present instance would be fatal.'

The risk was, if Mother Bernard failed to curb such trouble-makers, the Order would begin to crumble and the bishops would have grounds for again lobbying Rome for control. 'Be careful,' Mary warned Mother Bernard. 'Dr O'Reily is a good, disinterested friend – he has no pettiness about him – he likes the Sisters, sees their faults and their virtues. He does not interfere as long as he sees order maintained. But do not try him too far. For any other act such as Sister Borgia's – if repeated – he says he will follow up to the bitter end, that is, will lay all before the Cardinal [Moran] showing him the want of discipline and how it is – or will – ruin the [Order] if not checked.'

These divisions between Mary and Mother Bernard were clear to all, and fears were raised that Mary, unintentionally or not, was compromising Mother Bernard's authority. Archbishop Carr of Melbourne noted that the Sisters were unsure as to who they should take their orders from, and there was the danger of two distinct camps forming. He recalled with some concern that during one visit, a Sister told him that 'Mother Mary is our real Mother though Mother Bernard may be our nominal one...' Archbishop Carr firmly cautioned Mary, 'If the words mean that any number of Sisters wish to set you up against the Mother General and adhere to you, and to form a party of which you are to be the head, all I can say is that the [Order] is on the brink of a precipice from which only a miracle of God's grace can save it.'

No one believed that Mary was trying to wrest the leadership from Mother Bernard – she had been glad to offload the burdens of office, and it was highly unlikely that she would actively pursue these again now, at almost 60. But the Sisters could not help but be drawn to their wise, powerful and respected Founding Mother, and this certainly placed both Mary and Mother Bernard in difficult positions. Mary was aware of the Sisters' sentiments, and did all she could to encourage obedience and loyalty to Mother Bernard. '[Mary] did everything for Mother Bernard,' Sister Annette insisted. 'I did the management of business for her because Mother Bernard was no business woman. One day Mother Bernard cried to me saying, "If Mother Mary were here she would not allow the Sisters to speak so disrespectfully to me."

'[Mother Bernard] found fault with a couple of things done by Mother Mary,' Sister Annette admitted. 'From time to time, [Mother Mary] advised Mother Bernard against making certain appointments which she did not consider judicious. [Mother Mary] never formed a party of her own. She was very much against parties... Without Mother Mary,' Sister Annette maintained, '[Mother Bernard] would certainly have gone down. Mother Mary pitied Mother Bernard, but Mother Mary never had a party. A great many did not wish to have Mother Bernard but Mother Mary did not side with them.'

Mary worried for the future of the Order under Mother Bernard's continuing reign. She was so disheartened by the course being taken that in late 1897, not long after being notified of the decision to extend Mother Bernard's term, she wrote an emotional letter while still in New Zealand to her brother Donald, telling him she was 'tempted to give all up'.

What exactly she meant by this is open to interpretation. Perhaps it was her vision for the Josephites she was tempted to give up, or perhaps she wished to resign as Assistant General. Or maybe she actually considered quitting the convent. This would seem an extraordinary move at her stage of life, and yet her despondency and sense of hopelessness could well have bred such a drastic thought. 'I have fought so hard for so long for this Order, and for what?' she may well have asked herself. 'For it to crumble in a matter of years? For the Order to abandon the poor children it was intended to serve?'

Donald was shocked by the disclosure, and wrote a hurried reply to his sister, saying how concerned he was about her. Several weeks later, a somewhat calmer Mary wrote Donald a long letter, explaining away the dark thoughts she had had. 'I am so sorry for all the anxiety you must have had. I suppose that when I told you of the horrible temptations I had in the past I should have told you more, and this would have saved you some of the anxiety. Excepting that I lost my temper with Mother General on one particular occasion which I shall ever regret for I forgot what I owed to her in that position, and that I could not honestly feel that she was either true or just, I really did resist the temptations against submission and my vocation, though they were awful while they lasted,' Mary wrote frankly.

'I am truly sorry that Cardinal [Moran] has done this [extended Mother Bernard's term] as, unknowingly, he has done our poor [Order] a great wrong. He simply does not know the utter unfitness for her position... But oh, I dread Sydney,' Mary continued. 'You can have no idea of the falseness of my position there. I do not mean in the way of humiliations to myself, thought there are plenty, but in what I am expected to do and remedy. I do not and cannot approve of things I see done, or undone. I cannot bear to see the Sisters, especially the sick, in want, often of necessary medicines, and not procure them even the necessary food and clothing sometimes, and then I am left to find money to pay for all this myself. God only knows the torture I have endured over such things...

'Another thing, for I must tell you all,' Mary wrote with some urgency, 'any unfortunate Sister who would show me marked confidence, who, though not failing in any duty of submission to the Mother General, but who would not make much of her, has been a marked person and made to suffer in the end... Many do not trust Mother Bernard because she has a way of insinuating all she can against both Sister La Merci and me. You simply would not credit all we know in this way. I am so sorry to say it but, dear Donald, she is not my friend with the Cardinal. But oh dear, I am saying far too much...'

By early 1898, about six months into Mary's stay in New Zealand, Mother Bernard was feeling her absence and putting pressure on her to return. 'Mother General writes, wanting me home; everything in confusion, she says,' Mary wrote to Sister Bonaventure. 'She only says that she hopes I can come soon. I dread Sydney and what my being there means. May God help me to do what is right...' As it was, Mary began preparations to leave New Zealand in June 1898, but last-minute business, and an attack of measles, delayed her departure for two months, to the middle of

August. Just weeks before she was due to set sail for Australia, Mary received some sad and unexpected news from Australia – Mother Bernard, who had been in poor health since Christmas, had died. Mary immediately boarded the next available steamer for Australia.

'The shock of poor Mother Bernard's death prostrated me, but not until I got on board the steamer. I had only 25 minutes from receiving the cable, to catch the American Mail steamer. No time to think until I was alone in the cabin, and then my thoughts were too many for me. Poor dear Mother Bernard.'

Once back in Sydney, Mary began organising for the election of a new Mother General. She wanted the vote to be held at the fifth General Chapter meeting early in 1899, but she fully expected Cardinal Moran to oppose her in this, and to appoint a Sister to the position himself. If it would help secure the Cardinal's support, Mary was prepared to declare herself unavailable for election.

As it turned out, this was not necessary. Cardinal Moran proved to be just as eager for the Sisters to elect a Mother General as Mary, and offered his full assistance in helping to arrange a General Chapter as soon as possible. 'God's ways are truly wonderful,' Mary would have noted to herself, as she happily contemplated this unexpected backing from the Cardinal.

The fifth General Chapter was held in January 1899, and Mary was voted in unanimously as Mother General, with Sister La Merci as her assistant. Cardinal Moran seemed genuinely pleased with this outcome, and offered Mary his congratulations.

In the following years, Mary was based at the Mother House in Mount Street, North Sydney, but took regular excursions to Adelaide, Victoria and rural outposts in New South Wales to visit the Sisters. 'I mean to visit each convent myself before mid-winter,' she resolved in early 1899.

The Sisters were opening new schools and convents where there was the demand, and closing old ones where there was no longer the population to sustain them. They extended the orphanages at Kincumber on the New South Wales central coast, and at Lane Cove in Sydney's north, as well as the Kensington convent in Adelaide; opened a new refuge in South Australia, new schools in New Zealand, and a Foundling Home at Broadmeadows near Melbourne. Finally, on a momentous day in 1900, the Sisters moved back into Queensland, 21 years after Mary had withdrawn them because of the ongoing dispute with Bishop Quinn. Their first new school in Queensland was at Clermont, near Emerald, established with the full support of the bishop of Rockhampton, Dr Higgins.

Mary stayed in fairly good spirits during this time, although the years were beginning to take their toll. Constant travel and a heavy workload now left her 'tired to death'. '[However] the weather is bracing and keeps me up,' she wrote to Sister Patricia. 'Dean Hegerty, my old friend, has been here twice, and knowing what my early life has been, and what I have gone through, says he does not know how I keep up. It is only some of my own Sisters who appear to forget that I am human like themselves.'

Mary felt that the Sisters often expected her to have the stamina and vitality of a 20-year-old, and had little regard for her declining health. They loaded her up with small worries that could easily have been resolved some other way, and diverted her attention from the more pressing issues. 'At times I feel that too much is required of me,' she confided to

Sister Annette. 'I can bear any amount of bodily fatigue, but mental worry – or want of generosity on the Sisters' part in expecting too much of me – makes me ready to give up. I then get a queer crushed feeling that I cannot describe... Sometimes Sisters get so absorbed in their individual convents, schools and works, that they demand more help from me than I can give, and if I require any of them in the interests of the general good to make small sacrifices, they object and demur, and, thinking only of their individual cases, cause me intense pain, and that pain makes me almost lose heart and think my work for good amongst [our] children...is done...'

As much as Mary was frustrated with the Sisters for demanding too much of her, she was equally frustrated with herself for not being able to meet their demands. Age was slowing her down, and imposing limitations that she was finally having to acknowledge: 'To tell you the truth,' she told Sister Casimir, 'I am not well, and have not been so for some time, and it is so hard to brace myself up to writing anything... Don't think me desponding – I am not – but I feel so strangely weak, and yet look so well, that I am a puzzle to myself.' Mary confided, 'I feel that I require complete rest from worries, and some cheerful and cool change. Somehow many of our poor Sisters make too much of little everyday trials and, without reflecting, rush them on to me as if I can remedy all at once...'

The fact was, the Sisters revered Mary, and ran to her for advice because, quite simply, they always had. She listened when they wanted to talk, offered support when they were down, encouraged them when they were feeling disheartened, and laughed with them when they needed some light-hearted company. They went to Mary as naturally as a child goes to a mother, and would have been mortified at the thought that they were overtaxing her.

There were many qualities of Mary's which inspired this admiration and devotion, but certainly most of the Sisters have enduring memories of her unwavering dedication and drive. One nun, Sister Irene, recalled an incident which showed that Mary had no hesitation in putting her Highlander pride on the shelf if she thought the outcome was worthwhile. 'Cardinal [Moran] had asked her to form a class of adults [in an area where] there was no church or school. She agreed and said she would go herself, and appointed me as her companion…

'We went one afternoon to find a place to hold the class,' Sister Irene remembered. 'We knew no one out there but Mother saw a very pretentious looking mansion and said, "They should have plenty of room." I did not like the idea of asking, but Mother said, "We are doing God's work and he will help us." So in we went and she coolly said she wanted a nice large room in which to teach a Confirmation class three nights a week. The lady listened, told us she was Presbyterian, and went to get her husband. We prayed meanwhile.

'When the couple returned, Mother General again made her simple request and they evidently could not resist it for they told us the drawing room was the only room large enough and they would give us that but would cover the carpet. For some months,' Sister Irene concluded, 'we used that room for a crowd of about 30 grown men, and received the greatest kindness from the owners.'

Mary's love for children also endeared her to the Sisters, many of whom had little brothers and sisters at home whom they missed terribly. The Sisters came to learn that nothing could come between her and a child in need. This is illustrated in numerous incidents related over the years by friends and colleagues. Sister Lucy tells of one occasion, when Mary had driven some miles in a snow storm: '...But her first wish was to visit the school. There was a poor little bare-footed and ragged boy standing in class. Mother went straight to him, and putting her arms around him she kissed him, saying, "Ah, Sister, these are the children I love."'

Another time, Mary put her rusty skills as a horsewoman to work, to ensure she did not disappoint the children at the Kincumber Orphanage on the New South Wales central coast, who waited impatiently for her arrival. 'When they reached the waters which they had to cross, they found them in flood so that the coach was unable to cross. Mother Mary was not to be beaten when God's work was in question, so she mounted one of the horses and rode over to the other side.'

The Kincumber orphanage was a long-time favourite of Mary's, because there she could enjoy uninterrupted time with children who simply craved love and attention. 'Mother was devotedly attached to the orphans,' Sister Patricia observed. 'Her visits were always looked forward to by the boys who met her at Woy Woy in a small open boat and rowed her for over three miles across the Brisbane Waters, one little chap being employed the whole way bailing out the water. This happened frequently and on dark nights too when only the splash of the oar would indicate their arrival at the orphanage. Mother went on administrative business but always with bags of bread and meat. On one occasion,' Sister Patricia recalled, 'a little boy came to her crying – "Please, Mother, [Sister] sent me to tell you that I stole a loaf of bread."

'"Were you hungry, child? If so, go back and take another."'

Another time, she took in two homeless Aboriginal boys at St Mary's convent near Penrith, in Sydney's west, brought to her by her brother, Father Donald. 'Johnnie [the Aboriginal boy] is with me. We kept the two black boys when Donald went to South Australia. I feared they would never live the winter out unless very carefully housed during that time. They are dear boys and so good and intelligent.' Mary had great concern for the welfare of Australia's Aborigines, and at one point was considering sending Sisters to the Northern Territory, where Father Donald had begun a Mission, near the Daly River. However, the Daly River flooded, destroying all buildings and crops, and so the plans were shelved.

The Sisters always looked forward to any time spent with Mary, but her visits were becoming more and more infrequent, as the long-distance travel left her body weak and aching. In December 1900, she managed to get to New Zealand for the third time. She was there for only two months, to oversee the setting up of new schools in and around Auckland, and to find suitable living quarters for the Sisters. Unlike her other trips to New Zealand, this was full of 'worries and anxieties'. Mary could not even squeeze in visits to her favourite communities, such as Arrowtown. 'I cannot go to Arrow myself,' she told Sister Raymond. 'I won't be able to make any visitation beyond calling at the places en route. There is far too much going on in Australia at present for me to be long away. I am almost counting on the sea trip and the joy of seeing all my New Zealand Sisters as something to set me up for another year's hard work and anxiety over here.'

One of the new schools was at Paeroa, 130 km to the south-east of Auckland. The local priest, Father Hackett, had primed the parents for the Sisters' arrival – and stretched the truth just a little – by telling them that the nuns were the best teachers that the Sydney Training College had to offer, and that they would give their children a solid 'English' education, grounded in morals, manners and good conduct.

The school opened on 23 April 1900, with 84 children, and was a great success. But Mary was less than happy with the living arrangements at the convent – the Sisters were boarding children to help raise extra money, but the convent was 'open plan', and the children were running riot. Mary told Father Hackett that unless more suitable accommodation could be found, the children would have to be sent away. He eventually agreed to build a new convent.

Mary arrived back in Australia in early 1901, as the nation was celebrating the creation of the Commonwealth of Australia, in which the six colonies, renamed States, were brought together under a Federal Government. The country was also mourning the death of 82-year-old Queen Victoria, who had ruled the British Empire for 64 years.

Not long after Mary's return, one of the New Zealand Sisters wrote requesting that she 'cable' permission for a loan to be taken out for the new Paeroa convent. With hard lessons learned in the past, Mary had become a somewhat more astute money manager, and realised the implications of rash financial decisions – namely unwieldy debts and law suits. She replied that the request was out of the question: 'Of course I could not do this in a hurry like that and have written to say so. These impulsive movements must be restrained, and the general good considered. I have asked certain questions which must be satisfactorily answered before we can give the Deeds of one convent to be mortgaged in favour of another...'

Mary had a tough time adjusting to the summer heat back in Australia after the relative cool of New Zealand – more days than not, she felt quite ill and lethargic. 'My own health has failed very much,' she told one of the Sisters in February 1901, 'but I dare say when the great heat is over I shall be all right again. I had a hard, anxious time of it in Auckland.' Early the following year, 1902, Mary was again making preparations to travel to New Zealand – but this time it was on doctor's orders. Mary was advised to have 'rest and change', and to spend some time at the hot baths at Rotorua, on New Zealand's North Island, to help relieve her rheumatism.

She left for New Zealand on Australia Day, 1902, with her sister Annie, and a Sister Mary Winifrede. Some years later, Annie gave a brusque account of how she was 'ordered' to Sydney by Mary's deputy, Sister La Merci, and then to New Zealand, to be Mary's companion and nurse. Sister La Merci would not have intended to offend Annie by her manner, but she was no doubt preoccupied with Mary's deteriorating health.

Mary's first letter from New Zealand to Sister La Merci was sent from Matata the month after her arrival. The tone of it was noticeably more relaxed, and allayed her deputy's fears: 'Thank God I am having a grand rest and am getting strong. Everything is so peaceful here, and the Fathers and Sisters all so kind. Two masses every day, and perfect union between the Sisters...' In her follow-up letter a week later, Mary explained that she was preparing to begin treatment for her rheumatism. 'I am doing well, but for the rheumatism which is troublesome, especially in my right hand. I hope the Rotorua Springs won't be too strong for me, for if not, they are the ones most recommended for the rheumatism. Don't any of you fear the buggy ride for me,' Mary added. 'They get a special one with easy springs, good horses and careful drivers so that it is really more a pleasure trip than other, and I enjoy it.'

While in Rotorua, Mary and her two companions stayed at a guesthouse, Thirwell House, which was popular with the clergy – the Archbishop of Wellington, Dr Redwood, was a guest there at the same time as Mary (much to the chagrin of Annie, who on many evenings found herself providing piano accompaniment to his violin). Mary, though, was very contented with the arrangement: 'This is such a nice private house – boarding – where we have had a priest resident most of the time and very nice people as boarders, but Sister and I have our meals in our room and are made most comfortable.'

Mary stayed in Rotorua for almost two months, but did not write much – her rheumatism had badly affected her right hand, and a few lines every now and then was as much as she could manage. She did, however, jot a short note to her deputy, Sister La Merci, to tell her what a good job she was doing as Acting Mother General: 'I know the strain must be heavy on you, but you do not know the relief it is to me to feel that you are coming up to all my expectations of you.' The relief no doubt emerged from fears that Sister La Merci may have turned out to be another Mother Bernard – as it was, Mary was comfortable with the fact that if anything should happen to her, the Sisters would be in good hands.

She reassured Sister La Merci that she was getting the best of care from her 'watchdogs', and that the hot baths appeared to be working their magic: 'The Sisters are all so good and anxious about me, and Sister Mary Winifride and Annie watch me just like as if their lives depended upon it. I feel that the baths are doing me so much good – the rheumatism in my knees is becoming less and I can walk so easily now. Today my head is very painful which is counted a good sign…'

Throughout their stay in New Zealand, Annie wrote lengthy and quite colourful accounts of the ritual Mary underwent for her hot-bath treatment. One of these was to Sister Ethelburga, in March 1902: 'She does look comical…as only her head is to be seen and we always have a cold wet handkerchief tied around it, and a dry towel round her neck to keep the hot air from escaping. She has to sit in a place like a large wooden box, shut in all round with a very solid door and lid, you close first one side and then the other. The lids are very heavy. As soon as she is settled in it, we call the attendant who regulates the heat, counts the time and prepares the "douche" which is like a shower bath, only that it comes down like a stream instead of like a shower. They seem to be doing her a lot of good,' Annie continued. 'The heat comes up from underneath and is very strong with "sulphur" (in the Vapour ones I mean). The Sanatorium grounds are beautifully laid out and full of hot springs of clear water, muddy water, and all kinds of heat up to boiling.'

At the end of March 1902, Mary travelled to Auckland to spend Easter with the Sisters there, but a run of 'bad days' found her back in Rotorua within a month. '…I was not so well all the week as I had been here, and am only getting back to what I was. I was prepared for this by the Doctor here…that I might be worse before better, and so I have found it. Thank God, I am doing well again and this will be the final improvement. The vapour bath is naturally reducing me and removing the swelling out of my legs and hands, and makes me sometimes very weak...'

For her part, Annie began to have doubts about the benefits of the hot baths, and wondered if they might be doing more harm than good to a woman of Mary's age and fragile health. Early on, Mary had shared her fears. 'Mother Mary told the Dr that she was threatened with "Hemiplegia" (a stroke) and wanted to know if on that account it would be safe for her to take any of the Rotorua baths for her rheumatism,' Annie recalled. 'He told her to take the "Rachel" baths [the weakest] at a moderate temperature for 20 minutes and advised a mud bath for her rheumatic hand and arm.

'The Dr on our return [from Auckland] told her to take the Priests' bath – it was very hot and severe. She would never let me try it,' Annie wrote. 'Then he ordered her the Vapour bath, another very trying one even for strong men... We met the Dr the one day in the Sanatorium grounds, and I suggested that those baths were rather trying for her. He drew himself up and said, "But I approve and I'll have her take the 'Postmaster' yet [the strongest bath of all]." So he did, and she liked it very much – the water was so buoyant that she felt quite light when in it...'

By May 1902, Mary had almost completed her treatment, and although she felt much better for it, her rheumatism was proving stubborn. Whether it was the hot baths that delivered this slight improvement in her health is debatable – the rest, relaxation and cooler climate probably did her as much good as anything else – yet nothing could budge her conviction that a 'cure' to all her health problems was just around the corner.

'Thank God I am wonderfully well and able to take the strongest baths which are doing me a great deal of good,' Mary wrote to Sister Annette. 'I cannot say that the rheumatism is cured, but the symptoms are good and Dr thinks the real cure is sure to come after. Anyway, my general health is better than it has been for years. I eat well, sleep well, and can walk for miles on a level road...

'The day passes quickly. I have my mud bath for the hands,' Mary described, 'then a long walk to the "Postmaster" hot bath, the strongest of all, but which I now take with ease and safety. After coming back from it, I have to rest for an hour or so. Annie always comes with me, so her time is fully taken up. Between going to Mass and the two baths and back, we must walk quite 8 miles [13 km] a day. Fancy that for me, and you can judge how much I have improved in strength. Of course the weather is now cool or I could not do it, and there are no hills to climb.'

At night, Mary spent leisurely hours in front of the fire, reading books or enjoying the musical performances provided by Annie and Archbishop Redwood, who could not do enough for Mary. 'His Grace is very kind to me and to Annie whom he instructs to keep all worry from me, and cheer me up as much as possible,' Mary said. 'He discovered a new boiling mud pool in a very secluded part of the gardens, and brought us to it, offered me the use of his sitting room in which there is always a fire, and other little kindnesses.'

However, not all were as kind to her as the archbishop. The landlady of the boarding house showed herself to be a real tyrant, when she one day ranted at Mary for having a 'guest' in her room. 'We got home about four and were barely upstairs when the lady on whom we had called in the

morning came upstairs,' Annie said, recalling the incident.
'She had called shortly before and was told that we were
"out". She saw us come back so returned and came straight
up as the door was open. As soon as she was gone, the
landlady came to our room in a towering rage about her
impudence in walking into her house and into her drawing
room by herself etc... Poor Mother Mary was reading a
religious book, sitting near the window. I was lying down
near the door, but "sat up" and "gave it back" as Mother
Mary was silent. I told her that boarders had always a right
to have visitors but she said not in her drawing room. I said,
"Where then?" She said, "In the ladies' room." I said, "Yes,
and you've given *that* to a sick priest." That silenced her and
she went away.' Annie finished up: 'Poor Mother Mary said
she was pleased I spoke as she couldn't. It gave her a
headache and was, I am sure, the "beginning of the end".
She couldn't eat her dinner that night and felt more and
more heady...'

The following Sunday, on 11 May 1902, Mary and Annie
headed off to the baths as usual. '[Mary] was anxious not to
miss any baths, as we were going to leave for Auckland on
the following Wednesday,' Annie explained. 'We started for
the baths at the sanatorium while most of the people were at
Church. She had intended to have one of the severe baths,
but before she got there, she decided on having the
"Rachel"... She generally remained twenty minutes in the
bath, but this time she suddenly asked me how long had she
been in. I said, "Ten minutes, will you get out?" She said,
"No I'll stay the time". Immediately afterwards she said,
"I'll get out", and tried to do so. I helped her out and dressed
her and took her to the resting room and left her there while
I had a hurried bath. Then we went back so slowly, as she

said that she could hardly lift her feet, they seemed weighted.

'When we got to the house,' Annie continued, 'she went to see how Mrs W. [the landlady] was getting on – Mother Mary had helped to wipe up the breakfast dishes as Mrs W. was a servant short. I went on upstairs as I had to have my meals at the public table, and had to get ready. I [then] heard Mrs W. helping her upstairs, so feeling that something was wrong I opened the door and helped her to a seat. Instead of giving her a nice limewater drink, I asked her which she would have, limewater or whisky. I thought that, as she seemed so exhausted, whisky might be better. She chose it, but as soon as she took it, tried to take off her veil and guimp etc. [I helped her] and as she lay down she said, "I'm afraid it is – get a priest and send for a doctor." I rushed to a window and saw one of the Fathers and begged him to come up at once.'

Mary was diagnosed as having had a stroke, and there were doubts as to whether she would survive. One of the priests gave Mary the Last Rites in preparation for death.

CHAPTER 18

DEATH OF A SAINT

Bᴀᴄᴋ in Australia, hurried arrangements were made to get extra help to Mary. Sister Ethelburga, Mary's nurse during her illness in Melbourne 10 years earlier, was directed by her superiors to go to New Zealand immediately, 'as we have a feeling that you will bring her home alive'.

In New Zealand, it was decided that Mary should be moved to Auckland, to ensure that the country's best doctors should be available to her. Transporting her, without overtaxing her or causing her too much pain, was a logistical challenge, but with the bishop of Auckland, Dr Lenihan, in charge of operations, it was soon organised. A special invalid carriage would take her and her doctor to the railway station, where she would then be carefully lifted on board. 'They took her up so gently from the bed to the ambulance,' one of Mary's carers, Sister Patricia, described in a letter to Sister La Merci. 'Four priests carried her down very straight stairs, directed by the Bishop and the doctor – and then onto the station, so gently.

'But it looked so sad,' she said. 'Mother was in a flannelette dressing gown, a soft black shawl wrapped around her head and the Bishop's gold cross (with a relic of the Holy Cross within) which he placed around her neck on his arrival at Rotorua, and where it still remains. The whole side of the carriage opened and the Priests lifted her from the stretcher on to the bed prepared for her.

'We had a lavatory attached and another long carriage at the end all to ourselves,' Sister Patricia said. 'We were quite a large party coming up – the Bishop, three Priests, Doctor Annili and seven Sisters besides our darling Mother. The Doctor and Bishop came in at various stations along the line and were delighted to see her improving all the way up; she actually got us to prop her up to have a look at some of the lovely scenery along the line. The Sisters had a spirit lamp, made tea and coffee and boiled an egg for her lunch...

Sister Patricia then gave details on the effect the stroke had had on Mary's physical abilities. 'Of course she is very helpless as her right side is quite powerless. At first the doctors gave no hope; but now are more pleased with the progress she is making... When we arrived at the Newmarket station [in Auckland], Fathers Henry and McCarthy were again to the fore – removing Mother from the bed to the ambulance... Father Henry was so kind-hearted; he would say, "Doctor, come here and show us how we are to lift Mother and how we are to place her." The Bishop had four men to carry her to the Convent, Sister Augustine and I walking at each side. The Bishop's carriage was there to take the bed, bedding and parcels, himself packing all in. The men put the ambulance down in the hall and the priests again carried Mother into a bed a little tired after her 171 miles [275 km] but far better than when she had left in the morning...'

Sister Patricia remarked that for all the pain Mary must have endured, she never once complained. 'She is a wonderfully good patient. Two of us have always to be with her – she can do nothing for herself, not even turn in the bed...' In a note at the end of her letter, Sister Patricia described, as best she could, the doctor's prognosis. 'P.S. The Doctor has just been and thank God finds Mother much better. He says a blood vessel burst in her head – the sore is still there but if she is careful and does not sit up and is not excited in any way and the sore allowed to heal, she will be all right and able to run about once more. Is not that glorious news?'

Annie, meanwhile, had her own ideas about what brought on Mary's stroke, and the seriousness of her condition: 'She...got it in Rotorua through the impudent talking of the boarding-house keeper. The doctor thought she might die within 24 hours... In Rotorua I think she knew she was in great danger. I don't think she was afraid of death. She tried to live when she heard she was in danger, but she prepared for death. She was always cheerful and never gloomy.'

Seven months after her stroke, Mary was deemed to have recovered sufficiently to attempt the journey back to Australia. She was, however, still largely immobile, and could only manage a few steps, with the help of a walking stick. She made her return to Sydney in December 1902, after which she spent most of her time at the Mother House in North Sydney, and the Orphanage at nearby Gore Hill. She particularly enjoyed her time at the Orphanage, surrounded by the children she loved, all of whom looked forward to the visits of the Lady with the Lolly Tin. Mary found that in this cheerful environment, her health improved each day.

'I feel daily getting strength and can walk with a stick, and sometimes the length of the room alone,' she wrote in

September 1903. 'I sleep much better out here, and enjoy a drive now and then; and best of all, hear Mass and go to Holy Communion in the Oratory.' This was a very different life for Mary. She was no longer able to trot about from convent to convent, from one end of Australia to the other. Her deputy, Sister La Merci, took on the bulk of the travelling and most of the day-to-day administrative duties and general management of the Sisters. For Mary, these were quieter, more tranquil days. With the Order now almost 40 years old, the Sisters' affairs had comfortably settled, and the days of run-ins with rampaging bishops and fiery priests were thankfully a thing of the past.

While Mary was restricted in the duties she could now perform, she was by no means idle. It was a time for reflection, for introspection, for nurturing the soul, and a time which produced some of her most spiritually inspired writings. In verses which read like poetry, she reminded the Sisters to live their lives as one with God, and to rejoice in their calling, as she herself had from her earliest days as a Sister:

'And with this burning appeal of the Sacred Heart
[of Jesus] came such a rushing of longing desire on
my part to be Its lover and Its own true child that, in
a glance, the falseness of the world appeared to me;
the beauty, the pity, and the generosity of the Sacred
Heart in this loving appeal could not be resisted.
And in Its cause, since It deigned to raise me to It,
I have never known aught but true peace and
contentment of heart. Its love makes suffering
sweet, Its love makes the world a desert.

'When storms rage, when persecutions or dangers threaten, I quietly creep into its deep abyss, and securely sheltered there, my soul is in peace, though my body is tossed upon the stormy waves of a cold and selfish world.'

Her letters were short and every word precious – as she could no longer use her right hand due to paralysis, she wrote clumsily with her left. 'Words must be few – my left hand is unsteady and I cannot guide the pen.'

Mary put a brave front on her illness, but certainly there were days when she was overcome by despair at the hopelessness of it all. The Sisters, though, saw none of this – it was only from her brother, Father Donald, that she sought, and received, the little bit of sympathy and understanding she needed: 'Your children want you yet, dear Mary,' he wrote. 'Try to live for them. Heaven will be for ever! But are you to be a helpless cripple always? God's will be done!...

'I am so anxious to hear about your terrible illness. How you must have suffered! And how much, perhaps, have you still to suffer even if God wills to spare you to us. Mary of the Cross! What a glorious name, my sister. I hope in Heaven you will not be too proud for, you know, some of us would like to get near you sometimes,' he teased. Then, with great insight, Father Donald wrote, 'If you have had the cross as your portion, you have won also the love of Australia.'

Mary had indeed won the love of Australia. As champion of the poor and underprivileged, she provided them with education and social welfare at a time when few others considered these to be a priority. She lived an utterly selfless life, motivated by the needs of others in all that she did. She embraced a spirit of true egalitarianism, embodied in the Constitution of the Sisters of St Joseph. The homeless, criminals, prostitutes, the destitute, alcoholics; Jews and Protestants; Aboriginals, Irish, English, Chinese – she and the Sisters cared for all. With today's anti-discrimination laws and heightened social awareness, this perhaps does not seem so extraordinary. But 19th century Australia was an era of unashamed bigotry – racial and religious.

It is somewhat ironic that although Australians liked to think of themselves as egalitarian by nature, with lots of bravado about a fair go for all, this was tinged with more than a hint of white elitism and chauvinism. The country's convict heritage bred a distinctive Australian character, which was anti-authoritarian, bound by a spirit of mateship. However, the concept of mateship tended to support an 'us' and 'them' mentality, with women and non-whites, particularly the Chinese who came during the gold rushes and who later competed for limited jobs and wealth, very much on the outer.

That Mary was able to push beyond these barriers was evidence of her mature social conscience, her courage and fortitude, and her love for her fellow Australians.

In March 1905, the sixth meeting of the General Chapter meeting voted that Mary should continue as Mother General. This decision surprised some, who believed that the job deserved a young, fit and able body, and that Mary deserved rest. However, in the end, the Sisters were led by their hearts, their undying loyalty to Mary, and their reluctance to forego the wisdom and spiritual guidance that only she could provide.

Shortly after the General Chapter, Mary managed a brief trip to South Australia, at the urging of the Sisters who missed her terribly, and to oversee final work on the new wing of the Kensington convent. However, while there, she a had a relapse – at one time, her condition became so serious, she was again given the Last Rites. Desperately worried, Sister La Merci requested that Mary's doctor, Dr Isbister, send her a report on her condition: '...She is now remarkably well both bodily and mentally. The paralysis of the arm and the weakened power of the leg are both permanent and will not improve. Her mental condition is quite clear and there is no trace of blurring of her intellectual faculties – these are as bright as ever, and it is remarkable how clear and concise is her train of thought. At times she is emotional. There is always the possibility of another haemorrhage in the brain, and this is ever present. Excitement and worry are not good for her.'

Mary's return to Sydney was delayed for seven months while she regained her strength. In the meantime, she was determined to work on her writing skills: 'Again I have to dictate a typewritten letter,' she wrote with some self-disgust to Bishop Lenihan of Auckland. 'My last was dictated too, for as yet I cannot manage the type all by myself, as I have only the use of one hand. I may as well tell Your Lordship that it is my firm intention – as the duties of Mother General still devolve on me – to begin practising writing with my left hand and every day doing my copy like a little child. You will see by my next letter how I improve.'

Back in Sydney again in October 1905, Mary found herself largely confined to a wheelchair. For a woman who had led an active and independent life, these restrictions on her movement would have been enormously frustrating, yet there was no bitterness, just her usual good humour. 'One day Mother Mary was in her wheelchair down the garden,'

Sister Mary Protase recalled. 'When she needed anyone she would blow a whistle. I happened to be near at hand and heard it, so my companion and I ran to see what she wanted. Mother looked at us and then got a fit of laughing. When she recovered she said, "I wanted two big horses to lift me up and two little Shetland ponies ran to me."'

New Zealand's Sister Mary Ineen also remembered a visit to the wheelchair-bound Mary: 'Mother Mary was sitting in her invalid chair the morning we arrived in Sydney as postulants. I was so excited when I went to kiss her that I almost fell on her. She laughed outright and said, "My dear, you've come all the way from New Zealand to kill me!"'

By 1909, Mary's siblings, Annie and Father Donald, were also in poor health. Annie, now 60, was taking the hot-bath treatment in New Zealand for her aches and pains, while Donald was suffering from neuritis, an inflammation of the nerves. Mary was, he was sure, 'more patient with her cross than I am with mine. It may be, dear sister mine,' Father Donald wrote, 'that the end of your long sufferings is near at hand. Do you know if you do go to God soon I shall be quite disappointed if you do not manage to come to me, cure me and send me back to some more years of work.' (After Mary's death, Father Donald's health did, in fact, improve and he was able to give another 16 years to his work.)

By May 1909, Mary, now 67, had all but lost patience with her tired, worn-out old body. She knew she was close to death, but spoke of it only rarely. To Sister Annette, she revealed: 'As for my own health, dear child, my sufferings are increasing gradually, the nerves are giving me a great deal of trouble. I scarcely know any rest from them now at all. It is just seven years since the hand of God was laid so heavily upon me, and I often wonder how long more I shall be left in this weary world...'

The Sisters who nursed her knew the pain she suffered, and admired her courage and fortitude. 'During the last eighteen months of the life of our dear Mother Mary,' Sister Ignatia Rogan later told, 'she suffered a great amount of pain which, though she complained very little must have been intense. I was privileged to help to nurse her during that time, and on one occasion she said, "Have you ever had a toothache, dear?" I replied, "Yes."

'"Well, dear," she added, "the pain throughout my body is similar to a severe toothache."'

Sister Rogan said Mary's foot often moved up and down in spasms, and she would gently apply her weight to settle it. 'It was...something like gangrene set in in the leg... The right side was paralysed and it did not fully recover. Gangrene set in and she had to be constantly dressed. There was tremendous discomfort and pain I think really. I thought she was heroically patient, considering the bad nights she had.' In July 1909, Mary indicated in a brief letter to Annie in New Zealand, written falteringly with her left hand, that she believed she did not have much longer to live. Annie returned immediately to help nurse Mary, who was now confined to her bed.

News of Mary's decline soon reached the ears of her friends throughout Australia, many of whom made the trip to Sydney to visit her. Her mind still seemed alert, but her speech had deteriorated to the point where she could do little more than mumble a few faint words, nod or gently squeeze a hand. On Tuesday 4 August, after a particularly bad night, Cardinal Moran was called to Mary's bedside: 'His Eminence read the prayers for the dying, and gave our dear Mother the last Blessing, whilst the Sisters knelt around. He was quite moved, and, placing his hand on her head, he said: "Dear Mother General, God is about to take you to your reward. Have confidence and courage. You have a rich harvest before you and St Joseph will be there to meet you. Pray for me, dear Mother, and I will also pray for you. We will meet again in heaven. God bless you." Our dear Mother tried so hard to speak to his Eminence, but could not utter a word.'

Cardinal Moran then turned to the Sisters and said, quite prophetically: 'Her death will bring many blessings, not only on yourselves, and your Congregation, but on the whole Australian Church... I consider I have this day assisted at the death-bed of a saint.'

Some weeks later, Sister La Merci wrote to the Sisters telling them of Mary's last days, and of a quite remarkable occurrence: '[Mary] had only spoken in monosyllables for weeks; unable to swallow even a drop of water for days before she died; but [two days before her death] a marvel occurred... I sat near the bed; in a few seconds she looked at me; I asked if she were in pain; she bent her head in reply.

'For days previous,' Sister La Merci reported, 'she had not been able to swallow, and there was not hope of the consolation of Holy Communion for her, but hoping against hope I said, "Mother, do you think you can receive Holy Communion?" ...She looked at me very intelligently and said quite clearly and audibly, "Yes, dear." To be perfectly sure, I said again, "Did you say yes, Mother?" "Yes," she repeated.

'Imagine my delight. I ran to Father Smith. Father McGrath was just beginning Mass – the young priest went to get the Blessed Sacrament and we made a hurried preparation in Mother's room.

'Then a wonderful thing happened,' Sister La Merci said. 'What seemed an accident must have been arranged by Providence to give us all consolation in the sorrow so soon to be ours. A path of flowers was made all the way from the [Chapel] to the room; the Sister who carried the vases had let the flowers fall out on the way, though unaware of the fact. When I saw them I really thought one of the Sisters had strewn them to honour the Blessed Sacrament...'

By the end of the first week in August 1909, the Sisters were daily expecting Mary's death. 'Often we were sent to the Oratory to pray for her when she took a bad turn,' Sister Celsus McManus said. 'One of these occasions is indelibly impressed on my memory. It was one "Holy Hour" night and we were all in the [Chapel]. We were sent for as the Sisters thought that Mother was really dying. We were allowed to form a circle outside her window and look on and pray for her.

'I shall never forget the scene – the low bed, dear Mother lying there, some Sister kneeling by – one of them moistening [Mary's] lips occasionally – and two priests, Father Brennan and Father Smith. It was all like some wonderful picture.

'After a time,' Sister Celsus said, 'both priests left – each gave his blessing before leaving. Then we were allowed to enter the room in twos and kneel by our dear Mother and hold her hand. I am sure this made a great impression on each of us, it did on me and I always feel grateful to God to have been so privileged.'

Finally, on 8 August 1909, the sad announcement was made. In a letter to all the nuns, Sister La Merci wrote: 'This news will not be a surprise to you as we were all in expectation of the end for some days past. It came calmly and peacefully about half-past nine this morning. The change appeared about four o'clock... She seemed to be a little easier for a while, but at the hour mentioned she gently passed away, so quietly that we were hardly aware of it although all were watching.'

Sister Annette later said, 'There was no struggle at her death. As we said prayers her lips used to move in unison. She was conscious up to the moment of her death, and was able to press my hand. The blessed candle was in her hand all the time.'

At the time of Mary's death, Father Thomas Lee, who had helped Mary 'escape' the police many years earlier over an outstanding account for boots, witnessed something quite extraordinary. This is the story, as told to Sister Annette: 'It was related to me by Father Lee who was celebrating Mass in Adelaide when Mother died, that he paused at the Consecration and at the right side of the altar he saw Mother Mary standing in her habit and smiling most beautifully at him.

'When he arrived in the sacristy after Mass,' Sister Annette continued, 'the Sisters came and asked him if he had been ill. He replied, "No. Mother Mary is dead."

'"How do you know?" they asked.

'"I saw her," he said.

'This hesitancy [at the Consecration] was seen by all the Sisters,' Sister Annette said, 'and the lay congregation assisting at the Mass and was testified to by them afterwards.'

Within hours of Mary's death, expressions of sympathy poured in from across the country – from Sisters, bishops, Brothers, priests, even Pope Pius X. All honoured Mary for her invaluable contribution to the lives of the poor, and her role in establishing the Sisters of St Joseph, who would carry on her work.

Mary was laid out in the chapel of the Mother House in Mount Street, North Sydney, for people to pay their last respects. She looked serene and peaceful, just as if she were sleeping, so that even the children were not upset at the sight of her in her white coffin: 'During the day we were allowed to visit and pray by her dear remains...' Sister Celsus recalled. 'The [school] children, with the Sisters, visited the [chapel] in groups to pray, and to look on those dear features. I had the privilege of bringing groups of little ones and lifting them up to look at the dear face of one who had loved and done so much for them,' Sister Celsus continued. 'I remember persons taking soil from the grave when it was filled in. I thought at the time that people must have revered her as a saint.'

Members of the public filed in from dawn to dusk, and even those who did not know her well felt the need to touch her, or to take away something to remember her by, as if sensing that a very special person had died. 'The community was very...grieved, and as soon as they heard the news they crowded into her cell [room], never left the coffin, got their beads and crucifixes to touch her,' Sister Annette later told. The plain centre part of Mary's black shawl was cut into small pieces and sent to the longest-serving Sisters, while Annie, somewhat reluctantly, gave up the few articles of Mary's in her possession.

Those lucky enough to have some reminder of Mary were determined to hold onto it. 'After Mother Mary's death,' Sister Stanislaus Punyer recalled, 'I saw a photo of her in a shop and offered to buy it but the owner would not part with it on any account. "That kind lady," he said, "and holy nun that she was, saved my wife and me from starvation. She came to us in our direst need and brought food and clothing. She got me a good position in a large warehouse and from that time we prospered." The old gentleman was not a Catholic but he has always been a benefactor to our orphanages.'

Among the Sisters, there was the feeling that a very holy person had died. 'That seemed also to be the feeling of the older nuns who had been with her a long time,' Sister Ignatia said. 'I remember that a number of the older nuns came along with rosary beads to touch her hands with them before she died...'

There was, however, very little time for the Sisters to grieve, as Mary's funeral was planned for just two days' time, and the rush was on to get everything organised. 'Of course you will easily understand how sorrowful we all were and what a lot had to be done in a short time,' Sister La Merci said. 'We did not think of having the funeral so soon, but the Cardinal [Moran] arranged it for Tuesday and we did not get word of this till late on Monday afternoon; you may imagine how hard we worked to have everything ready; I am sure dear Mother helped us herself; all passed off in great order, and nothing seemed to be forgotten.'

On Tuesday 10 August 1909, the day of Mary's funeral Mass, St Mary's Church in Ridge Street, North Sydney, was brimming over – there were about 200 Sisters, more than 70 priests, not to mention all the school children, their parents and families. 'There was so much public interest at the Requiem Mass in the parish church, that the church was packed and I could not find a seat, though it was promised that one would be reserved for me,' Annie noted, just a little sourly. 'There was no comparison between the interest shown in her funeral and that of any other religious I ever knew.'

Sister Annette told of the unprecedented turn-out by ordinary Australians who usually shied away from any public display of their feelings: 'Sorrow was shown, and prayers were offered by great crowds present at her obsequies... Ridge Street Church, where the obsequies [were], was crowded inside, and outside in the grounds, and there was a big crowd at the cemetery.

'When the Sisters and children accompanied the remains to Ridge Street,' Sister Annette continued, 'the streets were lined with people. Both sides were crowded. When the Cardinal spoke, the people in the Church were moved to tears.

'There were crowds about while the funeral went to the cemetery,' Sister Annette said. 'In Adelaide, St Ignatius' Church was crowded for the Requiem. The people showed the greatest veneration; they sympathised with the Sisters, saying that their "saintly Mother has gone to heaven"... People looked on her as a saint. Not only the people but Sisters of other Congregations considered her a saint...'

Sister Mary Campion described the impact that Mary's death had on all sections of the community: 'Catholic Sydney was very stirred by it... Even the secular press featured her death. The parishioners from Ridge Street parish were all deeply moved by her death, though they had little contact with Mount Street [North Sydney]... It was something more than a Mother General would normally receive...'

Anyone who had ever known Mary, even for the briefest time, retained memories of this very special woman throughout their lives. All spoke of her goodness; many regarded her as a saint. The bishop of Rockhampton, Dr

James Duhig, was one of these. He had travelled many hundreds of kilometres to see Mary just months before she died. Some years after her death, Dr Duhig delivered a sermon in which he recounted this last conversation with Mary, in which he asked for nuns to be sent to Rockhampton: 'Sitting in her invalid chair, for she was then near her end, she said: "Yes Dr Duhig, I will send you a community of nuns. I could not refuse the appeal you have made to me." One of the Sisters standing near her said, "Mother, how are you going to give the nuns? You have no nuns to give!" Mother Mary replied, "God will see to that."

'She died in the following August and her death released about half a dozen nuns, so that by her own death she was able to send a community of nuns to Cloncurry,' Dr Duhig said. 'Mother Mary of the Cross was regarded by all her contemporaries as a living saint. This meeting with Mother Mary made a great impression on me which remains vividly with me until today. She was a very wise and saintly woman with a great trust in the Providence of God.'

Mother Mary of the Cross was laid to rest in the cemetery at Gore Hill, but within five years, her body was exhumed and moved to the Memorial Chapel just completed at the Mount Street convent in North Sydney, where thousands of people have since made a pilgrimage.

There were many qualities that made Mary the special woman she was – her utter selflessness, her kind heart, her gritty determination, her love and concern for her fellow Australians, her life of sacrifice, her dedication to making a difference. Always, she lived her life for a greater end – to help and encourage the 'underdog'. She valued individuals, and made it the priority of the Sisters to meet their needs – body, mind and soul.

The love that Mary showed those around her stemmed from the love of God she felt inside her. A priest and friend to Mary, Father Francis Clune, said his impression of Mary was that she was 'completely wrapped up in God. As far as any human being could, she was in union with God'. In her dying years, Mary wrote with great insight on what she had learnt about the 'strange' ways in which God worked in answering prayers for help. 'If anything should grieve me, it would be the fear that any might feel disappointed at so much devotion being apparently unanswered. Let me beg that no one will think so. The prayers will all be heard – if not as we wish – as God sees best.'

Where Mary made enemies through her life – notably the Bishops Quinn, Archdeacon Russell, and latterly, Archbishop Reynolds – it was not due to pettiness or maliciousness on her part. It was because they stood between her and the work of her and the Sisters, and this, invariably, brought out the steely and determined side of her character.

Those that loved and admired her most recognised this single-mindedness, without which the Order would never have survived. Sister Mechtilde once noted, 'Those whose views differed from Mother's and who opposed her, most of them afterwards left the Order.' Another acquaintance, a Mrs McCarthy, said, 'It was easy to talk to Mother Mary. She was not a dictator but kind and beautiful in her speech. But, mind you, I would not like to do something she didn't like.'

It is traits like these that show that while Mary was a very special woman, she was also human. Like the pioneering era into which she was born, she struggled with imperfections – her Scottish pride, her inefficiencies in financial management, her difficulty in accepting leadership styles different to her own, her despondencies. But with extraordinary courage, helped along by an almost heroic faith in God, she was in so many instances able to overcome these and make herself a better person.

In this way, Mary is a role model to us today. Overlooking the passage of time, the hardships we face as a society are not so different to Mary's – poverty, broken families, drug and alcohol abuse, depression, crime, homelessness, overwork and stress. Without exception, it could be said that some or all of these have touched the lives of every Australian, just as they touched Mary's.

The way in which Mary was able to rise to meet adversity, even when circumstances threatened to overcome her, is inspirational. Mary is a modern-day heroine and a saint not because she was faultless, but because she was able to draw on her faith and the strength and virtues of her character to mount seemingly impossible hurdles, not for her own ends, but to help ordinary Australians. Her suffering – the mental stress, the depressions, the constant strain on her health – is what makes her so real to us today. Many times, she was tempted to escape to an easier life, but she never did. She bore with the hard times, believing that God would bring her through them.

While we may not all be as good and holy as Mary, if we can take even the smallest part of her with us in our hearts and in our minds, then we may well gain a whole new outlook on the way in which we would like to lead our lives.

EPILOGUE

THE first steps towards Mary's Beatification were begun in 1925, by the then Mother General, Mother Lawrence, who had known Mary for some 40 years. Canonical investigations started in 1926, but were suspended just five years later, after accusations re-surfaced that Mary was an alcoholic. These accusations were found in three documents sent to Sydney's Cardinal Moran by Archdeacon Russell, Father William Kennedy and Bishop Reynolds after the Adelaide Commission in 1884. Requests were sent to Rome for a copy of Cardinal Moran's report on the Adelaide Commission, but nothing could be found (recall that Cardinal Moran had ordered his report to be hidden away as he believed its findings would reflect badly on Bishop Reynolds). Requests to Adelaide for a record of the Commission's proceedings also produced nothing.

The case was reopened in 1951, after Cardinal Moran's report was at last found buried deep in the Vatican archives, and an account of the Commission's proceedings was discovered in a secret repository in Adelaide. These, of course, cleared Mary of any charges that she was an alcoholic.

On 30 January 1973, a Special Congregation of Cardinals was held, to vote on the question of 'Whether the Cause of the Beatification of the Servant of God, Mary of the Cross MacKillop, should be introduced.' The cardinals decided that the Cause should be introduced, with the approval of the Pope. This approval was granted by Pope Paul VI on 1 February 1973.

Research was then begun into Mary's life – letters, photographs, documents held in Rome and at the Mother House in Sydney, and evidence given at different times by Sisters, priests, bishops, relatives and friends, was duly collected. From these, the Jesuit, Father Paul Gardiner, completed in 1989 the *Positio Super Virtutibus*, a three-volume work on the life of Mary MacKillop. A *Positio* is an official biography required by the Vatican prior to Beatification, to demonstrate the holiness of the candidate's life. (Father Gardiner's *Positio* was published in book form as *An Extraordinary Australian: Mary MacKillop*, in 1993.)

The acceptance by the Catholic authorities that Mary had lived a life of 'heroic virtue', as demonstrated in the *Positio*, together with the recognition by Pope John Paul II of Mary's part in the miraculous cure of a woman diagnosed with terminal cancer, led to the decision by the Pope, in July 1993, to approve her Beatification. This means that Mary is declared to be among the Blessed, and can be honoured as a saint within Australia, the first person to be officially recognised in such a way in this country.

The final step in Mary's journey towards sainthood will occur when she is 'canonised'. Her name will be placed in the canon (i.e. list) of saints who are celebrated in the official ceremonies of the Catholic Church throughout the world. Another miracle needs to be accepted by the Pope as performed in Mary's name before she can be canonised. Effectively, however, she is recognised as a saint within

Australia. As such, she is held up as a person of exceptional holiness, a model for others, and is recognised by the Catholic Church as being with God and as worthy of honour.

ACKNOWLEDGEMENTS

I gratefully acknowledge those many people who assisted me with this project: reading, correcting, suggesting and gently criticising. I am especially indebted to Margaret McKenna rsj and Clare Koch rsj from the Mary MacKillop Secretariat, North Sydney, for their guidance, encouragement and insight. Through them, and the archivists of the Sisters of St Joseph, I had access to many primary sources, including the letters of Mary MacKillop and the memoirs of some of her fellow Sisters, as well as a wealth of other research material. I would also like to acknowledge the work of Father Paul Gardiner SJ, the *Positio Super Virtutibus, Cause of the Canonization of the Servant of God, Mary of the Cross MacKillop, Foundress of the Australian Sisters of St Joseph of the Sacred Heart*, Volumes I, II and III (Rome, 1989), which proved to be a valuable reference. To all those other authors of books on Mary MacKillop and the Sisters of St Joseph, I also extend my thanks, for acquainting me with the life of a very special Australian. Finally, I record my gratitude to Marie Therese Foale rsj, who assisted in this project and whose book, *The Josephite Story* (Sydney, 1989), was a useful source.

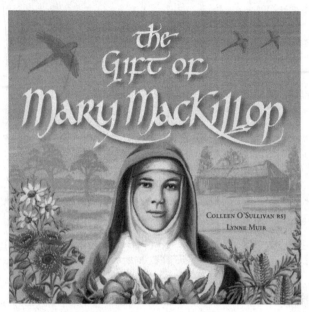